COLLUSIONS OF FACT AND FICTION

STUDIES IN THEATRE HISTORY AND CULTURE
Heather S. Nathans, series editor

COLLUSIONS
of FACT & FICTION

PERFORMING SLAVERY IN THE
WORKS OF SUZAN-LORI PARKS
AND KARA WALKER

ILKA SAAL

University of Iowa Press, Iowa City

University of Iowa Press, Iowa City 52242
Copyright © 2021 by the University of Iowa Press
www.uipress.uiowa.edu
Printed in the United States of America

Design by Kristina Kachele Design, llc

Printed on acid-free paper

Library of Congress Cataloging-in-Publication Data
Names: Saal, Ilka, 1970– author.
Title: Collusions of Fact and Fiction: Performing Slavery in the
Works of Suzan-Lori Parks and Kara Walker / Ilka Saal.
Description: Iowa City: University of Iowa Press, [2021] | Series: Studies
in Theatre History and Culture | Includes bibliographical references and
index. | Identifiers: LCCN 2020051372 (print) | LCCN 2020051373 (ebook) |
ISBN 9781609387785 (paperback) | ISBN 9781609387792 (ebook)
Subjects: LCSH: Parks, Suzan-Lori—Criticism and interpretation. |
Walker, Kara Elizabeth. | Slave trade in literature. | Slave trade in art. |
African Americans in literature. | African Americans in art. | Blacks in
literature. | Blacks in art. | African Americans—Intellectual life. |
Blacks—Intellectual life.
Classification: LCC PS3566.A736 Z83 2021 (print) | LCC PS3566.A736
(ebook) | DDC 812/.54—dc23
LC record available at https://lccn.loc.gov/2020051372
LC ebook record available at https://lccn.loc.gov/2020051373

For Tristan, Anselm, and Jan

CONTENTS

ACKNOWLEDGMENTS

This book has benefited from the critical insights and generous support of a great number of people. I would like to take the opportunity to thank them. First off, I am grateful for the support of the Alexander von Humboldt Foundation, its external reviewers and staff members, who enabled me to get this project off the ground with a prolonged research sojourn at the University of Toronto. In Toronto, I was welcomed by the Departments of History and English, which provided me with an academic home away from home. In particular, I want to thank Nicholas Terpstra, Jennifer Jenkins, Thomas Lahusen, and Tong Lam, as well as Paul Downes, Naomi Morgenstern, and Linda Hutcheon—thank you all for welcoming me, for sharing office space, coffees, and meals, and especially for being such generous critics and supporters of my work. My profound thanks also go to Elizabeth Wulff, Sangeeta Panjawi, and Jennifer Evans for working their logistic magic on my behalf.

I am also grateful to the staff at various libraries and archives for facilitating my research, in particular Jeremy Megraw and his colleagues at the Theatre Archives of the New York Public Library, Irene Wo at the Main Library & Museum Archives of the Royal Ontario Museum in Toronto, David Evans of the Magic Lantern Society, Sabine Ziebarth at the university library at Erfurt, and especially to Scott Briscoe at Sikkema Jenkins & Co. for his untiring and manifold support over so many years. Furthermore, I want to acknowledge the assistance of Yvonne Kirmse, Tobias Lebens, and Alina Russ at the English Department at Erfurt. Thank you all!

A number of people have read or listened to excerpts from this work. I would like to thank Tom Allen, Bert Ashe, Nassim Balestrini, Bill Decker, Jan Lensen, Jürgen Martschukat, Reingard Nethersole, Ralph Poole, Antonia Purk, Art Redding, Natalia Barykina, and David Savran for the rich conversations, helpful observations, astute comments and, above all, for their patience (and sometimes endurance). My thanks also extend to Jason Merchant and Marcus Folch for contributing their linguistic and classicist expertise. The editors and staff at the University of Iowa Press have been an invaluable source of support for me. I am deeply grateful for the conversations with Heather Nathans and Dan Ciba and their unwavering support of this project, and I deeply appreciate the constructive feedback from the external reviewers.

Finally, I raise my glass to friends, neighbors, and family members in Berlin, Toronto, New York, Leipzig, Eisenach, and Oostduinkerke, who have supported me in a myriad of ways throughout this endeavor: with meals and childcare, distractions and encouragement. Special thanks go to dear neighbor and friend, Meyer Brownstone, who alas is no longer with us to hold this book in hand. I will continue our conversations in my heart.

And last but not least, I would like to thank my three men, to whom I dedicate this book: Tristan and Anselm, you have been such troupers. I started this book when you were tiny babies; you toddled along to Toronto and New York and for many years waited so patiently for me to reemerge from my study to play. Thank you for being there throughout! And Jan, what can I say . . . without you none of this would have happened. *Toujours!*

PREFACE

Since the late 1960s, works engaging the traumatic experience of trans-atlantic slavery and its various material, psychological, and represen-tational legacies have emerged steadily—from Margaret Walker's cel-ebrated novel *Jubilee* (1966) and Betye Saar's iconic assemblage *The Liberation of Aunt Jemima* (1972) to the mini-TV series *Roots* (1977) and Toni Morrison's landmark novel *Beloved* (1987) to Kara Walker's monumental sculpture *A Subtlety* (2014), and Jeremy O. Harris's recent *Slave Play* (2019). Within this steady stream of cultural productions, important differences in the poetics and politics involved stand out. As British Guyanese writer Fred D'Aguiar explains, every generation needs "their own version of the past, to see the past in their own images, words. To have slavery nuanced their way" (1997, 126). *Collusions of Fact and Fiction* sets out to examine how one particular generation of African American artists, those coming of artistic age in the 1990s and 2000s, has "nuanced" the long history of slavery in its own way and to what effect.

The works of playwright Suzan-Lori Parks and visual artist Kara Walker are particularly suited to provide an entry into this kind of inquiry. Several parallels in their approach to slavery indicate the extent to which these artists share a certain poetic and political stance in relation to prevalent aesthetic, ethical, and political concerns of the particular cultural moment—the turn of the millennium. Both entered the art scene within a few years of each other with works focusing on the legacies of transatlantic slavery in contemporary American culture. Parks first attained public notice with her play *Imperceptible Mutabilities in the Third Kingdom,* which opened at BACA Downtown in Brooklyn in September 1989, and Walker made her debut with the silhouette installation *Gone: An Historical Romance of a Civil War as It Occurred b'tween the Dusky Thighs of One Young Negress and Her Heart* at the Drawing Center in New York City in September 1994. Both quickly garnered nationwide and international attention for their unconventional and provocative approach to the past, which they developed further in their subsequent work. They have been celebrated with a number of prestigious awards: for Parks, Obie Awards in 1996 and 1999 and a Pulitzer in 2002; for Walker, a nomination as the U.S. representative at the 25th Biennial de São Paulo in Brazil in 2002. Both have received MacArthur "genius" grants: Walker in 1997, Parks in 2001. At the same time, their works have also been vehemently debated and contested, particularly by African American critics. Many consider the artists' playful approach to the topic of slavery—particularly their use of stereotypes—to be detrimental to intraracial politics of respectability and racial obligation and disrespectful to the achievements of past generations of artists in battling negative images of Blackness. The polar nature and impassioned tenor of public reactions to Parks's plays and Walker's artworks indicates that at the end of the twentieth century the subject of transatlantic slavery continued to be a charged and contested topic in American cultural memory. In this regard, the debates over their art have set the tone for larger discussions about the form, politics, and ethics of memory work.

Parks's and Walker's oeuvres of the 1990s and 2000s also evince remarkable similarities in the aesthetic strategies they deploy in engaging the past of slavery and its various legacies. Both sets of work are marked by a provocative *gestus* of iconoclasm, at times even irreverence, with regard to established narratives and iconographies of slavery—those canonized in dominant historiographies, those revered in African American counterhistories, as well as those codified in popular and mass-cultural narratives. Riffing on well-known historical, literary, and pictorial antetexts, the two artists also share a frequently unsettling slapstick kind of humor in their representations of slavery and its afterlife. This often entails the calculated, confrontational use of cartoonish, racializing stereotypes, designed to draw the spectator/beholder into an affective relationship with the artwork. The playful, humorous engagement with racist stereotypes is not unique to Parks and Walker; it was so prevalent in African American art from the late 1980s to the early 2000s (such as in George Woolfe's 1986 play *The Colored Museum*, Spike Lee's 2002 film *Bamboozled*, and paintings by Michael Ray Charles) that it triggered vehement discussions in scholarship and public forums.[1] Shawn-Marie Garrett speaks in this context of the purposeful revival of tropes of minstrelsy as "the return of the repressed." Much of this work is "offensive, or, at best, strange and uncomfortable; it raids history and brings some of its deliberately forgotten scenes to light. It is painful and appalling. It is sometimes hilarious" (Garrett 2002, 32). For the most part, however, these works do not naïvely reiterate racist stereotypes of the past but defamiliarize them through strategies of parody and satire to interrogate their contemporary epistemological and affective valences and, ultimately, as Garrett and also Henry Louis Gates Jr. have suggested, to exorcise them.[2] This artistic praxis is also at the heart of Walker's and Parks's work with stereotypes, as I suggest in the chapters that follow.

The two artists also concur with regard to a pronounced entanglement of fact and fiction in their investigation of slavery. Walker admits to an "overzealous imagination" that persistently interferes with "the basic facts of history" (quoted in Armstrong 1997, 107). Parks similarly emphasizes her need to "make up" the figures and stories that she finds missing in established histories (Pearce 1994, 26). Although the use of the imagination is characteristic of any mnemonic or historiographic approach to the past, it stands out in Parks's and Walker's works in terms of its degree and purpose. As *Collusions of Fact and Fiction* argues, their works evince a *heightened* degree of imagination deployed not so much to reconstruct or correct the facts of slavery, nor to recuperate the interiority of the enslaved or enable an affective knowledge of their lives, which was typical for many earlier visual and verbal narratives of slavery, as to investigate the impact of established modes of knowing slavery on contemporary identities. Parks's and Walker's primary inquiry is not into the "truth" of slavery but into the complex ways in which the known facts of the past are always already intricately intertwined with the various fictions through which they have been articulated and mediated in word, performance, and image. Walker speaks on this score of the "collusion of fact and fiction" (quoted in Armstrong 1997, 107) that any access to the past entails, including her own. It is hence the history of the collusion of facts and fictions in our contemporary understanding of slavery as well as the impact of this collusion on contemporary perceptions of race in general and Blackness in particular that stands at the center of Parks's and Walker's artistic investigations into the past. This poststructuralist understanding of history, which foregrounds and riffs on the constructed and always already mediated nature of our knowledge of the past is, so I suggest in this study, a trademark of a generation of artists active in the 1990s and 2000s. We find it at work, for instance, in filmmaker Cheryl Dunye's self-reflective, made-up documentary about the Black actress Fae Richards, *The Watermelon Woman* (1996); in visual artist Glenn Ligon's provocative interrogation in the installation *To Disembark* (1993) of the various verbal and visual coordinates that seek to contain Black identity; and in playwright Young Jean Lee's perceptive probing of the impact of American theatrical history and dramatic form on contemporary presentations of Blackness in her unsettling play *The Shipment* (2009).

Importantly, Parks's and Walker's deployment of a poetics of playful Signifyin(g) on entrenched iconographies and narratives of slavery and the pronounced collusion of fact and fiction indicates a distinctive shift in attitude toward the past. As the two artists probe the continuing impact of slavery on the present by restaging its customary themes, motifs, images, and *lieux de mémoire*, they also assert the performative agency of word, image, and body in refiguring the prevailing representational grammar of slavery so as to enable new subject positions in the present. While, without doubt, the traumatic past continues to matter in the works of Parks and Walker, they no longer subscribe to the "melancholic historicism" characteristic of the interpretive paradigm preferred by a previous generation of artists, which insisted on the continuing affective identification with the trauma of slavery.[3] Instead, Parks and Walker assert the power of artistic agency and the generative force of poetic configurations in clearing a discursive space for fresh approaches to thinking about the past and its meanings for contemporary Black identities.[4] In tracing this shift in the artists' stance toward the past, my reading of Parks and Walker builds on recent scholarship in the field of African American literary, performance, and cultural studies.

There is yet another reason that motivates this comparative study of artworks by Kara Walker and Suzan-Lori Parks. Despite their primary work in different media (the performing arts and the visual arts),[5] the artists' interest in intervening in established histories of slavery ultimately cuts across artistic media and genre. Regardless of whether produced for the stage or the pictorial surface, ultimately their works examine how narratives of the past have been constructed and can thus be reconstructed. They do so by interrogating all three media recognized as crucial for mnemonic and historiographic practice: verbal narrative, visual image, and bodily performance.[6] For example, even as Walker's oeuvre seems to be primarily concerned with visual legacies of slavery, it is deeply invested in processes of narrative construction, as evident in the spatial arrangement of figures on the pictorial surface and the playful Signifyin(g) on the genre conventions of the slave narrative, which figures prominently as a key narrative intertext in her silhouette installations of antebellum plantation slavery. In her titles and visual compositions, Walker also plays with narrative constructs, such as narrative voice and (un)reliability. Parks, in addition to her interest in the work of language in constructions of the past, thematizes in several of her plays the visual dimension and scopic dynamics in which processes of racialization are embedded—most prominently in her use of photographs in *Imperceptible Mutabilities in the Third Kingdom* (1989) and her multilayered staging of processes of looking and performing in *Venus* (1996). Above all, both artists' works are decidedly theatrical in that through foregrounding the mediality and materiality of visual and dramatic performances of slavery, they interpellate their audiences into an awareness of the interpersonal, relational dimension of constructions, performances, and perceptions of race. In *Venus*, when an African American actress poses as the "Hottentot Venus," Parks not only plays on stereotypical perceptions of the Black female body but implicates her contemporary audience in the colonial fantasies that produced these stereotypes in the first place. Walker, similarly, provokes viewers with the display of life-size, black-on-white silhouettes that take on their particular racial meanings from the visual habits and stereotypical perceptions that spectators bring to bear on them.[7] The pronounced theatricality of these works creates a situation in which spectators are no longer mere beholders but are made complicit in performative and visual constructions of race. Parks and Walker thus share an interest not only in the constructed and mediated nature of verbal and visual narratives of history but also in the ways that theatricality draws viewers into affective encounters with the artwork. In this regard, too, their works echo a larger trend in late twentieth- and early twenty-first-century cultural productions dealing with slavery to foreground questions of materiality, mediality, and relationality.

There is sufficient evidence that Parks and Walker share a particular poetics and politics in approaching the past of slavery not only with each other but with a great number of other artists of the 1990s and 2000s. To the already mentioned works of Glenn Ligon, Cheryl Dunye, Michael Ray Charles, and Young Jean Lee, one could add the photographic work of Renée Cox (e.g., *Venus 2000*, 1994) and Carrie Mae Weems (e.g., *From Here I Saw What Happened and I Cried*, 1995), internet art by Keith Townsend Obadike (*Blackness for Sale*, 2001) and damali ayo (*Rent-A-Negro.com*, 2003), and literary and dramatic works by Robert O'Hara (*Insurrection: Holding History*, 1999), Alice Randall (*The Wind Done Gone*, 2001), Thylias Moss (*Slave Moth*, 2004), Branden Jacobs-Jenkins (*An Octoroon*, 2014), and Colson Whitehead (*The Underground Railroad*, 2016)—to name just a few. They all tackle the representational and affective legacies of slavery in similarly provocative, playful, and often theatrical ways. Any of these artists could have served as a starting point for inquiring how the generation of artists active around the turn of the millennium has rendered "the past in their own images, words" (D'Aguiar 1997, 126). I have chosen to focus on works by Parks and Walker as a gateway for this inquiry for their capacity to be both "exemplary and individual" (Saltzman 2006, 15). As *Collusions of Fact and Fiction* investigates the aesthetic specificities of some of Parks's plays and Walker's visual and sculptural work, it does so with an eye to their representativeness for a particular cultural moment. In delineating key formal strategies at work in Parks's and Walker's interrogation of the past, I hope to offer up an interpretative model for reading a variety of verbal, visual, and performance-based narratives of slavery at the turn of the millennium.

In conceptualizing an interpretative model of a particular generational engagement with slavery, this study is distinctly interdisciplinary in approach and transdisciplinary in intent. While my inquiry into visual and verbal narratives of slavery starts with a set of questions that emerged at the intersection of literary studies and historiographic/memory studies, it also draws on theoretical insights and methods from the fields of visual and performance studies to bring into focus the ways in which Parks and Walker engage, destabilize, subvert, and refigure codified narratives of the past. Ultimately, this inquiry is firmly embedded in the field of cultural studies, which—while emerging from the field of literary studies—is inherently interdisciplinary in its attempt to analyze, contextualize, and historicize cultural works.

My endeavor is much indebted to existing scholarship.[8] While there has been much discussion of Parks's and Walker's works,[9] very few scholars have so far attempted to read their works together or to read them with regard to generational similarities or differences.[10] Arlene Keizer's scholarship is an exception, and my analysis owes much to her insightful comments on the artists' shared aesthetics.[11] Keizer also underscores the ways in which Kara Walker's visual work connects with and builds on the work of such important literary predecessors as Gayle Jones, Caroline Herron, and Octavia Butler.[12] Moreover, she significantly expands our understanding of a large and diverse body of works addressing the legacies of slavery that has emerged since the late 1960s. Taking the antebellum slave narrative as their primary narrative model, these works have commonly been referred to as "neo–slave narratives."[13] Introducing the term "contemporary narratives of slavery," Keizer casts a "wider interpretive net" and alerts us to varieties in geographic scope and literary form (Keizer 2004, 2–3). Although Keizer does not specifically mention visual and performance-based work, her concept is wide enough to include these forms of artistic investigations into the legacies of slavery as well. Yet, because of their inclusive nature, neither the term "neo–slave narrative" nor the term "contemporary narratives of slavery" allows us to track important shifts of emphasis in poetics and politics during the evolution of this varied body of artistic work. To gauge the ways in which Walker and Parks might take the engagement with slavery in new directions, I turn to the work of Stephen Best, Judith Misrahi-Barak, and Margo Natalie Crawford, who have begun to point toward a paradigm shift in the poetics (Crawford 2016; Misrahi-Barak 2014) and ethics (Best 2012) of late twentieth-century narratives of slavery. As *Collusions of Fact and Fiction* builds on the work of these and other scholars, it does so with the specific interest of identifying and conceptualizing this paradigm shift more fully and exploring the ways in which changing social and political circumstances as well as cultural influences prompted artists at the turn of the millennium to ask different questions of the past of slavery and to render it in different ways.

Chapter 1, "Fictions of History and Historiopoetic Performances of the Past," sets up the conceptual and theoretical frame for my analysis. It investigates the prominent interplay of fact and fiction in the works of Parks and Walker by first situating them within a spectrum of what Marianne Hirsch (2012) calls "postmemory" approaches to a traumatic past and then differentiating the two artists' imaginative investment in the past from that of the authors of the neo-slave narratives of the 1970s and 1980s. The chapter focuses in particular on differences in archaeological praxis, especially with regard to changing attitudes toward questions of veracity, authenticity, and recuperability, as well as the concomitant shift in political attitude toward the past that this difference in poetic approach entails. The discussion of Parks's and Walker's poetics and politics is situated within a larger sociocultural frame of reference: the aesthetic praxis and overall ethos of a generation of artists who came of age after the civil rights movement, which critics have variously dubbed "post-soul" and "post-black." To highlight the particularities of this generation's imaginative approach to history, I introduce the term "historiopoiesis"—the making (*poiesis*) of history through poetic/formal means—as a new category of analysis that brings into focus the various processes of crafting and recrafting through verbal, visual, and performance techniques discourses—and with that, knowledges—of the past. This first chapter serves as a basic historicization and theoretical frame for the discussions of particular poetic techniques that follow in the next three chapters.

Chapter 2 focuses on Suzan-Lori Parks's historiopoetic method, identifying "digging," "Rep & Rev-ing," and "faking" as the three key techniques with which the playwright intervenes in established histories and makes up new ones. Digging is the primary tool in Parks's literary archaeology. In *The America Play* (1994) and *Venus* (1996), she implements this technique by having her figures literally unearth the absent identities, straying ghosts, and buried legacies of the past from what she terms "The Great Hole of History" and by figuratively digging up, in the spirit of a Foucauldian archaeology, the discourses with which Black subjects have been interpellated by dominant ideologies, past and present. Digging is closely interlinked with Parks's signature dramaturgy of Rep & Rev-ing, the playful and ongoing repetition and revision of motifs, words, and images, primarily on the level of verbal performance. Through the ludic process that literary scholar Henry Louis Gates Jr. (1988) calls "Signifyin(g)," Parks's figures dig into discourses, take digs at the meaning of words and phrases, and reassemble their morphological and/or syntactical bases so that new meanings can emerge. Along with faking, digging is one of the most powerful historiopoetic tools in Parks's dramaturgy for converting the melancholic haunting of history into ownership and possession. In close readings of the plays *Imperceptible Mutabilities in the Third Kingdom* (1989) and *Death of the Last Black Man in the Whole Entire World* (1990), I discuss how this technique refigures prominent themes, motifs, images, stereotypes, and narrative structures with which Black people have been inscribed into history. Finally, faking refers to the playwright's and her characters' liberal fusion of fact and fiction, the characters' penchant for playacting and the theatrical, for imagining otherwise. As I contend in my discussion of *The America Play* and *Topdog/Underdog* (2001), the art of faking is crucial for the capacity to refigure an arduous past and to forge an identity out of adverse circumstances. Refusing to adhere to an epistemic regime that stipulates that things are either true or false, fact or fiction,[14] figures like Brazil and Booth radically confound the dominant conventions of knowledge production, demonstrating that it is precisely in the process of playing and playacting—that is, in the imaginative performance—that moments of possibility flash up.

Chapter 3, "A Sidelong Glance at History: Unreliable Narration and the Silhouette as *Blickmaschine* in Kara Walker," considers two key techniques Walker employs in her engagement with the history of slavery: her use of the late eighteenth- and early nineteenth-century medium of the cut-paper silhouette and her parody of the autodiegetic narration of antebellum slave narratives. Both are used to take a sidelong glance at the ways slavery and notions of race (Blackness in particular) have been articulated in text and image from this period onward. In this context, Walker also problematizes the role these two media have played in shaping racial identities. Focusing on her curatorial and creative work for the exhibition *After the Deluge* (2006), which she put together for the Metropolitan Museum of Art to commemorate the victims of

Hurricane Katrina, the chapter discusses how Walker, through various techniques of visual and verbal Signifyin(g), defamiliarizes traditional uses of the silhouette and exposes it as a *Blickmaschine*, a perceptual apparatus, which from the eighteenth century onward has significantly shaped our gaze at racial identities. At the same time, she also deploys the art of paper cutting to intervene in hegemonic mechanisms of perception. The silhouette's inherent ambivalence of mimetic pretense and phantasmagoric projection, moreover, makes it an apt medium for the homodiegetic narrator that features so prominently in a number of Walker's visual and textual works: the figure of "the Negress." As the artist's fictional alter-ego, the Negress purports to chart and document with her silhouette work the troubled territory of slavery, she also professes to her profound desire to meddle with the past—not only through her idiosyncratic use of the silhouette but also by riffing on established themes of canonical slave narratives, such as authenticity, literacy, and freedom. Her parodic use of these themes brings into focus the ways in which the articulation of Black subjectivity has long been the result of complex processes of mediation. With the figure of the Negress, Walker demonstrates how the always already mediated body of the Black artist can be free to perform in *picara* fashion a number of unexpected, burlesque, and sometimes cruel roles that allow her to unmask and trouble the discourses and structures that seek to contain her as well as to seize the libidinal fantasies that prescribe her as the ground for a performative refashioning of the self.

Chapter 4, "Stereotypes and Theatricality: (Re)Staging Black Venus," focuses on Parks's and Walker's controversial use of racial stereotypes, particularly the affective force of the audience's encounter with stereotypes. In Parks's play *Venus* and Walker's sculpture *A Subtlety, or The Marvelous Sugar Baby* (2014), the artists deploy racializing stereotypes—particularly of Black femininity—in hyperbolic ways to tap into the psychic hold and various affective claims that stereotypes of the past continue to have on today's spectators. In teasing out the complex interplay of desire and phobia, fantasy and anxiety inherent in these stereotypes, Walker's and Parks's provocative and highly theatrical stagings of Blackness elicit the spectators' complicity with the stereotypes they behold and implicate them in a multilayered performance of racializing ascriptions and insurgent subversions. In many regards, the audience becomes the focus of these theatrical stagings of histories of racial representations. Drawing on Michael Fried's (1998) and Fred Moten's (2003) notions of theatricality, this chapter examines how the two artists probe the fundamental relational quality of perceptions and performances of race while also troubling and upsetting entrenched modes of seeing in order to open up possibilities of conceiving of new subject-object relations.

In a coda to this study, I ask about the relevance of a playful millennial poetics such as Parks's and Walker's, which advocates the performative force of individual, imaginative, and artistic agency over imposed or voluntary assertions of collective identity, in the contemporary period of the 2010s and the beginning of the 2020s—a period during which unrelenting state violence against people of color has called renewed attention to the ways in which "an *idea* of the black body has been and continues to be projected across actual physical bodies," as Harvey Young reminds us (2010, 4). Between 2008 and 2016, we have seen the election of both America's first Black president and its "first white president," in the words of Ta-Nehisi Coates (2017). Cheerful assertions of multiculturalism and post-racialism thus rub up against myriad manifestations of white supremacy. Given this climate, we might just now be witnessing the emergence of what Raymond Williams (1977) would call a new "structure of feeling" in Black cultural productions, one that underscores the ways Black agency, mobility, and freedom continue to be curtailed by an entrenched anti-Black racism. Yet, as I suggest in my close readings of Branden Jacobs-Jenkins's play *An Octoroon* (2014) and Colson Whitehead's novel *The Underground Railroad* (2016), while many contemporary narratives of slavery unflinchingly take stock of how the legacies of the past continue to impact contemporary discourses, representations, and ideologies, they also continue to affirm the role and force of the artistic imagination in troubling and undercutting these legacies and in opening up new conceptual horizons for inhabiting the traces of the past in the present.

This investigation into the poetics and politics of mnemonic cultures is certainly also inflected by my own cultural background as a scholar of American Studies from Germany. Growing up with the injunction never to forget the past, I have been greatly intrigued by how this mandate was interpreted differently on both sides of the wall during the Cold War as well as by how it has received fresh impulses with the fall of the Berlin Wall in 1989. In particular, I am struck by how my generation, often referred to as *Enkelgeneration* (the grandchildren's generation), influenced by the sweeping political changes that marked the final decade of the twentieth century, has begun to pose very different questions about the past than my parents and grandparents. This is not to say that I seek to draw a parallel between the memory of World War II and the Holocaust and the memory of New World Slavery; this is decidedly not the aim of this book. While I am mindful of my background as a German-born scholar of American Studies, my interest in the evolution of mnemonic and historiographic practices, particularly those addressing traumatic pasts, applies here exclusively to the analysis of developments in African American memory culture at the turn of the millennium. The playful, provocative works of Suzan-Lori Parks and Kara Walker serve as case studies for this investigation.

FICTIONS OF HISTORY AND HISTORIOPOETIC PERFORMANCES OF THE PAST

"I got her this ring today. Diamond. Well, diamondesque, but it looks just as good as the real thing" (10), a character named Booth declares in Suzan-Lori Parks's Pulitzer Prize–winning play *Topdog/Underdog* (2001). The smooth transition from the real to the fake and back again, the blurring of critical differences between the two ontological entities is indicative not only of this particular character's performative handling of a rather oppressive reality but more generally of Parks's (as well as Walker's) performances of history, particularly histories of the traumatic past of transatlantic slavery and its various material, affective, and representational legacies. *Topdog/Underdog* features two African American brothers, provocatively named Lincoln and Booth, who attempt to gain economic success and social status through various forms of performance and conmanship. Most prominent is the three-card monte hustle, which the two brothers consider their ticket to success. In addition, there is Lincoln's job at a penny arcade as a white-face impersonator of his presidential namesake, specializing in the spectacle of the president's assassination. And there is Booth's expertise in shoplifting. Booth's hustling skills also stand him in good stead when he attempts to brighten up the brothers' rather bleak housing situation by repurposing two plain milk crates as various pieces of missing furniture and when he seeks to revive a worn-out romance with the aforementioned "diamondesque" ring. Booth believes that when presented from the right angle, the fake / the make-believe is "just as good as the real thing" (10). What is more, because the proper performance of the fake will have a concrete effect in the world, it will become real. As Booth explains with regard to the salutary effects of wearing a stolen suit in times of economic depression and moral dejection, "just wear it around. Itll make you feel good and when you feel good yll meet someone nice" (30). It is in this spirit that the two brothers also regularly flip through their "raggedy family photo album" (13) in an attempt to reimagine a strenuous past marked by the trauma of parental abandonment as memories of happy childhood days. To the brothers, it is entirely irrelevant whether these memories are actual or imagined. What matters is that these fake/imagined memories enable them to inhabit usable post-traumatic identities in the present.

In light of the protagonists' evocative historical names, Lincoln and Booth, the play invites an allegorical reading as a reflection on the contemporary economic and psychological legacies of slavery in the United States. The insistence on the possibility of breaking with an oppressive past in the playful manipulation of the boundary between fact and fiction, history and (hi)stories also proves to be an effective strategy for a number of other characters in Parks's oeuvre. Many of her protagonists are poised performers, such as Venus in *Venus* (1996) and Billy Bead in *Getting Mother's Body* (2003); inspired impersonators and skillful storytellers, such as the Foundling Father and Brazil in *The America Play* (1994); or resolute historiographers, such as Aretha Saxon in *Imperceptible Mutabilities in the Third Kingdom* (1989)—all of them determined to refigure through verbal, visual, and bodily performances the official historical record to their own ends, to generate useable versions of the past.[1]

Kara Walker's artworks, especially her controversial silhouettes of the antebellum plantation South, present us, in the words of the artist, with a "purposeful misreading of historical texts."[2] Her momentous debut installation, *Gone: An Historical Romance of a Civil War as It Occurred b'tween the Dusky Thighs of One Young Negress and Her Heart* (1994), challenges conventional readings of history in all sorts of ways (fig. 1). Liberally drawing on mass-cultural genres, such as the historical

FIGURE 1. Kara Walker. 1994. *Gone: An Historical Romance of a Civil War as it Occurred b'tween the Dusky Thighs of One Young Negress and Her Heart.* Cut paper on wall. Installation dimensions variable; approx. 13 × 50 ft. (4 × 15.2 m). © Kara Walker, courtesy of Sikkema Jenkins & Co., New York. Installation view: *My Complement, My Enemy, My Oppressor, My Love,* Hammer Museum, Los Angeles, CA, 2008. Photo: Joshua White.

romance—Margaret Mitchell's best-selling novel *Gone with the Wind* (1936) and David O. Selznick's Academy award–winning film version of the same title (1939)—as well as on sentimental novels, Harlequin romances, and pornographic fiction, Walker contests the very notion of what constitutes the "historical" when approaching the past and its legacies. Referring to her imaginative silhouette installations, such as *Gone* or *The End of Uncle Tom and The Grand Allegorical Tableau of Eva in Heaven* (1995), as "pictorial histories" or "historical paintings,"[3] the artist provocatively puts fictional works such as Mitchell's and Stowe's on par with scholarly historiographies of slavery. In doing so, Walker not only mocks readers' faith in the historical truthfulness of fictional accounts like Stowe's or Mitchell's, but also underlines that, precisely because of their immense popularity and mass-cultural appeal, these works have significantly shaped late twentieth-century knowledge of slavery.[4] On this score then, Walker's made-up pictorial histories render a portrait of the various ways in which romanticized and mythologized representations of the American past continue to influence the popular historical imagination. It is in this sense that the artist considers *Gone with the Wind* as well as her own *Gone* "historical texts."

Having established the profound entanglement of fact and fiction in our understanding of history, Walker then sets out to "misread" both. Her works are replete with recognizable references to well-known figures, motifs, narrative themes, and received iconographies of plantation slavery: full moons, live oaks, and Spanish moss, ardent cavaliers and hoopskirted damsels, faithful retainers and mischievous children. Notably, these well-known clichés of history are presented somewhat out of focus, so that the familiar (*das Heimliche*) haunts us as the uncanny (*das Unheimliche*) of our own imagination. In *Gone* the amorous encounter between the Southern ingénue and her knight-errant appears on closer inspection to be a ménage à trois with a second pair of legs appearing from under the belle's skirt, most likely belonging to a slave.[5] While the hands and chests of the couple touch, their lips, expectantly parted for a kiss, do not. White heteronormative desire is deferred, on the one hand, to the belle's hoopskirted shenanigans and, on the other hand, via the gallant's sword aggressively pointing to a Black girl's behind to the violent assertion of the master's sexual power over enslaved women. The girl, however, seems quite oblivious to such advances, preoccupied instead with wringing a swan's neck. The swan itself is a keen reminder of mythologies of white patriarchal omnipotence as, for instance, rendered in the story of Leda's rape by Zeus in the body of the swan.[6] The little girl seems to make quick work of such powerful representational legacies. She offers up the dead bird to a Black woman riding the waters of an adjacent lake in boatlike fashion (possibly a reference to the Middle Passage) with what appears to be a bust of a founding father (possibly George Washington) in tow. Further on in this visual narrative, a replica of the bust is spit out by an older Black woman wielding a broom while she is sexually abused by another white cavalier figure (or perhaps the same?) in tailcoat as nearby a Black girl drops babies from between her legs. Meanwhile, center stage, we behold the silhouette of a third little Black girl fellating a little white boy, who yearningly reaches up to a young Black boy floating up into the air thanks to his ballooning phallus—another provocative allusion to entrenched mythologies of Blackness.

Each vignette in this wild carnivalesque silhouette installation thus indexes entrenched stereotypical figures, tropes, images, and mythological narratives of Blackness and whiteness embedded in mass-cultural historiographies of slavery. But ultimately the sequence of vignettes also refuses full legibility, throwing viewers back on their own devices, making them wonder what exactly it is they imagine seeing and for what reasons. In the end, Walker's "pictorial histories" of slavery seem to tell us more about our contemporary habits of reading history than about the past itself. Walker herself concedes that she persistently flounders in her "sincere attempt" to render the facts of history when encountering the various fictions articulating, shaping, and distorting them. She comments, "I am too aware of my overzealous imagination interfering in the basic facts of history, so in a way my work is about the sincere attempt to write *Incidents in the Life of a Slave Girl* and winding up with *Mandingo* instead" (quoted in Armstrong 1997, 107). In "coupling the real and the imagined" in her art (quoted in Lott 2000, 70), Walker aims to get at just this "collusion of fact and fiction" (quoted in Armstrong 1997, 107) that any access to history entails—including her own. The "offspring" of this collusion, so she contends, is vivaciously alive, is *real* in the sense of impacting perceptions and behaviors in the present, and is thus making history. Similar to Parks, she understands her role as artist-historian as intervening in entrenched collusions of fact and fiction to generate new kinds of offspring—new narratives and images of history that open up the field of possibilities for Black subject positions in past and present.

This introductory chapter aims to bring Walker's and Parks's performative collusions of fact and fiction into critical focus from a theoretical and contextual angle. In a first step, I contend that their imaginative engagement with the history of slavery differs significantly from that of other artists, especially those immediately preceding them—the authors of verbal and visual neo–slave narratives of the 1970s and 1980s. I trace this difference with regard to the kind and degree of imagination involved as well as with regard to a changing political interest in the past, focusing in particular on shifting notions of veracity, representation, and commitment. In a second step, I introduce the concept of "historiopoiesis" as a category of analysis for understanding the particularities of Parks's and Walker's creative processes. In contrast to historio-*graphy*, the term historio-*poiesis* is meant to draw critical attention to the various formal or, as I prefer to call them in this study for reasons delineated below, *poetic* devices at work in narrations of the past (e.g., narrative structuring, troping, framing, genre conventions, and intertextuality) and thus to the essentially constructed and mediated nature of knowledges of the past. Furthermore, it is to emphasize the performative *gestus* inherent in the work of Parks, Walker, and other artists of the time. As self-aware text and image makers, they claim the right to intervene in established processes of signification through formal revisions and to generate new significations of the past. In short, with the term "historiopoiesis" I wish to give expression to the *making* (poiesis) *of history through poetic means*. In a last step, I establish Parks's and Walker's historiopoetic work on the past as representative of a wider, generational ethos that begins to gain contours around the turn of the millennium and that has been variously dubbed "post-soul" or "post-black." This chapter then provides the basic theoretical frame and historicization for the discussions of concrete poetic interventions in the subsequent chapters.

IMAGINATIVE ARCHAEOLOGIES ON
A POSTMEMORY CONTINUUM

The collusion of fact and fiction, the purposeful interplay of established knowledges and the imagination in accessing and assessing the archive, is not new; in fact, it is quite typical for any postmemory approach (if not any mnemonic/historiographic approach) to the past. As Marianne Hirsch explains, forms of traumatic memory that are passed on inter- and transgenerationally well beyond any living recollection of the original experience are "mediated not by recall but by *imaginative investment, projection, and creation*" (2012, 5; emphasis added). Although originally developed in the context of Holocaust studies with regard to how the children of trauma survivors deal with their parents' past, Hirsch's concept of postmemory can be usefully extended to artistic productions in other historical contexts in which traumatic experience is passed on between and across generations, particularly when there is no longer a tangible proximity to the traumatic event—as is the case with the memories of slavery that have emerged continuously in verbal and visual form from the late 1960s onward.

Indeed, in the second half of the twentieth century, we witness what Paul Gilroy calls a "decisive turn to history" in African American literature (1993, 222). In the visual arts, scholars such as Huey Copeland and Krista Thompson (2011) have likewise pointed to the emergence of a great number of artworks dealing with transatlantic slavery in the same period.[7] Yet the continuing stream of cultural productions on slavery is far from homogeneous, comprising a wide spectrum of postmemory engagements with the past. Some striking differences in poetics and politics become apparent when the canon of works produced in the 1970s and 1980s—for instance, Ernest Gaines's novel *The Autobiography of Miss Jane Pittman* (1971), Faith Ringgold's *Slave Rape Series* fabrics (1972–73), and Alex Haley's TV series *Roots* (1977)—is compared to later works, such as Walker's provocative silhouette installations and sculptures and Suzan-Lori Parks's metatheatrical plays; Cheryl Dunye's 1996 mockumentary *The Watermelon Woman*; Branden Jacobs-Jenkins's 2014 metadrama *An Octoroon*; Paul Beatty's 2015 satirical novel *The Sellout*; and visual artist Titus Kaphar's playful Signifyin(g) on received images in, for example, *The Myth of Benevolence* (2014).

My inquiry into the shifts of emphases in artists' approaches to the history of slavery begins from the vantage point of literary studies because the field has traditionally asked pertinent questions about the nature and function of narrative structuring.[8] If history is what we know about the past, then this knowledge is always rendered in some form of narrative that unfolds events both in a temporal and causal sequence— whether in words, images, bodily performances, or a combination of these. Hence, due to their structural affinity with scholarly modes of writing history (historiography), narrative-based artistic reflections on slavery are particularly interesting with regard to changing emphases in conveying knowledges of the past. Literary studies can offer a set of useful tools for reading not only literary but also visual narratives of history.[9] It also points us to the inherent collusion of fact and fiction in any approach to history, including the discipline of history itself. As historians Reinhart Koselleck (1985) and Hayden White (1990) have compellingly shown, narrative structuring along recognizable story lines ("emplotment," as White calls it) is essential to turning an occurrence (*Begebenheit*) into a historical event (*Ereignis*) and a list of factual statements into a historical discourse.[10] History is in this regard intrinsically connected to the creative and persuasive arts (poetics and rhetoric in the Aristotelian sense). Paul Ricoeur speaks of the "mutual belonging" of history and literature (1981, 274), a notion that Koselleck underscores in his concept of the *Fiktion des Faktischen* ("fiction of facticity"): "Every event historically established and presented lives on the fiction of facticity; reality itself is past and gone" (2004, 111).[11] Koselleck hastens to add that this does not mean that scholarly historiography becomes arbitrary; it remains bound to the principal of verifiability by sources. But the source itself does not stipulate what can be said about it. Hence, he concludes, while historians remain beholden to the traces of the past, they also share in the function of the storyteller when they begin to interpret these traces on the basis of narrative structuring.[12]

By the same token then, verbal, visual, or bodily storytellers who rework the traces of the past also partake through their trade in the production of forms of historiography. These artistic historiographic productions tend to be more attuned to the noncanonical traces of the past than scholarly narratives—that is, they respond to the sounds, gestures, and movements of the past, record its commonplace (rather than exceptional) figures, quotidian spaces, and unremarkable objects, as well as the evanescent hints of felt experience. Diana Taylor differentiates on this score between the tangible and "supposedly enduring materials (i.e., texts, documents, building, bones)" of the archive and the more ephemeral forms of "embodied practice/knowledge" offered up by the repertoire (2003, 19). Due to the intangible nature of the latter, scholarship has tended to draw a line between the study of memory and that of history. Pierre Nora (1989), for instance, would insist that the unorthodox traces of the past contained in what Taylor calls "the repertoire" belong to the realm of a highly selective, affective, and mutable memory, which needs to be distinguished from the realm of the disinterested and scientific study of history. Yet, as Nora himself acknowledges with his influential concept of *"lieu de mémoire,"* these two modes of reconstructing the past cannot always be neatly separated; they frequently interact with each other in productive ways.[13] Precisely because "sites of memory" can take on concrete "material, symbolic, and functional" meanings (Nora 1989, 19), they can become historical in an objective and disinterested sense. In their pioneering study, *History and Memory in African-American Culture* (1994), Geneviève Fabre and Robert O'Meally assert that "more than ever, we saw novels, poems, slave narratives, autobiographies, and oral testimonies as crucial parts of the historical record" (9).[14] At the same time, Astrid Erll reminds us that the discipline of history is, after all, but "*one* mode of cultural remembering" operating alongside other modes, such as religion, myth, and literature (2011, 45). Regardless of whether we consider the realm of memory as historical or the discipline of history as a form of cultural/institutional memory, by now scholarship has effectively collapsed this binary opposition, which tended to value one disciplinary approach over another. What remains is a transdisciplinary interest in how and to what effect knowledges of the past are constructed, transferred, mediated, and refigured—whether through verbal, visual, or embodied practices. On this score, I see cultural productions, such as Walker's and Parks's, not simply as objects of inquiry but also as forms of epistemological practice. In short then, this study focuses on narrative-based productions and investigations of knowledges of the past in the literary, performing, and visual arts that draw on archive and repertoire alike and that also, if need be, freely invent figures, events, and stories to capture precisely those absences and possibilities that have not yet been articulated by the historical record and that might not even be articulable by traditional methods of research but that nonetheless are likely and plausible according to our accumulated knowledges of historical circumstances.[15]

To return to the matter of shifts in emphasis on the spectrum of imaginative historiographies of transatlantic slavery between the classical period of the neo–slave narratives of the 1970s and 1980s and turn-of-the-millennium narratives of slavery, the following discussion theorizes and contextualizes a significant shift through the lens of the metaphor of archaeology, which features prominently in the writing of Toni Morrison, whose novel *Beloved* (1987) is exemplary for this classical period, as well as in the works of Parks and Walker. In a well-known essay entitled "The Site of Memory," culled from a public lecture delivered around the time of publishing *Beloved*, Morrison describes her job as an artist in approaching the experience of slavery as "find[ing] and expos[ing] a truth about the interior life of a people who didn't write it (which doesn't mean that they didn't have it)" (1998, 193). To do so, she intends "to rip that veil drawn over 'proceedings too terrible to relate'" (191) and "to fill in the blanks that the slave narratives left" (193–94). She importantly adds that memories and recollections won't suffice in gaining "access to the unwritten interior life of these people. Only the act of the imagination can help me" (192). On this score, she understands her writing as a sort of "literary archaeology": "On the basis of some information and a little bit of guess-work you journey to a site to see what remains were left behind and to reconstruct the world that these remains imply. What makes it fiction is the nature of the imaginative act: my reliance on the image—on the remains—in addition to recollection to yield up a kind of a truth" (192). What is striking in this quote and elsewhere in her essay is that Morrison, while keenly aware of the role of the imagination ("a little bit of guess-work") in reconstructing past experience ("the world that these remains imply"), insists that it is the imagination that will allow her to recuperate "a kind of a truth" of the remains of the past. This truth claim is essential to how she approaches the past and how she sees her ethical relationship as an artist to the historical material at hand. To Morrison, the "crucial distinction . . . is not between fact and fiction but between fact and truth" (193). In other words, fiction allows her to reveal a truth about her subject that is not available through a purely factual approach. At the same time, she insists on remaining "deadly serious about fidelity to the milieus out of which I write and in which my ancestors actually lived" (192). She also vehemently rejects the labels of fantastic literature and magical realism for her writing: "I am not comfortable with these labels. I consider that my single gravest responsibility (in spite of that magic) is *not to lie*" (193; emphasis added).

I see Morrison's insistence on fidelity to the milieu of her ancestors and her faith in the "revelation of a kind of a truth" about the past through fiction as exemplary for her generation's imaginative approach to the history of slavery. Many of her peers are committed to the work of reconstructing and reclaiming the past through imaginative verbal and visual narratives. To be sure, there are variations in authors' understanding of "truthfulness"—ranging from realist, historical novels to the more fantastic fictions of slavery. But what they share is a sense of "truth" as something to be "found," "exposed," or "revealed" rather than something actively constructed and performed. Margaret Walker, author of *Jubilee* (1966), for instance, sees her role as that of a historian, insisting that "people will learn about a time and place through a historical novel" (quoted in Rowell 2002, 23). More than that, in rendering the oral memories of her grandmother, Walker aims "to set the record straight where Black people are concerned in terms of the Civil War, of slavery, segregation and Reconstruction" (23). Ernest Gaines's

The Autobiography of Miss Jane Pittman (1971), an entirely fictional account, similarly asserts the *gestus* of correcting the official historical record. The narrator, a history teacher, explains his desire for an interview from Jane Pittman: "I teach history.... I'm sure her life's story can help me explain things to my students." When a neighbor challenges him, "What's wrong with the books you already got?" he responds, "Miss Jane is not in them" (2009, vii). In a similar vein, Sherley Anne Williams acknowledges that while her novel *Dessa Rose* (1986) is inspired by two actual historical events (a pregnant Black woman helping to lead a slave rebellion in 1829 in Kentucky and a white woman in North Carolina in 1830 giving refuge to fugitive slaves), it "is fiction; all the characters, even the country they traveled through, while based on fact, are inventions" (Williams 1999, 6). Similar to Morrison, however, she adds, "what is here is *as true as if* I myself have lived it. Maybe it is only a metaphor, but I now own a summer in the 19th century" (6; emphasis added). In short, a pervasive sense of providing a more truthful account of slavery by correcting the dominant record, by supplementing it with untold stories, and by claiming authorship over historiography underlies many of the narratives of slavery written from the late 1960s to the 1980s.

Claims of veracity also play a substantial role in what Madhu Dubey calls "speculative fictions of slavery," a subgenre of the neo–slave narratives that "flouts the dictates of realism" (2010, 780). Embracing modes of fantastic literature, science fiction, and metafiction, writers such as Octavia Butler, David Bradley, and Toni Morrison clearly break with realist modes of storytelling. Dubey notes that these speculative fictions of slavery began to appear in the 1970s, when "the task of historical recovery seemed relatively far along" (783) and the historical archive was expanding with material "from below," such as fugitive slave narratives and survivor testimonies.[16] At this point, neo–slave narratives became free to take a "purposefully antihistorical approach to the past" (781), blurring the boundaries between past and present with the help of time-bending devices: anachronisms, time travel, ghostly hauntings, and, in Morrison's case, "rememory." Dubey explains, "Refusing to regard the past of slavery as history [i.e., as something that has passed], speculative novels suggest that the truth of this past is *more fully grasped* by way of an antirealist literary imagination that can fluidly cross temporal boundaries and affectively immerse readers into the world of slavery" (785; emphasis added). These speculative narratives, despite their obvious distrust of conventional academic approaches to history and their suspicion of "historiographic authority" (784), nonetheless affirm a faith in the "truth of this past." The truth, which is obfuscated, effaced, or marginalized in traditional historiographies, can be made available ("more fully grasped") through alternative modes of knowing, such as by imagining the visceral, affective, and bodily experience of slavery. In Octavia Butler's *Kindred* (1979), for example, it is only when the time-travelling protagonist Dana burns a twentieth-century history book that she becomes fully immersed in the experience of her antebellum ancestors, experiencing the emotional, psychological, and physical impact of slavery. In *The Chaneysville Incident* (1981), David Bradley similarly describes how the autodiegetic narrator John Washington, a professional historian who is investigating his father's death, needs to give up on his scholarly training in order to see the "truth" of the facts he had accumulated: "I had everything I needed, knowledge and time and even, by then, a measure of skill—I could follow a fact through shifts and twists of history, do it and love it. But I could not imagine. And if you cannot imagine, *you can discover only cold facts; you will never know the truth*" (1990, 146–47; emphasis added).

Despite the obvious difference between a corrective, revisionist approach to history (e.g., Walker, Gaines, and Williams) and an emphasis on nonhistorical modes of knowing the past (e.g., Butler, Morrison, and Bradley), both the realist narratives of slavery and the more speculative fictions of slavery assert a basic faith in the veracity of the experiences they imagine. The past is "real" and its essential truth can be located and revealed through various narrative strategies. This also applies to narratives influenced by postmodern theories of representation. As Carolyn Rody maintains, "though touched by the prevailing postmodern irony toward questions of truth and representation, fiction and history," contemporary novels of slavery continue to assume the "burden of communicating an authentic truth" about slavery (2001, 21).[17] In *Remembering the Past in Contemporary African American Fiction*, a study of such diverse authors as Sherley Anne Williams, Ernest Gaines, Toni Morrison, David Bradley, Charles Johnson, and Gloria Naylor, Keith Byerman fittingly sums up the neo–slave narratives' abiding investment in claims of truth and recuperability:

African American writers are more likely to demonstrate a belief in history as accessible, even if they agree on little else. They are less likely than white writers to be ironic, parodic, or overtly self-reflexive. The past is very real, though its patterns are not necessarily easily discernible. What they give special attention to is the falsity of previous descriptions of black experience, but they tend to assume that it is possible to provide a more accurate account. While they would not disagree with [Linda] Hutcheon's contention that "both history and fiction are discourses," they seek out or create discursive elements that have been suppressed or ignored (folk material, journals, letters, newspaper stories) that can open up and give voice to that which has been denied or silenced. They are more likely than white writers to privilege these texts as valid ways of knowing the past rather than as simply more texts to add to the mix. (2005, 10–11)

Many of the narratives of slavery that began to emerge in the late 1980s and early 1990s lack this interest in the knowability of the past—whether it is of a historical or ahistorical kind—and its attendant claims to authenticity and veracity. "I'm just going to say this right now so we can get it over with," playwright Branden Jacobs-Jenkins bluntly states in his 2014 play *An Octoroon*. "I don't know what a real slave sounds like. And neither do you" (2015, 17). With this he offers an apt contemporary rejoinder to an observation the fugitive William Wells Brown articulated in 1847 to his readers and audiences on the abolitionist circuit: "I may try to represent to you Slavery as it is; another may follow me and represent the condition of the Slave; we may all represent it as we think it is; and yet we shall all fail to represent the real condition of the Slave. . . . Slavery has never been represented; Slavery can never be represented" (W. W. Brown 2006, 4). Parks and Walker would agree. Their works do not attempt to render what slavery was like or felt like. Rather, when it comes to representing the past, their artworks and writings are marked by a pronounced degree of self-awareness and reflectivity with regard to the formal processes and techniques as well as the materiality and mediality at work. They are less concerned with the facts of the past than with the ways that these facts have been articulated, mediated, and repeatedly reiterated in word, image, and performance—to the point that these representations present us with a new order of facticity.

In her essay "Possession" (1995), Parks describes her method, not unlike Toni Morrison, in terms of archaeology:

A play is a blueprint of an event: a way of creating and rewriting history through the medium of literature. Since history is a recorded or remembered event, theatre, for me, is the perfect place to "make" history—that is, because so much of African-American history has been unrecorded, dismembered, washed out, one of my tasks as a playwright is to—through literature and the special strange relationship between theatre and real-life—locate the ancestral burial ground, dig for bones, find bones, hear the bones sing, write it down. (1995f, 4)

Note the striking parallels but also the differences between Morrison's and Parks's archaeology. Like Morrison, Parks seeks to locate the burial ground, excavate its remains, and record the world that these remains imply. Also like Morrison, she aims to intervene in the established historical record, to participate in the writing of history.[18] In marked contrast to Morrison, however, Parks attaches no truth claims to her archaeology. While she purports to record the songs of the "bones" she recovers, her oeuvre makes clear that she is not concerned with the authenticity of these bones or songs.

While Parks's works are replete with diggers—digging, both literally and figuratively, for corpses, treasures, memories—some of the "bones" they retrieve are real; others decidedly not. In *The America Play* (1994), a figure called Brazil, a gravedigger by profession, exhumes an actual bone of George Washington ("right pointer") alongside the president's wooden teeth (85). In *Topdog/Underdog* (2001), the brothers Lincoln and Booth dig up both real and imagined memories of their childhood past. And in the novel *Getting Mother's Body* (2003), it is the very undecidability of the question whether the fabled buried family treasure is "real" or "fake" that carries the plot. But regardless of their status as "real" or "fake," Parks's diggers indiscriminately listen to the "songs" of all the artifacts, memories, and desires they unearth. Moreover, more so than Morrison, Parks underlines the performative nature of these songs, their poetic and theatrical capacity to "make up history" (quoted in Pearce 1994, 26). I will address the performative aspects of this concept of history below; for now, I want to highlight another characteristic of Parks's archaeology.

In her dramatic and prose writing, Parks stresses that the very act of "locating the burial ground" and "digging for bones" cannot be separated from a host of expectations and projections brought to bear on them; neither an actual nor a figurative archaeology constitutes a disinterested practice. Depending on the particular method of excavation, one may locate quite different "facts on the ground." As contemporary theories of archaeology, such as Nadia Abu El-Haj's *Facts on the Ground* (2001), underline, the material practice of digging is always already embedded in a particular set of ideologies and narratives that one brings to bear on one's endeavor. Parks emphasizes this point in *The America Play*, in which, thanks to a rather performative method of digging and an expanded notion of what constitutes an artifact, the protagonist Brazil succeeds in retrieving from what Parks terms "The Great Hole of History" canonical artifacts, such as "peace pacts, . . . bills of sale, treaties" (1995a, 186) as well as objects typically overlooked, discarded, or simply considered unlikely, such as medals "for cookin and cleanin. For bowin and scrapin" (186). Brazil's archaeology—and, by allegorical extension, Parks's archaeology—evinces remarkably little concern for questions of authenticity or veracity, retrieving alongside a few genuine artifacts a plethora of "faux-historical knickknacks" (169), ranging from wooden teeth and sculptural reproductions (a bust of Lincoln) to hearsay and made-up stories. Hence, while Parks's plays might take digs at historical figures such as Abraham Lincoln (*The America Play*, *Topdog/Underdog*) and Sara Baartman (*Venus*) or historical events such as the Civil War (*Father Comes Home from the Wars*, 2014), at stake in these imaginative diggings is not the excavation or revelation of some kind of truth about this past "as it really was" but rather the excavation of the various legacies of its articulations and mediations. This is powerfully illustrated, for instance, in the playwright's rendition of Lincoln and Booth's ongoing quarrel with the Lincoln myth in *Topdog/Underdog* as well as in her theatrical exhumation of the "symbolic Venus" (Ford 2010, 99) rather than the actual Baartman in the play *Venus*.

Kara Walker similarly asserts her archaeological interest in "dig[ging] through the remains of historical stuff," but with the pronounced aim of "piec[ing] it all together *incorrectly*" (quoted in Boerma

2002, 168; emphasis added). In an interview with Silke Boerma, conducted on the occasion of the 2002 exhibition *For the Benefit of All the Races of Mankind: An Exhibition of Artifacts, Remnants, and Effluvia EXCAVATED from the Black Heart of the Negress* at the Kunstverein Hannover in Germany, Walker talks at length about what archaeology means to her as an artist. She starts by situating her work within a genealogy of creative archaeologies by Black women. Her primary point of reference is Alice Walker's "digging through the weeds" (165) of an overgrown cemetery at Fort Pierce, Florida, for the remains of Zora Neale Hurston's unmarked grave.[19] But she also stresses that she considers this particular model of restorative and affirmative digging, which she associates with the Black Arts movement of the 1960s and 1970s, as restrictive. Walker not only rejects this movement's injunction to produce socially progressive artworks for the Black community, she radically redefines the purpose of digging: "Normally one thinks of excavations as scientific events in which cultures are 'rediscovered' in the form of objects dug up at a specific site. But obviously the site I'm referring to is psychological, emotional, and physical" (165). The verb "excavate" resonates for her in terms of a "hollowed-out body" as well as "a body opened up"—particularly, a Black female body such as that of Sara Baartman, aka the "Hottentot Venus"—where "all that remains are projected fantasies" (165). Walker's playful subtitle, *An Exhibition of Artifacts, Remnants, and Effluvia EXCAVATED from the Black Heart of the Negress*, underlines the extent to which she (along with her fictional alter ego, "the Negress"), as artist-archaeologist, is interested in unearthing precisely the invisible, unsavory, frequently offensive, and hard-to-grasp emanations that accompany the remains of the past. Walker explains, "I believe I have a good, maybe an average working knowledge of African-American history, leaders, icons, events, a few dates, a couple of ideological perspectives, narratives etc. But what I'm interested in as far as art goes, is how contemporary value and individual neurosis project themselves into the blank spaces between the fact of (for instance) slavery's influence on the American system, and the power of its influence over the American imagination" (168–69). Accordingly, Walker, like Parks, targets in her work the various mythological, representational, and affective shadows that slavery continues to cast on the contemporary imagination. "It's silhouetting a fiction, the fiction of history; the fiction that has come out of history," she explains elsewhere (quoted in Saltz 1996, 82). And she makes it quite clear that she finds it difficult to ascertain "what truth is amid so much dreaming. And for that matter, how effective can art be at telling the truth, it's not really designed for it" (quoted in Boerma 2002, 169).

In short then, in sharp contrast to the artists of the 1970s to 1980s, the artists of the 1990s and 2000s, such as Kara Walker and Suzan-Lori Parks (and we might add Branden Jacobs-Jenkins, Cheryl Dunye, Glenn Ligon, and many others here), do not attempt to know or own the past, to tell it "as it really was" or to make it "yield up" a hidden truth. Rather, starting from the poststructuralist premise that the past can be known only "through its textual traces" (Hutcheon 2002, 75), they are invested in excavating, interrogating, and playfully engaging discursive traces of the past—the various narratives, verbal and visual tropes, as well as *lieux de mémoire*—that have been used by dominant, counterhegemonic, and popular imaginations alike to render the facts of slavery. In this regard, they also redirect our interest from questions of history (an interest in what we believe to constitute the past) to questions of historiography: an interest in *how* and *to what effect* these knowledges and imaginations of the past have been produced, articulated, and mediated in word, image, and embodied behavior.

SHIFTING ATTITUDES TOWARD THE PAST

The distinctive shift in the kind and purpose of imaginative investments in the past that we find articulated in the works of Parks, Walker, and others also signals a pronounced shift in the artists' ethical and political attitudes toward it. Stephen Best posits Morrison's *Beloved* as the text that most prominently anchors what he calls "the melancholic turn" (2012, 456) in late twentieth-century African American studies scholarship. Morrison's Nobel Prize in Literature in 1993, Best argues, "positioned *Beloved* to shape the way a generation of scholars conceived of its ethical relationship to the past" (459). He describes this relationship as being marked by "the commitment to remain 'faithful to the lost object'" (460) and the holding on to the narratives of loss that have come to constitute the history of the Black Atlantic. In Sethe's concept of "rememory," Morrison provides a powerful allegorical expression for what Best terms a "melancholic historicism" (460). As Sethe articulates it, rememory is a traumatic memory that will never go away but will always be there "waiting for you" (Morrison 1987, 36). Although Best coined the concept of a "melancholic historicism" in reference to a body of scholarship that arose in response to the *Beloved* moment," it can be usefully extended to describe a body of cultural productions leading up to and finding paradigmatic expression in Morrison's novel *Beloved*. As indicated earlier in this chapter, a great number of works of the 1970s and 1980s tend to hail their readers and beholders as witnesses to the losses sustained during slavery, to draw them into an affective bond with the past, and to point up how the time of slavery is essentially coeval with the present.[20]

My argument here is above all concerned with Best's reflections on possibilities for articulating and inhabiting a different relationship to the past, one less determined by affect and melancholia; one that, as the programmatic title of his essay suggests, "fails to make the past present."[21] In fact, he sees Morrison herself opening the door to such a possibility with her 2008 novel *A Mercy*. Here, the slave past is no longer depicted as a compulsory haunting, as an obsessive return as in *Beloved*, but "as that which falls away—a separateness resistant to being either held or read in melancholic terms" (Best 2012, 466). In contrast to *Beloved*, *A Mercy* does not hail us as witnesses but, as Best writes, "abandons us to a more baffled, cut-off, foreclosed position with regard to the slave past.... The past is here to be appreciated as a falling away—slavery to be appreciated in the failure to make its racial legacy present" (472, 474). Best reads *A Mercy* as the "undoing of the affective history project" (466) that has undergirded *Beloved*—and, so I would add, the majority of the neo-slave narratives of the 1970s and 1980s. He sees this assertion of a disjuncture between the history of subjection and contemporary notions of belonging as the necessary condition for beginning to imagine a different kind of ethical relation to the past, one that no longer hinges "on an assumed continuity between the past and our present and on the implicit consequence that to study that past is somehow to intervene in it" (454), one that enables a movement from melancholia to mourning, from an affective attachment to the past to an appreciation of its distinctiveness from the present.

Writing the "epitaph to the *Beloved* moment" (465), Best seeks to usher in a new body of scholarship. I suggest that works of Black cultural production began to undertake this desired shift toward a nonmelancholic engagement with the past much earlier, well before the 2008 publication of *A Mercy*. The shift is already evident in a great number of works of the 1990s, even the late 1980s: George Woolfe's play *The Colored Museum* (1986), Glenn Ligon's installation *To Disembark* (1993), and Cheryl Dunye's film *The Watermelon Woman* (1996). In fact, I suggest that Parks's plays and Walker's silhouettes of the 1990s anticipate the very paradigm shift that Best identifies in Morrison's *A Mercy*.[22]

In her 2016 essay, "The Inside-Turned-Out Architecture of the Post-Neo-Slave Narrative," Margo Natalie Crawford begins to describe this shift in aesthetic terms. In a response to Best, she contests his reading of Morrison's 2008 novel as effectively substituting mourning for melancholia, pointing up the comingling of these two modes in the liminal space of the unknown inhabited by the novel's protagonist, Florens. Yet, she also agrees with Best that precisely this antibinary, liminal space in *A Mercy* offers a "space-clearing gesture" (2016, 71) that is conceptually different from the ways that the past was articulated in the neo–slave narratives. Crawford posits this gesture as constitutive of what she terms "post-neo-slave narratives": "If the neo-slave narrative is revisionist history, the *post-neo-slave* narrative is a move from the literary imagination that fills in the gaps (what historians cannot know) to the refusal to fill in the gaps but to linger in the unknown. If the neo-slave narrative builds on the form of nineteenth-century slave narratives, the post-neo-slave narrative may be the narratives that stop building *on* and begin to improvise more fully in what *A Mercy* refers to as 'ad hoc territory'" (71). Like Best, Crawford sees the post-neo-slave narrative as "hail[ing] a future that does not have to be the past" (70). When the traumatized subjects in these narratives hold on to historical trauma, it is "to *repossess* the history that *possesses* them" (70). The central metaphor is no longer the haunting of rememory (as in *Beloved*) but the various spaces and architectures of the unknown that contain the "not yet formulated possibilities of the future" (81).[23] In this regard then, the post-neo-slave narratives function not so much as memorials to the past (as do the slave narratives and neo–slave narratives) but as an "antimemorial experimental form" (74) in which the history and legacies of transatlantic slavery can be read anew, against received epistemologies and pedagogies. Although with the term "post-neo-slave narrative" Crawford seeks to highlight a crucial conceptual rather than chronological difference from the neo–slave narratives, her examples— Morrison's *A Mercy* (2008), E. P. Jones's *The Known World* (2003), and

Monifa Love's *Freedom in the Dismal* (1998)—demonstrate (such early examples as Amiri Baraka's 1964 play *The Slave* notwithstanding) that the tendency to push away from an aesthetics of haunting to an aesthetics "of the not yet formulated possibilities of the future" appears to be much more prominent in the narratives of slavery emerging in the 1990s and 2000s.

In the visual arts, Huey Copeland traces a related "shift in emphasis, if not in kind" in conceptual artworks of the early 1990s from figurative works that seek to memorialize the trauma of slavery to what he calls "a-memorial" art forms (2013, 205). In his study *Bound to Appear* (2013), Copeland identifies a shift "from iterations of the peculiar institution that rest firmly on the plane of the image or give the body a recognizable human form" (14), such as in the works of Edmonia Lewis, Hale Woodruff, and Faith Ringgold, to the radical modes of "antiportraiture" (9) articulated in site-specific installation art by Fred Wilson (*Mining the Museum*, 1992–93), Lorna Simpson (*Five Rooms*, 1991), Glenn Ligon (*To Disembark*, 1993), and Renée Green (*Mise-en-scène: Commemorative Toile*, 1992), in which the human body signifies only in its absence, evoked by the material traces of slavery. "Although there is affect aplenty in these works," Copeland insists, "the primary impact is not of a replaying of the trauma of slavery" (14). Rather, these artworks foreground the structural and discursive coordinates of slavery and implicate the viewer in a complex theatrical situation by taking "the meaning of slavery out of the figure and ma[king] it a function of the viewer's relationship to the world" (17). In the visual arts, we thus encounter a related shift in attitudes toward the past along with a kindred shift in aesthetics.

The works of Kara Walker and Suzan-Lori Parks and other artists of the turn of the millennium share this interest in establishing a nonmelancholic—or at least no longer purely melancholic—relationship to the past. Parks in particular is keen on refiguring African American history from a "hole" to a "whole," even as this attempt does not always prove to be successful. As suggested in my discussion of *Gone*, Walker's carnivalesque silhouettes present slavery, similar to the post-neo-slave narratives that Crawford describes, as a radical antibinary, liminal space in which established modes of reading race and history no longer work, thus obliging "readers to gain a counterliteracy, to learn to read slavery against received epistemologies" (Crawford 2016, 71). Above all, the protagonists in Parks's and Walker's works continuously endeavor to possess what has possessed them, to turn haunting into some kind of ownership of the past—regardless of how provisional, vague, or pragmatic the solutions might be.

The work of artists such as Parks and Walker, unlike that of many of their predecessors, is also radically antimemorial in its orientation. They do not seek to orient the present toward the past but to open up possibilities for the present and future. Their self-aware poetics profoundly undermine any attempts to reify narratives of history, including their own. To be sure, the trauma of slavery and its various legacies continue to matter in the artworks of the turn of the millennium, but through ludic Signifyin(g) on established tropes, iconographies, and narrative conventions, these artists attempt to decenter it from its foundational position for African American identity. At play in these works is the insurgent act of "overthrow[ing]. . . . 'slavery' as *the* privileged text of Afro-American historical movement" (Spillers 1987a, 48),[24] so as to open up a space where Black identities can be performed, perhaps not independent of the trauma narratives of the past, but certainly in a fresh, nondeterministic relationship to them.

HISTORIOPOIESIS: POETICS AND PERFORMATIVES OF HISTORY

The term "historiopoiesis" provides a way to conceptualize Walker's and Parks's highly self-reflective and performative approach to history.[25] While the reference to "poetics" might seem unusual in the field of the performing and visual arts (in the field of literature it is a firmly established term), it can be made productive on a transmedial level for the following reasons. To begin with, in contrast to the more commonly used "aesthetics," which emphasizes processes of perception, "poiesis" emphasizes processes of production. The noun suffix "-poiesis," derived from the Old Greek ποιεῖν (*poieîn*: to make), underscores the various processes of crafting and recrafting, through formal means, discourses—and with that, knowledges—of the past. In conjunction with the word "history," *poieîn* —unlike the verb γράφειν (*gráphein*: to write)—clarifies the active, performative dimension of formal craft in the production of knowledge. Rather than suggesting that knowledge about the past is already in place, waiting to be made legible through various modes of recording, such as writing (graphy),[26] poiesis stresses that this knowledge is actively produced only in the process of signification itself. Variations in signification can thus produce different knowledges of the past.

My use of the term "historiopoiesis" bears an affinity to Hayden White's theory of historical representation, which stresses that stories about the past are always *made* and never just found and which, accordingly, exposes the various rhetorical devices (or in the case of visual or enacted narratives: stylistic devices and embodied behaviors) that typically partake in the making of history. Robert Doran fittingly summarizes White's understanding of historiography as "a poetic notion of history, understood in the twofold sense of *poiesis* as making (artistic creation, emplotment) and the revelation of its own constructedness in formal or generic analysis (poetics, metahistory)" (introduction to White 2010a, xxiv). In addition, so I might add, the shift of emphasis from a reproductive or mimetic notion of historiography to one that foregrounds the active configuration and refiguration of meanings of the past also refocuses our understanding of the word *historía*. In its etymological root, the Greek verb "ιστορειν" (*historein*) means "to inquire" or "to learn/know by inquiry."[27] Understood along the lines of such a reorientation, historiopoiesis, then, foregrounds the poetic processes at work in our diverse verbal and visual inquiries into the past along with the directedness and purposefulness of these inquiries.

A second reason motivates my use of the term "poiesis": Along with bringing into focus the concrete poetics (i.e., formal processes and techniques) at work in verbal, visual, or embodied figurations, mediations, and refigurations of our knowledges of the past, historiopoiesis serves to highlight the pronounced performative *gestus* manifest in the works of Parks and Walker as well as other artists. They emphatically express their faith in the illocutionary force of their art, their intention, to borrow J. L. Austin's phrase, "to do things with words" and images, to accomplish change through poetic intervention.[28] The word "poiesis," in the sense of making / creating / bringing forth, therefore also provides a useful vocabulary for describing the performative force at work in a number of artistic productions of the period. Subsequent chapters will attend to this force in the work of Parks and Walker in detail, but for this more general introduction, Cheryl Dunye's film *The Watermelon Woman* serves as a compelling illustration.

In her 1996 documentary, Dunye renders a moving portrait of Fae Richards, a young, gifted Black lesbian actress consigned by the racist casting policies of the early Hollywood studio system to play the role of subservient side characters, such as slaves and maids. Dunye's highly self-reflective film interlaces Richards's biography with Dunye's own struggle as a fledgling lesbian filmmaker. As "Cheryl" in the film explains, she becomes interested in the woman who in old film footage is identified simply as "The Watermelon Woman" because black women's stories "have never been told." The film focuses on Cheryl's efforts to piece together Fae's story from sparse and eclectic archival material, which she does successfully. Yet, at the very end, as we watch the film's closing credits, we unexpectedly encounter the editorial note: "Sometimes you have to create your own history. The Watermelon Woman is fiction. Cheryl Dunye. 1996." What we took as the filmmaker's faithful effort of enlarging the existing historical record by filling in its blank spots with previously hidden but now successfully recovered archival material suddenly turns out to be a fake, a mockumentary. And yet, as the closing credits admit to the documentary's fictionality, they nonetheless claim historical validity for this imaginative creation: "Sometimes you have to create your own history." Throughout her film, Dunye has humorously mocked the whimsicality of the archive, the arbitrariness of definitions of what constitutes archival evidence. If existing visual and verbal documentation is open to political interpretation, as the film repeatedly underlines, then the artist-historian (Cheryl) is free to stitch it together in such ways as to render an artistic as well as communal genealogy that can adequately represent her in the contemporary moment. At times, this might require a more imaginative, performative approach to the question of archival evidence, such as the inclusion of oral testimonies, faulty memory, gossip, and communal legends.[29]

Dunye's insistence on historiopoetic authority and a more performative understanding of archaeology closely echoes Suzan-Lori Parks's endorsement of the artist's right to use the theater to "make up" history. In an interview with Shelby Jiggetts, Parks explains, "if you looked back into the past or looked up onto a screen, a film screen, or looked into a show, or looked on the shelf in the library, you don't see enough of you. Or even if you do see enough of you, I do think you have the right to put some of you up there by any means necessary. . . . If that means inserting some of you back in the early 1800s, why not? I think it's just as valid as what we are told happened back then" (quoted in Jiggetts 1996, 317). Importantly, for Parks, as well as Dunye, the performative force of their art goes beyond the task of historical recovery, of "filling in the gaps" of mass-cultural and canonical historiographies (those available on screens and library shelves); they see their art as valid ways to generate ("create" / "make up") events and figures that they consider just as "historical." Historical validity is here anchored not in demands of veracity but in plausibility and necessity. Dunye's autodiegetic narrator Cheryl makes up the biography of a struggling Black lesbian artist of the 1930s to produce a queer artistic genealogy that can serve as a platform for her own creative and professional ambitions as an African American filmmaker as well as for her community of lesbian friends. In a similar though more abstract way, Parks creates in *The America Play* in the story of a gravedigger family's quest for history an arresting allegory of the salutary effect of a performative approach to the past. While the father, in his attempt to create a place for himself in the nation's history, gets stuck in the melancholic reenactment of canonical clichés of History with a capital *H* (to borrow Édouard Glissant's phrase), the son, thanks to a rather resourceful and imaginative archaeology, assembles his own idiosyncratic version of history—a history of miscellaneous bits and pieces that can accommodate him as well as his lost father. Parks clearly models her own dramatic archaeologies on the example of Digger Jr. As she states on various occasions, through the theatrical process she intends to create histories that "serve" her (quoted in Pearce 1994, 26), that enable her as a Black woman to firmly inhabit past, present, and future. Chapter 2 discusses how Parks works both the performative force of language and what she calls the "special strange relationship between theatre and real life" to generate new historical events "ripe for the inclusion in the canon of history" (1995f, 4). Kara Walker, though less outspoken with regard to the performative force of her work, similarly insists that her fabricated interventions into contemporary hegemonic and mass-cultural historiographies serve to undo the historical damage done by mythological conceptions of history and to create a history that "resemble[s] me, Kara" (quoted in Subotnick 2002, 26). Her homodiegetic narrator, "The Negress"—who appears in a number of Walker's silhouette installations, interviews, and written texts as a sort of fictional alter ego—is crucial to this performative endeavor. In chapter 3, I discuss how, with a sidelong glance and unreliable narration, this narrator destabilizes and flips popular and mythological knowledges of the past and asserts her creative authority in scripting and performing her own history. In short, at stake in these highly imaginative interventions in popular, dominant, and counterhegemonic histories are always concrete needs in the present as well as "the conditions of a possible future" (Koselleck 2004, 113).

How feasible is the claim to create history through art? The answer to this provocative question hinges on our understanding of the terms "create" and "history" and entails several levels of interrogation. On a pragmatic level, a play, once performed, or a story, once shared with the public, becomes "historical" in the sense that it leaves traces in the institutional archives and/or collective memory of the community. Through these traces it impacts human consciousness, affecting not only our thinking about the past but also our actions in the present. It is in this sense of influencing our being in and acting on the world that the work will "make the change," as Parks writes (quoted in Wetmore 2007, 139). On a more abstract level, these works interrupt the facile equation of history with the past and intervene in established practices of knowledge production. On this score, historiopoetic works share characteristics with a body of works that Linda Hutcheon terms "historiographic metafiction": works of prose fiction that thematize in content and demonstrate in form the narrative construction of the past. According to Hutcheon, historiographic metafiction sets out to "'de-doxif[y]' received notions about the process of representing the actual in narrative—be it fictional or historical," underlining that "like fiction, history constructs its object" (Hutcheon 2002, 75). In this regard, Walker's and Parks's (and Dunye's) claim to "making history" is to be understood primarily as an epistemological intervention, as an attempt to alert readers/spectators to the discursive character of knowledge production and the concrete poetics and politics involved. But historiopoetic work also departs from historiographic metafiction in that it moves beyond problematizing "our confidence in empiricist and positivist epistemologies" (Hutcheon 1988, 106). Taking their cue from poststructuralism's insight into the constructed nature of any knowledge of the past, Parks and Walker (along with Dunye and others) insist that if an occurrence becomes a historical event by being narrated, as poststructuralist historians Koselleck and White maintain, then art, particularly the narrative arts, can accomplish such bringing forth of the "historical" just as well as its scholarly cousin.

From a cultural and political point of view, in challenging established regimes of representation and knowledge production, the historiopoetic work of Parks, Walker, Dunye, and many other contemporary artists partakes in the African American tradition of what critics have variously called "storying" and "counterfeiting" (K. Young 2012) or "afro-fabulation" (Nyong'o 2014, 2019). These terms designate the liberal use of fiction to break the bounds of the factual and create new possibilities of being and imagining oneself in the world. They refer to a long-standing tradition of using the imagination, as Kevin Young writes, "not as a mere distraction from oppression but as a derailing of it" (2012, 19), as a means to "forge—both 'create' and 'fake'—black authority in a world not necessarily of their making" (24). Tavia Nyong'o understands the task of the afro-fabulist similarly, as a teller of tales who, in upsetting "a key demand of representational mimesis: the demand that representation be either true or false, either history or fiction" (2014, 77), intervenes in the existing aesthetic-political order to investigate different possibilities of representation. Elaborating on his use of the term in his monograph *Afro-fabulations: The Queer Drama of Black Life* (2019), Nyong'o presents afro-fabulation as "the tactical fictionalizing of a world that is, from the point of view of black social life, already false. It is an insurgent movement—in the face of an intransigent and ever-mutating anti-Blackness—toward something else, something other, something more" (2019, 6). And while it might not yet be possible to spell out this "something" concretely, in tethering together "what was with what might have been" (Nyong'o calls this synthesis "the incompossible"), afro-fabulation presents "a necessary step toward investigating possibilities outside our present terms of order" (6).

Nyong'o's articulation of afro-fabulation builds on Saidiya Hartman's concept of "critical fabulation." In her seminal essay "Venus in Two Acts" (2008), Hartman underscores the intrinsic dilemma encountered by the historian of slavery (whether of academic or artistic provenance): "How does one revisit the scene of subjection without replicating the grammar of violence?" (4). How does one avoid reproducing the power structures inherent in the archive of slavery when trying to recuperate the lives of the enslaved? In her own writing, Hartman attempts to tackle this aporia by developing the method of "critical fabulation," a subjunctive mode of writing that allows her to "strain against the limits of the archive" (2008, 11) in order to envision the humanity of the enslaved outside the discourses that constrained, subjugated, commodified, and ultimately destroyed them, while simultaneously "enacting the impossibility of representing the lives of the captives precisely through the process of narration" (11). While Nyong'o's study is interested in a different kind of archive (queer Black performance), his notion of incompossibility, the simultaneous performance of what can and cannot be, echoes Hartman's temporality of critical fabulation.

Granted, Walker's and Parks's interest in the archive of slavery is different from Hartman's. Their imaginative engagements with the past do not seek to "liberate" the enslaved from the "death sentence" of the archive (Hartman 2008, 2) by recuperating their humanity or to bear witness to their suffering (all this is very much the project of the melancholic historicism of cultural works of the 1970s and 1980s). Rather, their fabulations are primarily concerned with intervening in the afterlife of the archive, in the various articulations it has found in hegemonic, counterhegemonic, and mass-cultural representations.[30] In terms of method, however, they would certainly share Hartman's insistence on the need for intervening on the poetic level of narrative: "By playing with and rearranging the basic elements of the story, by re-presenting the sequence of events in divergent stories and from contested points of view, I have attempted to jeopardize the status of the event, to displace the received or authorized account, and to imagine what might have happened or might have been said or might have been done" (Hartman 2008, 11). Parks and Walker (along with their peers) are just as interested as Hartman in the work of poetic restructuring, in playing with and rearranging the available visual and verbal components of entrenched histories to imagine different narratives *of* the past and, above all, *for* the present. Similar to Hartman's critical fabulation or Nyong'o's afro-fabulation, their historiopoetic interventions ultimately seek to challenge and destabilize existing representational regimes, which historically have produced—and in the present continue to produce—"disposable lives" (Hartman 2008, 11). Parks and Walker share Hartman's goal, "to illuminate the contested character of history, narrative, event, and fact, and to topple the hierarchy of discourse, and to engulf authorized speech in a clash of voices" (2008, 12).

Beyond using fabulation to critique entrenched epistemes and representational regimes, Parks and Walker, with their manifest disinterest in getting the past "right" and "piec[ing] it all together incorrectly" (quoted in Boerma 2002, 168), also engage in the afro-fabulist impetus to forge—in the double articulation of creating and faking proposed by Kevin Young—an identity from the traumatic traces of the past and create new possibilities for the future. The opening chiasmus of Parks's *The America Play* compellingly asserts the playwright's faith that through art the past can be refigured on behalf of the present and future: "He digged the hole and the whole held him" (159). The performative movement from "whole" to "hole" is accomplished through a series of poetic refigurations, such as homophonic pun and chiasmus.

Walker similarly puns on a small note card that opens the collection of her works *Kara Walker: Narratives of a Negress* (Berry et al. 2003, 7):

African
African't
Africouldn't
Afrishouldn't
Africould've
Africould

Deliberately misreading the third syllable of the adjective for the possibility modal verb "can," Walker refigures the word "African" along the lines of a grammatical conjugation, moving the verb "can" through three inflections for tense and polarity in English that express negation and impossibility ("can't," "couldn't") and deontic modality ("shouldn't") to two affirmative modals: the past counterfactual "could've," followed by the present possibility modal "could."[31] Although all these expressions are still *irrealis* (indicating something that does not represent a fact), the affirmative modals also entail and set the stage for the possibility of bringing forth not-yet-existing facts, the possibility that something that is currently unreal may become real. Such grammatical punning is not vain word play. With the playful movement of a marker of geographic identity from factual statement via negative modalities to affirmative possibility meanings, Walker renders a subtle yet potent dig at Hegel's notorious erasure of Africa from world history by moving the adjective "African" from the realm of negativity to that of possibility.[32] I see this playful verbal and visual refiguration of established discourses of the past in pursuit of useable knowledges for the present and future at the heart of historiopoetic praxis.

In sum, the crucial cultural and political work of historiopoiesis consists in the imaginative and often playful engagement with entrenched histories (dominant, counterhegemonic, and mass-cultural narratives of the past), deploying a liberal collusion of fact and fiction and a pronounced degree of self-reflectiveness with regard to formal principles of construction, the materiality and mediality of the work, as well as audience relations to lay bare processes of narrative construction and thus denaturalize/defamiliarize (in the Brechtian sense of *Verfremdung*) established modes of knowledge production. While historiopoiesis is not a unique technique of Black cultural production, it takes on particular salience in light of its capacity to destabilize oppressive regimes of representation, to trouble entrenched notions of Blackness (both those articulated by white supremacy and those put forth by African American communities), and to create through a performative fabulation of the past possibilities for forging a variety of identities in the present and with an eye to the future.

GENERATIONAL NUANCES

As indicated throughout this introduction, Parks and Walker share important aspects of their poetics with other contemporaries. The purposeful collusion of fact and fiction is a pronounced strategy not only in Dunye's film but also in Jamaica Kincaid's writing. In her biographically inflected prose works *Autobiography of My Mother* (1996) and *Mr. Potter* (2002), Kincaid's narrators liberally blend fact and fiction, established and made-up knowledges, to fabricate family histories that are otherwise not available to them. Concomitantly, they generate genealogies and memories that can bestow identity on people who, because of a long colonial experience of physical and representational exploitation, are, as the narrator in *Mr. Potter* repeatedly states, of little or "no account" in the established historical record (121). Kincaid's narrators thus effectively fabulate a Black history of the Caribbean.[33]

Kincaid's fiction also shares Walker's and Parks's concern with excavating and intervening in the various layers of mediation through which our knowledge of the past is articulated. Similar to Dunye, who humorously deconstructs documentary's claims to narrative authority and veracity, Kincaid probes the conventions of narrative realism that sustain the genre of biography and autobiography. Interrogation of the politics of form is also at the heart of such contemporary plays as Young Jean Lee's *The Shipment* (2009) and Branden Jacobs-Jenkins's *Neighbors* (2010), *An Octoroon* (2014), and *Appropriate* (2014). Both playwrights use the mediality of theater to performatively excavate and interrogate the racial legacies of theatrical form—the stereotypes of minstrelsy and melodrama anchored in slavery as well as the codified and restrictive notions of Blackness that undergird realism.[34]

In the visual arts, a number of artists have likewise tackled the representational legacies of slavery to underscore how entrenched perceptions of race continue to inform contemporary scopic habits. In the lithograph series *Runaways* (1993), Glenn Ligon provocatively combines the formulaic imagery of antebellum runaway broadsheets (the stereotypical figure along with the typeset) with descriptions of his own persona rendered by friends. The clash of modern subjectivity with the visual language of slavery is both disconcerting and humorous. On the one hand, Ligon's parody effectively unmasks the violence effected by a particular genre (the "Wanted" poster), which, not unlike strategies of racial profiling, reduces identities to easily recognizable stereotypes. On the other hand, the verbal dwelling on details (such as the repeated, admiring references to Ligon's smart glasses, silver watch, and "cute" eyebrows) resists generic confinement and effectively queers and undermines efforts at normative representation.[35] Similarly, photographers Carla Williams in *How to Read Character* (1990) and Renée Cox and Lyle Ashton Harris in *Hottentot Venus 2000* (1994) challenge with their theatrical restagings of the "Hottentot Venus" pose the persistence of colonial stereotypes in contemporary perceptions of the Black female body. Examining the works of Williams, Cox and Harris, and others in her essay "Playing with Venus," Kianga Ford points to an entire body of work in the visual arts of the 1990s dedicated to examining and deconstructing the various layers of contemporary racial fantasies. This performative archaeological effort continues well into the 2000s. Hank Willis Thomas, for instance, in a series of high gloss photographs draws attention to the ongoing commodification of the Black body; in one example, *Cotton Bowl* (2011), he provocatively juxtaposes an African American athlete with an African American cotton picker.

Many of these millennial interrogations of what Ford calls "the constitutive elements of contemporary [racial] fantasy" (2010, 98) are deliberately confrontational. In a bid on the internet auction platform eBay, artist Keith Obadike, for instance, offers his Blackness for sale (*Blackness for Sale*, 2001), while damali ayo sets up the website *rent-a-negro.com* (2003), where clients could "rent" the services of African Americans, for instance, to enhance their "coolness" at work.[36] Although both websites were quickly taken down, they nonetheless managed to underline in a rather piquing manner how notions of Blackness continue to be reified in the present. Even when the ironic nature of these projects is evident to many viewers/consumers, works by ayo, Obadike, Cox, Ligon, and certainly Parks and Walker tend to elicit a range of affective responses from their audiences, including laughter, discomfort, and anger.[37] As I suggest in my discussion of aspects of theatricality in the works Parks and Walker in chapter 4, affective responses take center stage in these provocative performances of racializing stereotypes and clichés of history, for they effectively underscore the relational quality of constructs, perceptions, and performances of race and reveal the complicity of the viewer/consumer with the transactions they stage. This list of parallels and intersections between the works of Parks and Walker and other artists of the 1990s and 2000s working in the visual and performing arts, in film, literature, or internet art could obviously be extended.[38]

Indeed, there is sufficient evidence of a shared generational poetics that endeavors to render slavery according to a specific sociocultural age cohort's attitude toward the traumatic past of transatlantic slavery and its various legacies. While I consider Parks's and Walker's works to be exemplary for the poetics and politics that this generation brings to bear on the topic of slavery, I do not wish to suggest that the concept of historiopoiesis, which describes a particular performative approach to the past, is fully applicable to all other millennial artistic productions addressing the legacies of slavery. Historiopoiesis serves not as an umbrella term for a common poetics but rather as a loose mold or matrix, in which the millennial works I am interested in partake in varying degrees. Some might foreground the collusion of fact and fiction and the performative *gestus* of their engagement with history; others, the playful Signifyin(g) on established narratives, themes, and motifs, as well as the self-reflective engagement with issues of narrative construction, mediality, and/or materiality; and yet others again, the

theatricality of their work, the various ways that they draw their beholders into an affective encounter with entrenched perceptions, desires,
and anxieties. Or we might encounter a combination of some or all of
these aspects. What these works have in common, however, is an investment in challenging, through formal/poetic intervention, entrenched
orders of representation and knowledge production so as to refigure the
link between contemporary Black identities and slavery.

By embedding my analysis of Parks and Walker in a generational
frame, I am taking my cue from British Guyanese writer Fred D'Aguiar's assertion that "each generation of blacks demands more of the past.
Not because they are suffering short-term memory loss or some such
syndrome (after all, didn't the generation before have lots to say about
slavery) but because they need their own version of the past, to see the
past in their own images, words. To have slavery nuanced their way"
(1997, 126). I find it productive to think of the works of Parks, Walker,
and their contemporaries in generational terms for several reasons. In
Karl Mannheim's sense, the term "generation" refers to the particularities of the shared social experience of a group of people that is distinct from that of other periods (1998). Walker, Parks, Jacobs-Jenkins,
Dunye, Ligon, Cox, Obadike, and ayo were all born or came of age *after*
the civil rights movement and thus came to maturity in a society in
which de jure racial segregation had been abolished and full citizenship
for African Americans guaranteed. Such legal achievements allowed
for the emergence of notions of identity and freedom that were very different from those of the preceding generation, whose experience had
been prominently marked by the struggle for civil rights and the Black
Power movement.[39] Mark Anthony Neal (following Nelson George) uses
the term "post-soul" to acknowledge and describe these drastic changes
in political, social, and cultural experience.[40] He refers to the members of this particular generation as "children of soul . . . , who came of
maturity in the age of Reaganomics and experienced the change from
urban industrialism to deindustrialism, from segregation to desegregation, from essential notions of blackness to metanarratives of blackness
without any nostalgic allegiance to the past . . . , but firmly in grasp
of the essential concerns of this brave new world" (2002, 3). Neal's list
of changing experiences includes both concrete economic and social
markers (such as desegregation and deindustrialization) as well as the
less tangible markers of shifts in experience, such as the desire to for-

mulate new notions of Black identity. Neal thus gives expression to the ways in which changes in social experience are always intertwined with changes in thought and feeling that might not be fully articulate and coherent yet, but nonetheless index the emergence of what Raymond Williams calls a "structure of feeling." Not a worldview or an ideology, a structure of feeling indicates "meanings and values as they are actively lived and felt"; it bespeaks "social experience still *in process*" (Williams 1977, 132), which typically finds semantic and formal expression in the cultural productions of the period. To be sure, as Astrid Erll (2014) reminds us, the concept of a generation remains a discursive construct, one that tends to reduce the complexities of a given historical moment for the sake of enabling the auto- or heteroidentification of a cohort of people. Nevertheless, together with its companion concept, structure of feeling, it enables us to focus key elements of processes of experience and their attendant feelings that are crucial to how a group sees itself or how it is seen by others. As a structuring device, it, moreover, allows us to trace cultural evolutions so that shifts in emphasis and perspective can be perceived more clearly. This is not to suggest that the term "generation" demarcates one period from another in a clear-cut way as independent from or even in marked opposition to each other. Rather, as in any genealogical use of the terms, the concepts of generation and structure of feeling bring into focus relevant lines of descent and continuity along with moments of transition.[41] The particular generational attempt of working out a new version of the past, of rendering slavery in one's own words and images that I am interested in here begins in the post-soul moment of the late 1980s.

According to Neal, one of the core aspects of the generation "post-soul" is the "radical reimagining of the contemporary African-American experience, attempting to liberate contemporary interpretations of this experience from sensibilities that were formalized and institutionalized during earlier social paradigms" (2002, 3). It articulates this new sensibility in several, interrelated ways. Artist and cultural critic Greg Tate notes in a 1986 *Village Voice* article the emergence of a younger generation of artists "for whom black consciousness and artistic freedom are not mutually exclusive but complementary, for whom 'black culture' signifies a multicultural tradition of expressive practices . . . . No anxiety of influence here" (1992, 207). He adds that in many regards these "black artists have opened up the entire 'text of blackness' for fun and games" (200).[42] A couple of years later, novelist Trey Ellis likewise describes the emergence of a new sensibility toward Black art and Black identity, which he terms the "New Black Aesthetic," or NBA. NBA is "disturbatory art—art that shakes you up," Ellis explains (1989, 239). It is "an open-ended aesthetic as opposed to a rigid canon, which is what [Maulana] Karenga and some Black nationalists were trying to argue for. In the sixties they were trying to codify Black art. And now more than any other time, it's uncategorizable."[43] Looking back from the vantage point of the early 2000s, scholar Bertram D. Ashe later theorizes this emergent post-soul aesthetic by delineating three characteristics: First, "a hybrid, fluid, elastic, cultural mulattoesque sense of blackness," which, according to Ashe, was either "unlikely or unseemly in earlier black artistic eras" (2007, 614).[44] Second, the prominent use of "allusion-disruption strategies" (614), which simultaneously cite and disturb received narratives and iconographies of Blackness. A form of what Henry Louis Gates Jr. calls "Signifyin(g)," these iterations with a "signal difference" (Gates 1988, xxiv) disrupt existing semantic orientations and hegemonic meanings, along with established reading habits, and expose the fundamental constructedness and changeability of the sign. In the post-soul aesthetic, artists often use such Signifyin(g) strategies to "'make fun' of their nationalist elders" (Ashe 2007, 616), to disrupt sacrosanct texts, icons, and *lieux de mémoire* of Blackness, particularly those codified during the Black Power and civil rights movements. Ashe refers to this process as "blaxploration," the third and crucial characteristic of the post-soul aesthetic: "These artists and texts trouble blackness, they worry blackness; they stir it up, touch it, feel it out, and hold it up for examination in ways that depart significantly from previous—and necessary—preoccupations with struggling for political freedom, or with an attempt to establish and sustain a coherent black identity" (2007, 614). Ashe hastens to add, however, that ultimately these blaxplorations indicate "a dogged allegiance to their communities, however non-essentialized and gorged with critiques said allegiance might be" (614). They are undertaken "in service to black people" (614), for they stress that definitions of Blackness continue to be in flux, subject to change.

This sense of necessarily changing notions of Blackness also motivates and undergirds art curator Thelma Golden's and visual artist Glenn Ligon's 2001 collaborative coinage of the term "post-black," which has largely come to replace the older "post-soul." Like the related term, post-soul, which precedes it by about a decade, post-black was coined to give a name to a structure of feeling that increasingly found expression in the works of young artists who began to emerge on the cultural scene in the late 1990s. Golden explains that "it was a clarifying term that had ideological and chronological dimensions and repercussions. It was characterized by artists who were adamant about not being labeled as 'black' artists, though their work was steeped, in fact, deeply interested, in redefining complex notions of blackness" (2001, 14). This definition clearly does not regard post-black as post-racial; rather, it emphasizes an evolving understanding of the meanings of Blackness. It has nothing to do with the semantic fields of "post-race" or "color-blindness" with which, unfortunately, the term "post-black" has been incorrectly aligned in some scholarship as well as in the mass media, particularly during Barack Obama's presidency.[45] Similar to the scholarly advocates of the term "post-soul" (e.g., George, Neal, and Ashe), Golden and Ligon, along with journalist-critic Touré (2011), artist-scholar Ytasha Womack (2010), and art theorist and historian Derek Conrad Murray (2016), use "post-black" to indicate significant political and artistic shifts in the works of artists who were either born or came of age after the civil rights movement. I consider post-black and post-soul as more or less synonymous, although the term "post-black," thanks to its provocative positioning of the marker "Black," tends to bring questions of identity into sharper focus.[46] Murray, for instance, uses post-black to signal resistance to and departure from normative understandings of Blackness, especially those that "negate forms of difference, particularly the subjectivities of women and those that are queerly identified. For many in the African American community the visual and ideological emblems of normative Blackness have not spoken to the complexities of their experience" (2016, 2). He understands post-blackness not only as an aesthetic but also as a "generationally-specific ethos" (25) or consciousness that challenges "the hegemony of hetero-patriarchal expressions of blackness that, in their essentialist logics and racial nostalgia, relegate African-American identity to a series of limiting scripts" (3).

An important way of troubling normative scripts of Blackness is post-black art's engagement with the history of slavery. As Michelle M. Wright points out in *Physics of Blackness* (2015), contemporary discourses of Blackness in the United States and the Caribbean tend to be anchored in what she calls the "Middle Passage epistemology": an understanding of history that links "cultural practices and expressions, our politics and sensibilities, to the historical experience of slavery in the Americas and the struggle to achieve full human suffrage in the West. These histories are both constructed and phenomenological: they are chosen arrangements of historical events (spaces and times) perceived to be the defining moments of collective Blackness" (2015, 7–8). She insists that while this particular epistemology continues to matter, it "exclude[s], isolate[s], or stigmatize[s]" (5) the experiences of Blackness of large groups of people by favoring the heteropatriarchal male body engaged in the long, linearly perceived collective struggle of overcoming obstacles; it does not exhaust contemporary understandings of Blackness. Rather, Wright argues, it needs to be supplemented with another epistemology, anchored in different conceptions of time that locate Blackness at the intersection with other categories of belonging at the particular moment of interpretation—"the 'now' through which all imaginings of Blackness will be mediated" (14).

For many post-black artists and scholars, the project of troubling delimiting scripts of Blackness and producing more inclusive definitions entails connecting the linear historical time of slavery (the epistemology of the Middle Passage) with Wright's understanding of the "multifarious dimensions of Blackness that exist in any one moment," whose "valences will likely vary from those of a previous moment" (2015, 20). In *Who's Afraid of Post-Blackness*, Touré includes, in addition to reflections on his own experience, several interviews with contemporary African American artists, scholars, and public personalities that inquire about the meanings of the past of slavery for contemporary Black identities. He quotes Derek Murray, who speaks of "the dogmatic transference of trauma" from one generation to the next in his family and the attendant "mandate that we have to feel this kind of trauma and then carry that with us through our lives" (2011, 22). Murray goes on to explain that while his generation certainly honors "the history of the struggle of Black people in America, we still want to construct our own notion of Blackness that is separate from that of our parents and grandparents" (22). Touré also quotes literary theorist Wahneema Lubiano's similar sentiment: "Post-Black is what it looks like when you're no longer caught by your own trauma about racism and the history of Black people in the United States. Then everything is up for grabs as a possibility. . . . It's not a disavowal of history, it's just the determination that you're not wearing all that trauma anymore and you're not waiting for the world to be different to live your life in more interesting ways" (21). I see artists such as Kara Walker and Suzan-Lori Parks (and, for that matter, Cheryl Dunye, Glenn Ligon, Brandon Jacobs-Jenkins, and all others mentioned so far) as sharing this post-black ethos of challenging established narratives (Black and white) of Blackness anchored in slavery. Clearly, they continue to engage with the trauma of slavery in complex ways and attempt to give it a place in contemporary understandings of Black identities and race relations, but they no longer place it front and center. Rather, their work indicates the manifold attempts in contemporary Black cultural production to decenter slavery from its privileged position in conceptualizing Black identities. This is where the work of historiopoiesis—the poetic excavation, destabilization, and refiguration of entrenched practices of representation—comes into play. While it is not synonymous with the post-black/post-soul aesthetic, it features prominently in this generation's attempt to engage the legacies of slavery in playful and provocative but nonetheless quite sincere ways.

To be sure, this shift in poetics and attitudes toward the past does not come out of nowhere. Earlier, I mentioned relevant socioeconomic and political changes and shifts in structures of feeling. But there have also been important artistic predecessors for engaging slavery on the grounds of a post-black imagination, and, in particular, for a historiopoetic engagement with the legacies of slavery. As Hortense Spillers reminds us, Ishmael Reed's ludic metafictional novel *Flight to Canada* (1976) constitutes the original "insurgent act" of overthrowing slavery "as *the* privileged text of Afro-American historical movement" (1987a, 48). Parks, for her part, acknowledges the influence of Adrienne Kennedy, while Walker credits the pioneering work of Robert Colescott.[47] One could also point to the performative force of some of Zora Neale Hurston's writing as well as the humorous theatrics of Williams Wells Brown's antislavery play, *The Escape; or, A Leap for Freedom* (1858). None of the characteristics delineated above are new per se, but in the work of Walker, Parks, and others they come together with unprecedented force and visibility to indicate a fresh direction in the engagement with slavery, one that seeks to articulate a new structure of feeling that differs in significant ways from the one articulated in the neo–slave narratives of the 1970s and 1980s.

As we move further into the twenty-first century, to a point where we encounter various forms of an emboldened white supremacy in the United States and across the Western world, we need to consider the continuing viability of the post-black imagination and a historiopoetic take on the past. I will take up this issue in a coda to this study. From our current historical vantage point, it is not yet possible to assert a definitive end point to the millennial poetics that I sketch out with the examples of Parks and Walker because a number of artists have continued to work in this vein into the 2020s. At the same time, we have begun to witness since the 2010s the emergence of another artistic generation in reaction to both mass-media celebrations of an alleged arrival in a post-racial or color-blind era and the continuing use of state violence against people of color and various manifestations of anti-Black racism in everyday life. This emergent generation, developing a different set of questions about the past and also preferring different poetic forms, once again changes the conversation about the continuing relevance of the past. Addressing the particularities of this emerging generation would require another study.

The main emphasis of this book is on describing and conceptualizing a shifting attitude in the engagement with transatlantic slavery that began to emerge around the turn of the millennium. The readings of selected works by Suzan-Lori Parks and Kara Walker are intended to offer an interpretive model for approaching the works of a group of artists who gained prominence in the 1990s and 2000s, one that might help us understand how a particular generation attempted to nuance slavery their own way—and to what ends.

DIGGING, REP & REV–ING, AND FAKING

Suzan-Lori Parks's Historiopoetic Praxis

GHOSTS AND POSSESSIONS

From her early plays, *Imperceptible Mutabilities in the Third Kingdom* (1989) and *The Death of the Last Black Man in the Whole Entire World* (1990), to *The America Play* (1994), *Venus* (1996), and *Topdog/Underdog* (2001), as well as the more recent *Father Comes Home from the Wars (Parts 1, 2 & 3*, 2014) and *White Noise* (2019),[1] Suzan-Lori Parks has persistently thematized the legacies of slavery to examine questions of historiography and re-membering, identity, and race relations. Her performative investigations into the past focus in particular on its enduring material, representational, and psychological afterlife. "History is time that won't quit," Parks insists (1995e, 15). This statement accurately reflects the experience of many of the characters in her plays. "How dja get through it?" a woman named Chona asks her roommate, Mona, at the start of *Imperceptible Mutabilities*, and Mona responds, "Mm not through it" (25). *The Death of the Last Black Man* opens with the announcement that the death of the last Black man is recurring and ongoing: "Yesterday today next summer tomorrow just uh moment uhgoh in 1317 dieded thu last black man in thuh whole entire world"

(102). In *Venus* a figure called the Negro Resurrectionist declares at the start of the play that "the Venus Hottentot iz dead. / There wont b inny show tonite" (3) but then proceeds to resurrect her life and death in the ensuing vaudeville act. Finally, in *The America Play*, an African American figure called the Foundling Father is obsessed with his likeness to Abraham Lincoln and keeps reenacting the Great Emancipator's death, while in *Topdog/Underdog* two brothers named Lincoln and Booth are doomed to act out the legacy of their historical namesakes. In short, in Parks's plays (and also in her 2003 Faulknerian novel, *Getting Mother's Body*) the past is never past; refusing to be put to rest, it continues to haunt the present in body, word, and image.

A potent gothic strain thus runs through Parks's oeuvre. Her plays are populated by ghosts of the past returning to challenge the present—whether in the shape of a revenant, such as in *Last Black Man*, or undead ideologies, cultural legacies, and racial perceptions, as in *Imperceptible Mutabilities*, *The America Play*, and *Venus*, or the reenactment of traumatic events as in *Topdog/Underdog* and *White Noise*. These ghosts make manifest a latent melancholic strain in contemporary attitudes toward the past, calling attention to an open wound that continues to unsettle Black identities. The wound finds its most powerful expression in Parks's signal allegory of the Great Hole of History, emblematic of the African American experience of alienation, dismemberment, erasure, and absence. This hole of history (another ghost) materializes quite literally center stage in *The America Play*, which, as the stage directions instruct, is set in *"A great hole. In the middle of nowhere. The hole is an exact replica of the Great Hole of History"* (159). In other plays, it exerts its haunting powers in more subtle ways—for instance, in Parks's dramaturgical penchant for what Marc Robinson calls "a perforated landscape," stages "pockmarked with ditches, pools, and graves; the text with lacuna: the bodies with wounds; the narratives with secrets and other recesses" (quoted in Kalb 2004a, n.p.). Furthermore, as indicated by her choice of names—Black Man with Watermelon, The Foundling Father, as Abraham Lincoln, The Venus, Lincoln and Booth—the playwright tends to conceive her dramatis personae not as realistic characters but as what she calls "fabricated absence[s]" and embodied echoes of the great hole (quoted in Drukman 1995, 67). They are "ghosts" from "PastLand," Parks writes. "They are not *characters*. To call them so could be an injustice" (1995e, 12).

With such proliferation of gothic motifs, figures, and landscapes, Parks playfully takes up what several critics have recognized as the preeminent narrative in American literature's engagement with the past. Leslie Fiedler, in *Love and Death in the American Novel* (1960), identifies American literature as "almost essentially a gothic one" (142). He considers the gothic mode the most popular and potent manner of charting the newly founded nation's dreams of innocence and nightmares of violence.[2] And because the dream of freedom and democracy for some has, from the start, been premised on the unfreedom and disenfranchisement of many others, "certain special guilts awaited projection in the gothic form" (143). The gothic thus became an apt medium for articulating white America's anxieties over racial categorizations, boundaries, and transgressions. As Eric Savoy states, the "entire tradition of American gothic can be conceptualized as the attempt to invoke ... the specter of Otherness that haunts the house of the national narrative" (1998, 13–14).[3] Other scholars, however, have noted that the gothic has also proven to be a powerful tool in the hands of those "Others" for addressing "the shifting meanings of race and the white effort to contain and control it" (Weinauer 2017, 92). In this regard, Parks not only takes a parodic stab at the white literary imagination but also joins an eminent tradition of Black subversive Signifyin(g) on the gothic that extends from the early slave narratives to the contemporary period.[4]

If we read the gothic with Fiedler and Savoy as a particular mode of historiography in which "history controls and determines the writer" and the narrative "returns obsessively to the national pasts to complicate rather than to clarify them, but mainly to implicate the individual in a deep morass of American desires and deeds that allow no final escape from or transcendence of them" (Savoy 2008, 169), then Parks turns this long-standing historiographic tradition on its head to emphasize the possibility of taking control, of opening up the past, along with the present, toward the future. In her plays, the ghostly encounter with the past results neither in a deadly clasp, as it does for Fiedler (2003, 141), nor in what Savoy identifies as "the flight from that unbearable and remote knowledge" of America's "monstrous history" (2008, 169). Rather, in Parks's plays, the perforated landscapes of the gothic imagination become "the arena of action" (Marc Robinson quoted in Kalb 2004a, n.p.) in which protagonists engage this "monstrous" history head-on and appropriate and refigure it in the process. When asked in

2005 what, in her opinion, constitutes a "black play," Parks responds, "A black play knows all about the black hole and the great hole of history and aint afraid of going there" (2005, 578).

Ghosts, so Parks would agree with Avery Gordon, not only haunt us but present us with an opportunity. For Gordon a ghost is a "form by which something lost or barely visible, or seemingly not there to our supposedly well-trained eyes, makes itself known or apparent to us" (1997, 8). Ghosts thus have the capacity to challenge established historiographies and to demand a departure from entrenched modes of perceiving and knowing. Joseph Roach speaks on this score of the "revolutionary potential" of ghosts (1996, 34), of the ways they enjoin the living to reorder memory and rewrite history. Along similar lines, Kathleen Brogan maintains that ghosts allow for an "imaginative recuperation of the past" in the service of the present (1998, 4). Parks similarly asserts in a number of interviews and essays that she considers her plays not only challenges to established narratives of the past but active interventions in them; she understands them as a way "of creating and rewriting history" (1995f, 4).

The medium of theatrical performance and the stage are not incidental to this endeavor. Parks speaks of working "the special strange relationship between theatre and real life" for the purpose of creating "'new' historical events" (1995f, 4).[5] Her claim that theater can "'make' history" (4), as bold as it may seem, finds support in a number of theories of theater. Richard Schechner, for instance, views performance in the theater as "twice-behaved behavior" (2002, 29), while Joseph Roach points to the act of "surrogation" that is intrinsic to performance (1996, 2). As an iteration of an ever-elusive prototype, the nightly repetition of the memory of previous performances can never quite duplicate what went before, either falling short of or exceeding the "original." In either case, each theatrical performance refigures and transforms the past model in the process of citing it. More than any other medium, theater is thus haunted by its own past; in the attempt to bring this past alive, it generates ever new versions of it.[6] As Roach reminds us, performance, like memory (or history, for that matter), "operates as both quotation and invention, an improvisation on borrowed themes, with claims on the future as well as the past" (1996, 33). This remark also succinctly captures Parks's historiopoetic praxis: her endeavor to generate in the performative engagement with the past new possibilities for the future.

This chapter distills three poetic techniques in Parks's historiopoetic praxis that feature prominently in many of her works: (a) digging: the literal and figurative excavation of dead, lost, forgotten, dismembered bodies, artifacts, and discourses of the past; (b) Rep & Rev–ing: Parks's signature dramaturgy of repeating and revising words, phrases, motifs, and tropes; and (c) faking: her liberal fusion of fact and fiction, her figures' penchant for playacting, acting out and up, and for the theatrical. The three techniques are instrumental to the playwright's working of the "special strange relationship" between theater and history; they point us to three distinctive yet also interrelated possibilities for a performative engagement with the past. Although I examine them separately in this chapter, in Parks's oeuvre the three techniques typically work together and alongside each other. Parks's innovative use of language proves crucial to the uncovering of the psychic hold of the past exerted through words and images as well as to their appropriation in performative acts of autopoiesis. Language thus partakes in both digging and faking. Likewise, just as performance takes its force from digging, digging tends to involve a good amount of performance. Working in concert, these three strategies often succeed, as Parks suggests with regard to the dual meaning of the word "possession," in converting "the condition of being possessed" into the "action or fact of possessing" (1995f, 3); or put differently, they succeed in converting the haunting *by* the past into ownership *of* the past. In sections that follow, I work out how the techniques of digging, Rep & Rev–ing, and faking accomplish this transformation with examples from Parks's early works (*Imperceptible Mutabilities, The Death of the Last Black Man, America Play, Venus,* and *Topdog/Underdog*), in which we encounter these techniques in their most distinctive and compact articulations. They recur in Parks's later works, for instance, in the playwright's use of Rep & Rev and forms of faking in *Father Comes Home from the Wars* as well as in *White Noise.*

DIGGING

Many of Parks's plays involve digging in a quite literal sense: from her first play *Sinner's Place* (1984), which "had a lot of dirt on stage which was being dug at" (quoted in Jiggetts 1996, 310), to the "spadework" of professional gravediggers in *The America Play* and of a resurrectionist in *Venus*, to a family's amateur endeavor to unearth the remains of the deceased mother and recover her fabled treasure in *Getting Mother's Body*. These figures dig for ancestors, for an inheritance, for origins, or simply as a way of making a living. On a more metaphorical level, they also dig through the past to derive, as one figure puts it, "some benefit" from it (1995a, 180), some evidence or story to validate who they are as an individual person, as a member of a family or a group. "You find your voice by digging," Parks comments; "lots of my characters dig" (quoted in Fraden 2005, 40). Digging is also part of the author's process of writing: "They put things together as I was putting things together" (quoted in Savran 2014, 96). Moreover, because Parks considers large parts of African American history to be "unrecorded, dismembered, washed out" (1995f, 4), digging functions for her, as discussed in chapter 1, as a tool of literary archaeology, as a means "to locate the ancestral burial ground, dig for bones, find bones, hear the bones sing, write it down" (4). It serves as the principal method for accessing the past and dealing with its legacies—both on the diegetic (the digging *in* the play) and nondiegetic level (the digging *by* the play).

At the same time, Parks emphasizes her multivalent understanding of the verb "dig." In her various uses, it refers to a number of figuratively related processes: the process of thrusting down beneath the surface in search for something, but also of unearthing and bringing to light, as well as, in a more vernacular sense, the process of understanding and appreciating something (do you dig it?) and of making fun of something (taking digs). In Parks's dramaturgy, digging can refer to absences (the quest for something missing) as well as presences (excavation and resurrection); it can be affirmative (as in taking possession or claiming ownership) as well as critical (as in deconstructing and reassembling something). Her dramatic figures implement digging in all of these forms in their persistent endeavors to transform absence into presence, haunting into ownership, and melancholia into mourning. "He digged the hole and the whole held him"—this potent chiasmus, proclaimed at the opening of *The America Play* (159), succinctly captures not only the overall poetic and dramatic movement of this particular play but also of Parks's composite archaeological method. It can be read as the overarching motto for her historiopoetic praxis.

The America Play illustrates the composite nature of Parks's archaeology in an exemplary manner. Throughout the play, two gravediggers are constantly digging on stage—first the father, later the son. They do so in a place named "The Great Hole of History," a hole "in the middle of nowhere" (159). The father's digging leads nowhere—rather than unearthing the grand meaning he is searching for, he ends up reproducing his own fears and frustrations, disappearing in the process. The son's digging, however, thanks to a set of special excavation techniques, yields wondrous "inheritances," including his father's ghost, which become the basis for a new archive of history: The Hall of Wonders. In the play's movement from "hole" to "hall" (or "whole," as the chiasmus indicates), Parks implements two forms of digging and, by extension, allegories of historiography: digging as the self-destructive reiteration of absence and digging as the self-conscious, performative production of meaning. For now, let us focus on the first form of digging. The second form intersects closely with another technique, faking, which will be discussed later in this chapter.

In the first part of the play, "The Lincoln Act," a Black man called "The Foundling Father, as Abraham Lincoln" is possessed by a past that seems to have forsaken him. A gravedigger by trade and bearing a striking resemblance to Abraham Lincoln, "taking into account of course his natural God-given limitations" (163), the Foundling Father profoundly regrets not having been given the chance to make national history alongside the sixteenth president of the United States: "Being told from birth practically that he and the Great Man were dead ringers, more or less, and knowing that he, if he had been in the slightest vicinity back then, would have had at least a chance at the great honor of digging the Great Mans grave" (161). Despite his claims to "virtual twinship with greatness" (164) and his dreams of himself becoming "of interest to posterity" (162) by virtue of his profession, he remains relegated as the "Lesser Known" to the margins of this particular history centered around Lincoln, watching "the Greats" parade by (180). A visit to a theme park called "The Great Hole of History" drives home this sense of erasure and relegation to mere spectatorship: "You could look intuh that Hole and see your entire life pass before you. Not your own life but someones life from history, you know, someone who'd done somethin of note, got theirselves known somehow . . . uh face on uh postal stamp, you know, someone from History. *Like* you, but *not* you. You know: *Known*" (196). Haunted by "The Hole and its Historicity" (162), the Foundling Father travels out West to dig his own historical theme park, which is to be "an exact replica of The Great Hole of History" (159). But for the Foundling Father, digging this hole only reiterates and amplifies the sense of alienation and loss he experienced earlier. In a melancholic reenactment of his own erasure from history, he begins to reenact President Lincoln's death by assassination. Putting on a top hat, fringe beard, and a false cheek wart, he has himself "shot" over and over again by paying customers and becomes "famous overnight" (171). His brief local fame notwithstanding, he eventually disappears into the void of the Great Hole: "The Lesser Known forgets who he is and just crumbles. His bones cannot be found. The Greater Man continues on" (172–73).

As this brief plot synopsis illustrates, the figure of the Foundling Father stands as the quintessential "fabricated absence" (Drukman 1995, 67) that Parks seeks to index with many of the figures in her plays. He is literally a figure who "comes from a hole" (67), lives in a hole, and disappears into a hole. His very name indicates his existence in the "shadows, . . . margins, gaps, and crevices" of established, "known" history (Parks, quoted in Savran 2014, 96). He is the foundling, the orphan, the perpetual "Lesser Known"—always already relegated to the invisible supporting cast of the national drama. His arduous digging of his own Great Hole of History, in which he eventually disappears, aptly captures this melancholic relationship to dominant national historiographic narratives.

With Abraham Lincoln as the central historical persona with which the Foundling Father has to contend, Parks excavates a popular and persistent mythology of American memory culture.[7] While widely memorialized as "the Great Liberator" (in monuments, museums, plays, novels, pageants, names of parks, schools, libraries, etc.), the sixteenth president of the United States left a rather fraught legacy. His interest in freeing slaves was secondary to his interest in preserving the Union; he was both the author of emancipation and a defender of slavery. Frederick Douglass discerningly summarized the dual nature of his presidential legacy on the occasion of the unveiling of the Emancipation Memorial in Lincoln Park, Washington, DC, in April 1876 (funded by formerly enslaved people, the monument also became known as the Freedman's Memorial). While applauding Lincoln for the abolition of slavery, Douglass takes the occasion to sketch out the problematic relationship African Americans have with the historical person they have come together to venerate: "He was pre-eminently the white man's President, entirely devoted to the welfare of white men. He was ready and willing at any time during the first years of his administration to deny, postpone, and sacrifice the rights of humanity in the colored people to promote the welfare of the white people of this country. . . . You are the children of Abraham Lincoln. We are at best only his step-children; children by adoption, children by force of circumstances and necessity" (2018, 344–45). Douglass reminds his audience of the president's supremacist views and political deeds that were often far from beneficial to African Americans: his support of the Fugitive Slave Act, his repeated delays in proclaiming emancipation, and its partial enactment only in rebel territory. But he concludes that with Lincoln's assassination and with the unveiling of a memorial on the occasion of the tenth anniversary of his death, the nation (and Douglass includes his fellow African American citizens in this term) chooses to remember and mythologize him as "our friend and liberator." Douglass thus underscores how a collective actively selects at a particular historical moment for political expediency one narrative over another and chooses to reify this narrative in certain sites, such as the Freedman's Memorial. In this manner, *a narrative of a person* (or a place, a date, an artifact) becomes invested with symbolic significance that will resonate through the following decades and centuries as "history."[8] It is therefore not surprising that when the post-soul artists of the late twentieth century set out to "liberate contemporary experience from sensibilities that were formalized and institutionalized during earlier social paradigms" (Neal 2002, 3), they would also tackle Lincoln as a prominent *lieu de mémoire* of entrenched cultural memory and mythologized historical discourse.[9]

In "The Lincoln Act" of *The America Play*, Parks emphasizes how the symbolic Abraham Lincoln (rather than the actual person) continues to impact contemporary perceptions of the past.[10] As suggested by the protagonist's full name, "The Foundling Father, as Abraham Lincoln," the figure's identity remains tightly linked to this national mythology. His entire life is spent in its overwhelming shadow: he digs (in vain) for its meanings for his own personal life and quite literally digs a stage on which to reenact parts of this mythology. Echoing Douglass's critical remarks on Lincoln, Parks turns her "lesser-known" protagonist into a foundling of the Great Man, "a child by adoption" and "by force of circumstances and necessity." The oxymoronic alignment of the contradictory words "foundling" and "father" in his name not only riffs on the notion of "Founding Fathers,"[11] it also brings to the fore how Lincoln's celebrated paternalism was both nourishing and stifling to his progeny. In the Emancipation Memorial, as in other popular iconographies of Lincoln, "the Great Emancipator" is rendered by sculptor Thomas Ball as a benevolent father figure towering over a kneeling slave, his right hand holding a copy of the Emancipation Proclamation, his left hand extended in a gesture of benediction and uplift over the head of the kneeling figure. Lincoln appears as a kind and just figure. Yet the vertical arrangement of the two figures, along with their bodily positioning in relation to each other, also clearly conveys relations of power, with the white man standing tall in a posture of authority and the Black man crouching low in a posture of submissiveness. This arrangement renders freedom/emancipation not as something achieved in a collaborative effort of equals but as a gift bestowed by a white man. Only two small details in the sculptural ensemble—the remains of a whipping post and the shackles around the African American's hands—remind the observant beholder of the prior, violent theft of "the black man's unalienable right" to freedom. Even as the memorial is designed to speak of equality and full citizenship, it inadvertently corroborates in its form the racial formation of slavery. With the provocative appellation "Foundling Father," Parks visually and sonically digs up and takes digs at the historical dissonance and violence of representations embodied in the canonical representation of white history, such as the Emancipation Memorial.

Parks, furthermore, Signifies on Lincoln's mythological omnipresence in the protagonist's life with a large Lincoln bust and pasteboard cutout. In the 1994 production of *The America Play*, directed by Liz Diamond, the two objects were prominently placed on the left- and right-hand side of the stage. Along with a large inscription of Lincoln's name against the back wall, they visually create a sort of psychological and ideological frame that contains and determines the Foundling Father's actions.[12] He repeatedly acknowledges their presence with "a nod" to the bust and "a wink" at the cut-out. At the same time, the Foundling Father's selective performances of well-known "crowd pleaser[s]" (188), such as the Gettysburg Address and the spectacle of the presidential assassination, underline the profoundly commodified nature of the Lincoln myth. Even in commodified form, however, Lincoln's death figures as a deeply traumatic event for the Foundling Father, who repeatedly invokes "thuh great black hole that thu fatal bullet bored" (189). The president's deadly wound reinforces the Foundling Father's personal sense of abandonment and irrelevance, his not being called on to share the Great Man's history. When the Foundling Father aligns the wound with "[t]hu freeing of the slaves" (189), he, moreover, Signifies on the collective trauma of abandonment experienced by many African Americans after the end of Reconstruction (a period ushered in by Lincoln) and the ultimate failure of full emancipation. Despite the Foundling Father's manifold efforts to "catch up to the Great Man" (171), "to equal the Great Man in stature, word and deed" (162)—by digging his own personal "Big Hole" for reenactments of history, by digging into the trauma of Lincoln's assassination through repetitive performance—he does not succeed in shaking his own sense of historical insignificance. At some point, he wonders whether he might not be "running too fast in the wrong direction," whether his approach to history might not have been wrong all along, and whether perhaps the Great Man should have been catching up with him, but he dismisses these musings as "ridiculous" (171). His digging techniques do not enable him to break up the dominant representational frame that delimits his possibilities for self-creation.

While in the "Lincoln Act," the prevalent motif of digging serves to articulate the playwright's frustration with the non- and mis-representation of African Americans in American history, in the second part, "Hall of Wonders," Parks transforms it into a tool for intervention. In a reverse movement (a sort of structural chiasmus analogous to the verbal chiasmus that opens the play), the Foundling Father's wife, Lucy, and son, Brazil, set out to recuperate the father's remains from the Great Hole of History. Unlike the Foundling Father, they consider the site not a "chasm" but an "inheritance of sorts" (185). They are determined to "dig up something" (174), and thanks to the mother's perseverance and the son's own digging skills, they eventually succeed in unearthing the Foundling Father—not his body but his ghost and his various belongings. Thanks to another set of skills, faking, which the son also inherited from his father (and which will be discussed later in the chapter), Brazil succeeds in converting the Great Hole of History into a Hall of Wonders. Here, he provides his father's revenant with a proper resting place, installing him as "One of thu greats Hisself!" (199).

In the play's overall dramatic movement from hole to hall, absence to presence, haunting to ownership, we see how Parks turns the motif of digging from a tool of melancholic iteration into a tool of autopoiesis. Parks does not simply revise the dominant historiographic narrative of

African Americans as orphans of national history, she also generates a new narrative of belonging. Her approach to history is a reparative one; it effects a restructuring of the symbolic order that enables African Americans to take up different subject positions in relation to national history—no longer as spectators but as actors and creators.[13] To be sure, *The America Play* resembles on this score other African American history plays that similarly trace how characters succeed in overcoming the traumatic pull of the past and in claiming ownership over their history, such as August Wilson's famous Pittsburgh cycle. What distinguishes Parks's plays about history from those of Wilson and other playwrights working in the realist mode—and what makes them historiopoetic and not just historical in a conventional sense—is the high degree of self-reflectivity that the author as well as her dramatic figures bring to their investigations of history. Parks does not simply make up a reparative counterhistory of "lesser known" figures, but she thematizes and foregrounds time and again the various processes at work in the art of history-making: the particular forms of digging, the performative force of narrative, the concrete poetics at work in the verbal and visual structuring of discourse, the body's entanglement in these discourses, as well as the capacity of language and bodies to refigure them. Like playwrights working in the realist mode, Parks deploys fictional characters and stories to make up a history that addresses the ways that the past of slavery continues to inform contemporary Black experiences. Unlike realist history dramas, however, her plays do not mask but rather foreground the various processes of construction involved, and they do so in a highly self-aware, theatrical manner. Parks is interested not in countering one history with another but in instilling awareness (not skepticism) of the discursively constructed and mutable nature of any historiography. In her historiopoetic approach to the past, digging is therefore always tightly intertwined with techniques of verbal (re)-figuration (Rep & Rev) and performance (faking).

Before taking a closer look at these crucially related techniques, it warrants stressing that in Parks's oeuvre digging does not always serve a reparative function—as seen in its literal implementation in the protagonists' actions in *The America Play*. Digging also comes into play in other more figurative, less straightforward ways, such as in the playful deconstruction of verbal meanings (which will be the focus of the following section) as well as in the excavation and refiguration of hegemonic discourses that have interpellated African Americans as Others into the dominant white historiography, such as the already mentioned Lincoln myth.

The 1996 play *Venus* provides a compelling example of Parks's archaeologies of discourse. *Venus* features another digger by profession, the Negro Resurrectionist, who used to make a living by digging up human corpses for medical experiments and now specializes in the nightly resurrection of the spectacle of "The Venus Hottentot" in a vaudeville show. This theatrical resurrection takes its cue from the story of Saartjie Baartman, a Khoikoi woman from South Africa, who in the 1810s was put on public display in England and France as the "Hottentot Venus."[14] Although the Negro Resurrectionist promises to stand watch over Baartman's theatrical revenant, The Venus, and to "put her safely in the ground when she dies" (1997, 150), as the show's emcee, he also partakes throughout the play in the perpetuation of the spectacularization and commodification of Venus's body. Unlike in *The America Play*, the overall movement of Parks's archaeology in *Venus* is not a straightforwardly reparative one (from hole to whole), but leaves us with what Marc Robinson calls a "deliberately unresolved tension between exhumation and burial—or, more generally, exposure and concealment" (quoted in Kalb 2004b, n.p.). Because of this tension, a number of critics have objected to what they perceive as the ongoing reification and victimization of the historical person Saartjie Baartman by Parks's drama.[15] Other critics, however, hold that Parks's archaeology is concerned not with the recovery of an actual woman but with the excavation of the various verbal and visual discourses of nineteenth-century racial ideology that produced the symbolic body of "the Hottentot Venus" in the first place and that continue to affect perceptions of Black womanhood well into the twenty-first century.[16] According to this reading, which I here build on, The Negro Resurrectionist's digging work consists not in recovering the historical Baartman but in exposing the various discourses that conjoined to produce "the symbolic Venus" (Ford 2010, 99). In *Venus*, Parks thus pursues a second kind of digging, which is also central to her historiopoetic praxis: a Foucauldian archaeology of contemporary perceptions and discourses of race.

The play opens with the Negro Resurrectionist hailing the protagonist in the fashion of a vaudeville barker as "The Venus Hottentot"—an appellation immediately reiterated by the supporting cast and later adopted by the protagonist herself. From the start, the central figure is thus presented as first and foremost a discursive construct: a show business commodity offered up for spectatorial consumption. Throughout the play, the Negro Resurrectionist reinforces the essentially constructed nature of the figure of "The Venus Hottentot" by marshalling a series of "Historical Extracts" and "Footnotes" that reveal how the protagonist is created, assessed, appraised, and disciplined by various discourses. They include snippets of advertising bills for the historical Baartman exhibition, diary entries from people who saw the exhibition (such as by Scottish writer Robert Chambers, who records the visit under the rubric "Oddities of Human Life and Character"), quotations from newspaper articles of the time protesting the display as a form of slavery, and the reenactment of the legal inquisition into Baartman's labor status. In addition, excerpts from two popular street ballads about the "Hottentot" from 1810 and 1812 are performed, and scenes from a popular French vaudeville act of the time are reenacted. Most prominent, however, are the lengthy quotations from anatomist Georges Cuvier's lecture notes concerning the autopsy of Baartman's body, which are read out by a character named Baron Docteur.[17] These various popular, scientific, commercial, legal, and moral discourses collude to project onto a woman named Saartjie Baartman a mixture of colonial and erotic fantasies and to qualify her body in moral and aesthetic terms as the quintessential Other to European standards of beauty, morality, sexuality, and femininity.[18] They conjoin to produce, contain, and control an abstract, symbolic body of Black femininity as it figures in the white colonial imagination. Parks thus demonstrates how "The Venus Hottentot" is ultimately the product, in Michel Foucault's words, "of a set of practices that systemically form the object of which they speak" (2010, 49).

Chapter 4 will discuss in more detail the various ways in which Parks makes use of the medium of theater and performance to lay bare and examine the various discursive and scopic mechanisms that produce the symbolic Venus as well as how she uses theatricality to undercut the spectatorial desire underwriting these mechanisms. Noteworthy here is that with *Venus*, Parks realizes the motif and technique of digging not only with regard to the resurrection and re-membering of marginalized and subordinated bodies (as practiced in *The America Play*) but also with regard to the iteration and dissection of discourses.

"Diggidy-diggidy-diggidy-diggidy" (161), the Negro Resurrectionist and other figures scat in the play's "Final Chorus." Debby Thompson suggests that this scat should be read as the rhythmic announcement of "an aesthetics of digging" (2007, 172), an aesthetics that performs both literal and figurative archaeologies of racial history. A closer look at how Parks's dramatic figures work language will show how this aesthetics of digging works not only to expose but also to dissect discourse.

"WORDS WORKIN"

Language plays a crucial role in Parks's archaeological endeavors. The playwright uses it as her primary tool for digging up as well as taking digs at the discursive basis of constructions of history and identity and for reassembling them in the process: "95 percent of the action, in all of my plays, is in the line of text," Parks remarks (quoted in Ong 1994, n.p.). Director Liz Diamond comments, "Her words are actors, performing virtuoso feats of transformation, reconfiguring new meanings right before our very eyes" (1993, 86). Parks's development and refinement of this particular historiopoetic technique is particularly evident in her early plays, *Imperceptible Mutabilities in the Third Kingdom* (1989) and *The Death of the Last Black Man in the Whole Entire World* (1990). Both plays focus on the investigation of the link between language, power, and identity, on the ways language is used to control and contain Black subjectivity but also the ways it can be reconfigured to enable a self-fashioning of identity and history. The phrase "words workin" (1995c, 26) from *Imperceptible Mutabilities* provides a useful shorthand expression for conceptualizing both the hegemonic work of language and Parks's figures' persistent reworking of language to resist and break free of the stranglehold of a dominant sign system. This section focuses on how Parks's performative excavations are intrinsically linked to her figures' (and plays') verbal work.

Diamond describes Parks's first professional production, *Imperceptible Mutabilities in the Third Kingdom*, which she directed at BACA Downtown in Brooklyn in the fall of 1989, as a play that condensates "meaning in form" (1993, 86). Indeed, Parks approaches her theme—the profound sense of displacement, fragmentation, and alienation that has long marked Black experience in the United States—in a highly experimental and abstract dramatic form. In *The Souls of Black Folk* (1903), scholar-activist W. E. B. Du Bois poignantly comments on what he calls the "peculiar sensation" of being an African American in a nation ruled by white supremacy: "this sense of always looking at one's self through the eyes of others, of measuring one's soul by the tape of a world that looks on in amused contempt and pity" (1989, 5). In *Imperceptible Mutabilities*, Parks thematizes how verbal discourses are deployed as measuring tapes with which a dominant culture produces, defines, controls, disciplines, and contains its Others. She also shows how these "Others" appropriate the tools of power and refigure them for their own purposes. In both cases, it is language that acts. With her unconventional, non-Aristotelian form, Parks successfully shifts spectators' attention from questions of character and plot development to the playful and creative workings of language.

Like the later *America Play, Imperceptible Mutabilities* starts with a negative space—here configured not as a hole but as the interstice or chasm opened up by double consciousness. Parks calls this the "Third Kingdom." She develops this metaphor especially in two eponymously entitled choral passages, which link the three dramatic parts of her play. The choral figures describe this space as a "world . . . cleaved intuh 2" (37) and articulate the sense of fragmentation and alienation that marks their experience of inhabiting this space. "My new Self was uh third Self made by thu space in between" (39), one figure states, while another frantically attempts to wave and holler across this space "at my uther me who I could barely see. . . . but my uther me could not see me" (38). The Third Kingdom thus emerges, alongside the Great Hole of History, as another powerful metaphor for African American experience in Parks's work, denoting the uneasy, liminal space inhabited by a people violently abducted from their homeland (the space of the Middle Passage) as well as the conflicts of identity resulting from such displacement. Du Bois describes these conflicts as the "unreconciled strivings" of "two souls, two thoughts . . . two warring ideals in one dark body" produced by the sense of being both African and American (1989, 5). Throughout the play, but particularly in the choral passages, Parks's figures untiringly sound this gap between autoidentification and heteroidentification through and in language. As we will see, it is also through language that they manage to refigure this gap, for the Third Kingdom is also the site where meanings shift and mutate—imperceptibly at first, but with astonishing effects later on.

Parks enhances her verbal explorations with various visual strategies that draw attention to what she calls "the gap" between "preconceived images of African-Americans and real people" (quoted in Solomon 1990, 75). Throughout the play, she includes projections of photographs and other images to visualize the discrepancy between her figures' perceptions of themselves and how they are seen by the white gaze. In addition, the process of taking photos and posing for photos is repeatedly emphasized. Although issues of visuality play a significant role in Parks's first professional play, they take second place to the playwright's verbal sounding of double consciousness, which I here focus on.[19]

In the 1989 BACA Downtown production, the performance starts with six minutes of complete darkness during which it is not bodies but language that is at play. Through audio projection we hear the opening dialogue, in which a figure called Mona tries to understand the power of "words workin" (1995c, 26).[20] We learn that Mona recently lost her job as a telephone operator because of her persistent use of Black vernacular rather than standard (white) English. "'Speak correctly, or you will be dismissed,'" her manager reprimands her (26). Asked to undergo mandatory linguistic training, she finds it difficult to abide by the imposed rules of grammar and pronunciation when they fail to correspond to her lived experience: "'S-K' is /sk/ as in 'ask.' The little-lamb-follows-closely-behind-at-Marys-heels-as-Mary-boards-the-train. Shit. Failed every test he shoves in my face. He makes me recite my mind goes blank," Mona complains. "Aint never seen no woman on no train with no lamb. I tell him so. He throws me out. Stuff like this happens every day y know? This isnt uh special case mines iduhnt uh uhnn" (25). Her clash with the dominant sign system leads, in addition to unemployment, to a profound crisis of identity, as she now considers suicide: "What should I do Chona should I jump should I jump or what" (25). Her sense of constantly being measured "by the tape of a world that looks on in amused contempt and pity" (Du Bois 1989, 3) is further enhanced when she, along with her two roommates Chona and Verona, encounters a white "naturalist," who insists on hailing the women by different names:

LUTZKY: You must be Charlene.
CHONA: Char-who? Uh uhn. Uh—It-is-I,-Dr.-Lutzky,—*Chona*.
LUTZKY: Ha! You look like a Charlene you look like a Charlene, you do look like a Charlene (32)

The opening section of the play stresses how these three African American women find themselves entrapped in a language they do not consider their own and which, furthermore, constructs and interpellates them as linguistic and racial Other to the dominant white subject. Dr. Lutzky is quite intent on observing and describing the three roommates as specimens of what he calls "*mundus primitivus*" (29) and contemplates how to "accommodate the presence of such subjects in our modern world" (29).

While the first part of Parks's play emphasizes the hegemonic work of language on people, the subsequent parts demonstrate the ways individuals can work language to trouble and refigure dominant ideologies. This is most evident in the two choral passages, "Third Kingdom" and "Third Kingdom (Reprise)," interspersed between the three dramatic sections of the play. During these sections there are once again no actors on stage. Projected through the sound system, their voices present—similar to a Greek chorus—an extended lament on the systemic condition of alienation, rupture, and displacement thematized in the dramatic sections. They render, in the words of Liz Diamond, a poignant "portrait of a people lost in middle passage, floating in the hyphenated space between Africa and America" (1993, 87).[21] Parks, however, does not abandon her characters in a "perpetual state of middle passage" (Solomon 1990, 79). The choral figures actively work language, shuttling words and phrases back and forth between speakers and between sections of the play. Taking up various fragments of dialogue from the other parts of the play, the chorus not only gives expression to the historical chasm of African American identity, of a world cleaved in two, but attempts to fill it. For instance, Mona's desperate opening question from part 1, "What should I do Chona should I jump should I jump or what?" (1995c, 25), is taken up several times: tentatively in the first choral part by a figure called Kin-Seer as "Should I jump? Shouldijumporwhut?" (40), then repeated more forcefully by the same figure in the choral reprise as "Should I jump? Should I jump?? Should I jump shouldijumporwhat?" (55), and shortly after refracted by yet another figure, Shark-Seer, as "Should I jump shouldijumporwhut? Should I jump shouldijumporwhut?" (56). Altogether the phrase is reiterated, in variations, nine times.[22] Mona's existential question thus gains in intensity and scope and begins to reverberate on a collective level. At the same time, its manifold iterations also emphasize the sonic qualities of the phrase, gradually turning it into a tune sounded alongside other, similarly amplified phrases, in a polyvocal oratorio: "Shouldijumpshouldijump or whut?" (57). The materiality of language becomes apparent in this process of constant refiguration through choral song; language becomes pliable, transformable on a material (sonic and phonetic) level. Eventually, by the end of the choral reprise, this reworked language enables the singers to take surprising new attitudes toward the existential condition they find themselves in: in place of lamenting the chasm of the Third Kingdom, Kin-Seer begins to throw "Kisses" across it (57).[23]

Parks refers to this poetic technique of repeating and revising language until it begins to yield new meanings as "repetition and revision," or "Rep & Rev" (1995e, 8–9). Like a jazz piece, Rep & Rev moves words, phrases, themes, motifs, and tropes through a series of playful iterations and variations; an individual tune is reshuffled, enhanced, played back, shuttled forward again—sometimes individually, sometimes collectively. This process is far from straightforwardly linear; it pushes forward in a complex, dynamic process, without apparent teleology. Besides adding a profound musical quality to Parks's early plays, Rep & Rev functions as the principal tool for refiguring meanings along with experience and attitudes toward experience. As the playwright explains, "Characters refigure their word and through a refiguring of language show us that they are experiencing their situation anew" (9). For Parks there is a marked difference, for instance, between the use of Mona's "what" and the chorus's "whut." "The 'uh' requires the actor to employ a different physical, emotional, vocal attack" (Parks 1995e,12). And because a change in language provokes a change in attitude, it also enables a different experience of the world. Put differently, for Parks, language does not merely record experience but actively shapes it. On this score then, Rep & Rev also enables the characters in Parks's plays to refigure their relationship to the past and to articulate history differently.

In the continuous process of repetition and revision, the link between signifier and signified is loosened; seemingly hard-and-fast signs become destabilized and opened up for new meanings. Even the central metaphor of *Imperceptible Mutabilities*, the Third Kingdom, does not remain immune to such changes. Its original figuration as a liminal space, as a chasm and wound—"thu world had cleaved intuh 2" (37) and "Half the world had fallen away making 2 worlds and a sea between" (39)—morphs in the course of the play into a reflection on the world-creating capacities of language: "2 cliffs where the Word has cleaved. Half the Word has fallen away making 2 Words and a space between. Those 2 Words inscribe the third Kingdom" (55–56). On the one hand, this refiguration of a cleaved "world" into a cleaved "word" refers us back to the play's opening theme of linguistic alienation, to Mona's being torn between two language systems. On the other hand, the cleaved word now also indicates the opening up of established signs, of seemingly fixed meanings, signaling the mutation of meanings.

While Mona and her roommates remain caught in a dominant sign system, the protagonists of part 2 (Aretha Saxon) and part 3 (Sergeant Smith) begin to appropriate the alienated word for the sake of constructing workable representations of the past and of asserting their place in these representations. Sergeant Smith, for instance, a soldier who, despite his dreams of greatness, remains throughout his military career relegated to maintenance chores, takes charge of the word (along with the photographic image) to construct his own sense of distinctiveness. When he eventually receives an honorary distinction, he refigures the official narrative of the award as compensation for a wound received in an accident into one of a heroic deed: "I saw that boy fallin out thu sky. On fire. . . . Made a wish. Opened up my arms—was wishin for my whole family. He fell on me. . . . I broked his fall. I saved his life" (71). Such narrative refiguring of a wound into a symbol of deliverance and pride, of the motif of falling (Mona's opening question "should I jump" is echoed) into a motif of rescue and revival, indicates the extent to which Parks's play with words is integral to her historiopoetic project.

If Parks's historiopoetic deployment of language is still somewhat tentative in *Impossible Mutabilities*, it develops its full force in her next play, *The Death of the Last Black Man in the Whole Entire World*. Here Parks establishes Rep & Rev as the backbone of her dramaturgy and as her primary tool for digging up the past and refiguring its meanings in the process. The play renders the dilemma of a figure called Black Man with Watermelon. Having suffered a violent, racially motivated death, he is stuck in the limbo between life and afterlife, unable to move on. In this liminal space, he is condemned to reenact various versions of his own death—all of them linked to historical acts of racial violence:

by blood hounds, drowning, lynching, and electrocution. The singular death of a single man thus becomes an ongoing experience and comes to symbolize the violence committed against people of color more generally. In this manner, the play draws a direct line between past and present, emphasizing how the violence intrinsic to slavery continues to determine contemporary experience. Black Man succinctly captures the ongoing temporality of such systemic violence by coining a new grammatical tense with which to project the past into the future: "Thats how it has gone. Thats how it be wentin" (119). The main goal of the play, then, is to put Black Man, along with all the dead men he embodies, to rest so as to undercut the temporality of slavery. "Make me uh space 6 feet by 6 feet by 6. Make it big and mark it so as I won't miss it. If you would please, sweetness, uh mass grave-site. Theres company comin soonish," Black Man asks of his wife, Black Woman (109).

The digging of Black Man's grave involves both the unearthing of a collective history of violence and the uncovering of delimiting significations of the Black body. As Black Man adds to his request for a grave, "I would like tuh get up and go. I would like tuh move my hands" (109). The inability to move stands in metonymically for the inability of this man's dead body to pass on into the afterlife. It also signifies, on a more abstract level, what Hortense Spillers calls "the powerful stillness" of the Black body as "a signifier that has no movement in the field of signification" (1987b, 66). Not incidentally, the figures in *Death of the Last Black Man* all carry names evoking racial stereotypes or mythical notions of Black culture: besides Black Man with Watermelon and Black Woman with Fried Drumstick, there is Lots of Grease and Lots of Pork, Yes and Greens Black-Eyed Peas Cornbread, Queen-Then-Pharaoh Hatshepsut, And Bigger And Bigger And Bigger, Prunes and Prisms, Ham, and Old Man River Jordan. All these names are charged with a host of assumptions or abstractions that bear no relation to living beings.[24] As And Bigger And Bigger And Bigger (an echo of Richard Wright's protagonist in *Native Son*, Bigger Thomas) remarks, "I would like tuh be fit in back in thuh storybook from which I camed" (Parks 1995b, 116). In a similar vein, Black Man with Watermelon wonders why he has been stuck with a watermelon in his hand: "This does not belong tuh me. Somebody planted this on me. On me in my hands" (105). Parks's figures, in other words, impersonate what Spillers refers to as the "mythical prepossessions" that have buried Black agents so deep that "there is no easy way for [them] to come clean" (1987b, 65). The main goal of the play then is to return movement to these frozen significations and temporalities so that Black Man can be put to rest; it accomplishes this through the work of verbal digging.

"We getting somewheres. We getting down. Down down down down down down down down—," Black Woman intones during *Death of the Last Black Man*'s overture (104). She invokes the collective digging work of a chorus of what Parks calls "spirit people" (quoted in Geis 2008, 58), who convene nightly in a ritual of re-membering Black Man. The three main sections of the play (in an analogy to a religious triptych, Parks refers to them as panels) focus on the encounter between husband and wife, with Black Woman bearing witness to the ordeal of Black Man, attempting to nourish his body with food, and assisting his soul's passing through voodoo work. The important digging work is accomplished in the four chorus sections interspersed between panels and framing the play as a whole. These choral sections are highly abstract. Lacking in dramatic action, they present, similar to the chorus in *Imperceptible Mutabilities*, a polyphony of voices in which various themes and phrases are shuttled back and forth between speakers and slightly revised with each new utterance. Together with Black Man and Black Woman these "spirit people"—"all kin" to Black Man (Parks 1995b, 112)—dig into, dig up, and dig at the grammar and ideology that prescribe Black Man's body and history.

These digs are diverse and versatile, covering vast ground with regard to African American history and identity. One particular angle of inquiry focuses, just as in *Impossible Mutabilities*, on the link between language and power. A figure named Before Columbus refers to "uh tiny land mass just above my reach" (116). His words are immediately reshuffled by another figure, Lots of Grease and Lots of Pork, as "uh tiny land mass just outside my vocabulary" (116). With such Rep & Rev, the inherent link between journeys of discovery and linguistic practices of appropriation and subjugation is revealed. Consider, for instance, how early American explorers and settlers, such as Christopher Columbus, John Smith, and William Bradford, used not just the more obvious praxis of naming but also writing (in diaries, reports, and chronicles) as an instrument for the domestication and appropriation of the New World for their respective empires.[25] Not surprisingly, as Diamond observes, it is "the least enfranchised figure" (quoted in Kalb 2004b, n.p.), Yes and Greens Black-Eyed Peas Cornbread, who is most alert to the relevance of written discourse in the production of sociopolitical realities and repeatedly demands of Black Woman and the spirit people to record Black Man's history: "You should write it down because if you dont write it down then they will come along and tell the future that we did not exist. You should write it down and you should hide it under a rock. You should write down the past and you should write down the present and in what in the future you should write it down" (1995b, 105). Two other figures, Before Columbus and Queen-Then-Pharaoh Hatshepsut, extend this reflection on the role of language in the production of knowledge and in the articulation of power when musing on the difference between a "roun worl" and a "round world" in pre- and postconquest cosmology:

> BEFORE COLUMBUS: The popular thinking of the day back in them days was that the world was flat. Them thinking the world was flat kept it roun. Them thinking the sun revolved around the earth kept them satellite-like. They figured out the truth and scurried out. Figuring out the truth put them in their place and they scurried out to put us in ours. (103)
>
> QUEEN-THEN-PHARAOH HATSHEPSUT: Before Columbus thu worl usta be *roun* they put uh /d/ on thuh en of roun makin roun*d*. Thusly they set in motion thuh end. Without that /d/ we coulda gone on spinnin forever. Thuh /d/ thing ended things ended. (102).

Their exchange not only draws out the difference between a Black vernacular articulation of "roun" and the (white) received pronunciation of "round." It also shrewdly ties this difference to a hegemonic use of language. The imposition of standard grammatical rules (the sharp articulation of the final consonant) signifies to them the end of a holistic cosmology and the implementation of an ideology that thrives on the demarcation of difference and the concomitant subjugation and immobilization of alterity.

In *The Signifying Monkey*, Henry Louis Gates Jr. conceptualizes the complex and self-reflective awareness and articulation of Black linguistic difference as the key technique of Black vernacular culture and African American literature. According to him, the "blackness of the tongue" (1988, xiv) derives from various speakerly and tropological processes of repetition with a signal and identifiably Black difference. Gates refers to these processes of formal repetition and revision as "Signifyin(g)." Much like Parks's omission of the d in "roun," he marks the complex semantic and political relation and confrontation "between two parallel discursive universes" (45) by bracketing the final consonant in Signifyin(g). "The bracketed or aurally erased g, like the discourse of black English and dialect poetry generally," Gates explains, "stands as the trace of black difference in a remarkably sophisticated and fascinating (re)naming ritual graphically in evidence here" (46). The self-reflective act of Signifyin(g) not only exposes the hegemonic uses of standard English, it also actively intervenes in the imposition of power through language—revealing, resisting, and undercutting it. According to Gates, the homonymic iteration of standard English in the Black vernacular basically empties the signifier of received concepts and fills it with new meanings. In the process, the established nexus of signified/ signifier is loosened, the sign itself put in question, and its arbitrary and thus essentially mutable nature revealed.

Parks's signature dramaturgy of Rep & Rev is a close cousin to (if not a direct offspring of) Gates's notion of Signifyin(g). In deploying a stylized, poetic version of the Black vernacular, which she presents as her choice to "Signify on the Signifyin(g)," the playwright emphasizes the self-reflective and complex daily interaction of "a people oppressed by language" with that very language (quoted in Solomon 1990, 76).[26] As seen in the exchange between Before Columbus and Queen-Then-Pharaoh Hatshepsut, the presence or absence of the final d in the word "round" makes all the difference to the figures in her play with regard to their sense of history and identity. In addition, Parks's signifying Rep & Rev also undermines the violent symbolic order imposed on Black subjects; it destabilizes what Spillers calls the "American grammar" (1987b, 68) and reorders it.

Another example from *Death of the Last Black Man* illustrates how Parks's historiopoetic Signifyin(g) refigures imposed significations and opens up new possibilities of meaning. In the choral passage, which recounts how the fugitive Black Man jumps into a body of water to deflect the scent of the dogs on his track, a figure called Old River Jordan begins to riff on the various meanings that the motif of crossing water has accumulated in African American culture and history. He evokes the mythological meaning of rivers as marking the boundary between earth and the underworld, life and death (e.g., the mythical rivers Styx and Acheron), but also their concrete geopolitical meaning in demarcating slave states from free states, as did the Ohio River. Meanwhile, the biblical connotation bestowed on the Ohio River in slave narratives is invoked in Old Man River Jordan's very name.[27] In a reference to a path "worn out by uh 9 million paddin bare footed feet" (Parks 1995b, 114), water finally also takes on the collective experience of crossing the Atlantic Ocean in the Middle Passage. The various meanings that amass to water come to stand as a massive and multifarious symbol of fugitivity and death. As Old Man River, however, rehearses this heavy cultural history of water, he accentuates his story, over and over again, with the onomatopoeic words "drip" and "drop," which he combines in phrases such as "Dribblin by droppletts. Drop by Drop" (112). As the meanings of water grow in complexity, so does Old Man's scat: "Do drop be dripted? I say 'do'" (112) and "Do in didly dip didded thuh drop" (114). Like the Negro Resurrectionist's scat in *Venus* ("Diggidy-diggidy-diggidy-diggidy"), the onomatopoeic phrase gathers performative force, (re)enabling the flow of meanings and returning movement to a static text. Not long after Old Man Jordan's Rep & Rev on the meanings of the motif of water, Black Man realizes: "My text was writ in water" and asks "tuh drink it down" (116). He literally incorporates the troubled history of water into his body, appropriating it as a source of sustenance and life rather than anxiety and death. Old Man River Jordan approves with a final scat, "Do in dip diddly did-did thuh drop? Drop do it be dripted? Uh huh" (116).

Through the collective verbal digging work of the chorus, Black Man, and Black Woman, flux and flexibility are restored. "Somethins turnin" (128), several figures comment repeatedly in the Final Chorus, referring to the renewed movement in signification and body: "Uh blank page turnin with thu sound of it. Thu sound of movin hands" (129). Just as the dramatic figures' Rep & Rev work has enabled the refiguration of words, meanings, and narratives, it has also broken up the frozen, "mythical prepossession" of the Black body and enabled it to move of its own account in the field of significations. "Melon: mines," Black Man now declares (126), deciding to take ownership of the stereotypical attributes that used to possess him.[28] Most importantly, as Black Woman notes at the end, "Thu black man he move. He move. He *hans*" (131; emphasis added). The movement of the Black body is enabled by a Black vernacular signifying order: "hans." With this movement in a language of his own, Black Man can finally be put to rest.[29] Through speakerly and tropological digging work, the play thus generates its own performative force. It excavates restrictive significations (e.g., watermelon and water) and grammars (e.g., "round") and refigures them in "a remarkably sophisticated and fascinating (re)naming ritual," to use Gates's memorable phrase again (1988, 46). Through the playful digging work of Rep & Rev, the world of Parks's figures is made "roun" again and the world-making capacity of Black articulation, epistemology, and identity asserted.

All this then underlines Parks's faith in the performative capacity of poetic language. She means to do things with words, taking up J. L. Austin's assertion that words not only have the capacity to describe but also the force to perform, to bring about the thing they say. Austin denies this performative power to literature; he regards language "in such circumstances" as "used not seriously" (1975, 22), as not meaning what it says. But this is where Parks firmly disagrees.[30] Clearly, she is quite serious about the illocutionary work her words are to accomplish—on stage and off stage. They are to destabilize dominant grammatical structures and narratives of history and undermine their hold on identities that officially or traditionally have been written out of history or relegated to its margins, gaps, and chasms; they are to generate new grammatical structures and narrative possibilities for acting in the world.

FAKING

As we have seen, verbal dexterity and wit are crucial to Parks's protagonists in refiguring the signifiers that restrict them. Several of them stand out for their knack for Signifyin(g), telling a tall tale, and outsmarting their opponents with wordplay and tonal semantics. Their skill in manipulating language often proves to be part of a larger performative repertoire—playacting, impersonating, make-believe, a flair for the theatrical. Not incidentally, one of the most virtuoso speakers in *Death of the Last Black Man*, Ham, delivers his brilliant verbal dig at the epistemic violence inflicted on Black people through the abuse of biblical scripture (e.g., the story of Ham) in a parodic reenactment of a minstrelsy stump speech, a classic piece of "ham" performance.[31]

Parks emphasizes the beneficial nexus of verbal and bodily performance in the encounter with the past in a number of her plays, most prominently in *The America Play* and *Topdog/Underdog*, the focus of discussion in this last section. Before taking a closer look at faking techniques in these two plays, let us return briefly to a character in Parks's *Imperceptible Mutabilities* who presents one of the most compelling examples of how new narratives of the past are engendered in verbal as well as bodily performance. Aretha Saxon, the protagonist of "Open House," the third part of *Imperceptible Mutabilities*, is a former slave whose work as a caregiver for the children in the white Saxon family has been discontinued thanks to her belated emancipation. But even now her life continues to be determined by the authority of "the book," the established historical record. "The book says you expire. No option to renew," Miss Faith, the authoritative keeper of the book, informs her (45). Aretha's perception of herself and the world around her, however, differs so widely from the "facts" (47) recorded in Miss Faith's book that she begins to suspect that "we got different books" (51). While Aretha believes her small flat can accommodate three guests, Miss Faith insists on squeezing in six hundred, citing the precedence of the slave ship *Brookes* from "the book" as historical evidence for her calculation. At the same time, however, Miss Faith's book contains no record of the millions of Africans abducted from their homeland, prompting Aretha to protest, "Nine million just disappeared! That's uh fact!!" (52). By the end of the act, we find Aretha fed up with being misrepresented by the official record in word and image. She resolutely takes hold of the photographic apparatus with the help of which Miss Faith and her former master, Charles Saxon, had previously inscribed her into their "great chronicle" (46). Reversing the terms of her relationship, Aretha now stages her own representation of Charles and his children, arranging them for a photo session:

ARETHA: Don't care what you say you done, Charles. We're makin us uh histironical amendment here, K? Give us a uh smile. Uh big smile for thuh book.
CHARLES: Historical. An "Historical Amendment," Ma'am.
ARETHA: Smile, Charles.

. . .

ARETHA: SMILE. Smile, Charles, Smile! Show us them pretty teeth. Good.
CHARLES: I can't get the children to smile, Ma'am.

. . .

ARETHA: Smile! Smile! SMILE!! There. That's nice.

CHARLES: They're crying.

ARETHA: Don't matter none. Don't matter none at all. You say its uh cry I say its uh smile. These photographics is for my scrapbook. Scraps uh graphy for my book. Smile or no smile mm gonna remember you. Mm gonna remember you grinnin. (53–54)

This brief interaction and dialogue reveal Aretha's determination to put together her own historiography, to take control of what and how she chooses to remember and be remembered; in short, to create her own book. This entails, first of all, taking over the media of historiographic production—in this instance, camera, framing, and language, which had been instrumental in fixing the Black subject against a white background, as seen in part 1 of *Imperceptible Mutabilities*—and restaging the crucial events according to her own script. If Aretha's project of historical self-fashioning proves to be as selective and willful as that of Miss Faith and Charles Saxon, it is because she has understood the fundamentally constructed and essentially unstable nature of historiography. Her careful punning on historical/"histironical" and historiography / "scraps uh graphy" suggests as much. Aretha's claim to a "histironical amendment" is evidence not of her lack of education and understanding, as Charles Saxon suggests with his correction, but of her astute awareness of the uses to which even "scraps of graphy" can be put by the one who controls the means of historiographic production. In this particular situation, she makes up an enabling history from carefully selected and creatively interpreted scraps of experience. Hayden White refers to such selective, pragmatic historiographic production as the making of "a practical past" (rather than historical past). At stake is not a disinterested approach to the facts of the past for their own sake but the elaboration of select "memories, illusions, bits of vagrant information, attitudes and values . . . to justify, dignify, excuse, alibi or make a case for actions to be taken in the prosecution of a life project" (2010b, 16). Aretha is such a "practical" maker of her own past. But she is also more than that. Her hist-*ironical* amendment is marked by the deliberate "interpretive and intentional move" of irony (Hutcheon 1994, 11). According to Linda Hutcheon, irony is "the making or interfering of *meaning* in addition to and different from what is stated, together with an *attitude* toward both the said and the unsaid" (11). It asserts its emotional and political edge by taking away the certainty "that words mean only what they say" (14), that meaning can be fixed securely. Aretha's performative speech act accomplishes precisely that. Her declaring a cry to be a smile, a smile to be a grin does not simply invert a past representational regime (the stereotypical attribution of the smile or grin to the enslaved);[32] it keeps the old meaning visible even as it generates a new one. In this regard, Aretha's intervention posits an amendment of history, rather than a counterhistory.[33] It foregrounds the relational character of the historiographic process along with its continuously evolving nature. At the same time, "the simultaneous perception of more than one meaning" (Hutcheon 1994, 58) also alerts us to the very process of meaning-making, the various techniques of performance and the power constellations involved in it. In short, Aretha's statement is performative and ironic at one and the same time. In the Austinian sense, she intends to do things with words, to usher in a new understanding of history. The irony at work, while playful and humorous, does not undercut the seriousness of intent. Aretha means what she says, but at the same time she also articulates her awareness that meaning is contingent on speakerly authority and virtuosity of language. Aretha Saxon's producing new meanings through verbal and bodily performance while also being aware of what these processes entail and how they operate make her Parks's historiopoet par excellence.

With *The America Play*, Parks develops her figures' knack for fabulating practical pasts most fully. We have seen how digging plays a central role in reconfiguring the Hole of History into a Hall of Wonders. In addition to being avid diggers, Parks's protagonists, the Foundling Father and Brazil, also prove to be passionate performers—or, as Parks calls them, "fakers" (180). "Diggin was his livelihood but fakin was his calling. Ssonly natural heud come out here and combine thu 2" (79), Brazil remarks on his father's encounter with the Great Hole of History. This comment succinctly captures the dual nature of Parks's engagement with history—both archaeological and performative. Recall her oft-quoted statement that with her plays she attempts to "dig for bones, find bones, hear the songs, write it down" (1995f, 4). As any archaeologist knows "there is nothing more silent than a piece of archaeological evidence. Pots, stones, bronzes and bones do not speak to us" (Gamble

2008, 45). Hence, while Parks's figures strain to "hear the songs" of the past—the "echoes" and "whispers," as Lucy calls them (1995a, 174, 177)—the language in which they record what they hear is decidedly their own.[34] Like any other artifact, the pieces dug up by Parks's diggers "only acquire significance when interpreted" (Gamble 2008, 45). The past is thus not only the site of excavation but also of interpretation—at times, highly performative ones. In *The America Play*, the Great Hole of History quite literally serves as a stage on which the protagonists can transform the traumatic possessions of the past from ghostlike haunting into ownership. They do so with varying degrees of success, which, so I suggest, are related to varying degrees of performativity.

The Foundling Father's reenactment of Abraham Lincoln's speeches and assassination is a cautious and conservative one. Although he impersonates his "virtual twinship with greatness" (164) with quite some zest, adding a yellow "fancy" beard (163) and matching shoes to his Lincoln outfit, he remains overall loyal to the conventional Lincoln iconography, including its accepted historical inaccuracies, such as the stovepipe hat ("Never really worn indoors but people dont like their Lincoln hatless," 168). "If you deviate too much they won't get their pleasure," the Foundling Father explains. "Thats my experience. Some inconsistencies are perpetuatable because theyre good for business. But not the yellow beard. Its just my fancy" (163). The possibilities for making the history that haunts him on his own are thus limited. The Foundling Father finds some satisfaction in grooming his various Lincoln beards: "The beards were his although he himself had not grown them on his face but since he'd secretly bought the hairs from his barber and arranged their beard shapes and since the procurement and upkeep of his beards took so much work he figured that the beards were completely his. Were as authentic as he was so to speak" (159–60). Note that even as the metonymy of the beard suggests a certain degree of appropriation of the Lincoln myth, this partial ownership remains suspended in the rhetorical figure "so to speak." Moreover, even as the Foundling Father occasionally ventures to wear his fancy beard ("Ev-ery once in a while," 163), he remains hesitant to put on the matching shoes: "Its a little *much*" (161). Overall, the Foundling Father remains trapped in the shadow of the founding father, losing himself in his efforts to catch up with him: "The Lesser Known forgets who he is and just crumples. His bones cannot be found. The Greater Man continues on" (173).

By contrast, the Foundling Father's son, Brazil—another digger for history—remains unimpressed by the grand narratives of the past. Gone from his archaeological site are the Lincoln bust and pasteboard cutout. When Brazil digs up his father's marble bust of Lincoln, he considers it just as wondrous as any other artifact he retrieves from the hole. Placing it alongside artifacts such as a "glass tradin bead," "lick-ed boots," and "uh dried scrap of whales blubber" (185), Brazil deflates the Lincoln myth in the bathos of enumerating the trivial and ordinary. Above all, unlike his father, Brazil refuses to keep his actual and figurative digging for ancestral bones "tuh scale" (185). He liberally draws on "hearsay" (179) and popular legends alike in fashioning his father's life story from the traces of the past. "Come out here all uhlone. Cleared thuh path tamed thuh wilderness dug this whole Hole with his own 2 hands and et cetera" (179), he theatrically declares to his audience in a playful invocation of the frontier myth. In the same vein, he readily accepts the imitation for the original, the fake for the real. Recounting his parents' honeymoon at the historical theme park out East, he claims that "at thuh original Great Hole . . . Mr. George Washington, for example, thu Fathuh of our Country hisself, would rise up from thu dead and walk uhround and cross thuh Delaware and say stuff!! Right before their very eyes!!!!!" (179). All this is reinforced by exuberant exclamations, hyperbolic expressions, and histrionic gestures, prompting his mother, Lucy, to intervene: "That iduhnt how it went. . . . Thu Mr. Washington me and your Daddy seen was uh lookuhlike of thuh Mr. Washington of history-fame, son. . . . Keep your story to scale" (179–80). Brazil, however, remains undeterred by such repeated admonitions to keep the story "to scale." Again and again, he interrupts his digging by breaking into song ("Loook onnnnn thuhhh briiiiiiight siiiiiiiiide!!!," 178) or performing various comedic acts, such as punning on the loss of his "Pa" by pretending to have lost his "paw" (181)—his hand.

Brazil's archaeological method differs significantly from his father's and, therefore, not surprisingly, also yields very different results. As Nadia Abu El-Haj, an archaeological studies theorist, points out, the production of archaeological data occurs not only, as commonly held, through interpreting the artifacts on the ground but also through the concrete material practice of excavating them in the first place. What kind of objects are "discovered"—that is, actively carved out of the ground—and what kind of objects are recognized as significant and thus recorded and preserved will depend on the specific excavation techniques deployed as well as the ideologies and interests guiding them. Each set of practices hence yields a different set of data.

With his performative digs, which favor the imitative just as much as the original, the known just as much as the "lesser known," Brazil succeeds in retrieving, alongside a few actual bones of the past ("Mr. Washingtons bones, right pointer, so they say," 185), several "faux historical knickknacks" (169): Washington's wooden teeth, his father's beard box and Lincoln bust, a bag of Lincoln pennies. All, indiscriminately, receive a place in Brazil's very own historiography, his Hall of Wonders. Here he proudly shows off to the audience a rather unconventional archive. It includes items that have been traditionally accepted as "historical" and "authentic," such as "peace pacts, writs, bills of sale, . . . freein papers, summonses, declarations of war, title deeds, obits, long lists of dids" (186) as well as medals "for bravery and honesty; for trustworthiness and for standing straight; for standing tall; for standing still" (186). But it also includes items that have so far been ignored and dismissed, such as medals "for making do. For skills in whittlin, for skills in painting and drawing . . . For cookin and cleanin. For bowin and scrapin" and even "uh medal for fakin" (186). Thanks to such a shift in excavation and archiving practices, Brazil eventually succeeds in digging up from the Great Hole of History, not the Great Man, but the revenant of his imitator and "lookuhlike," the Foundling, the Lesser Known, who at long last returns from the void of history to assume his "designated place" (176) in his son's new history: "To my right: our newest Wonder: One of thu Great Hisself!" (199).

Once again, Rep & Rev is crucial to Brazil's archaeological praxis. In addition to his performative pun on "Pa/paw," Brazil also verbally digs through various homophonic connotations of the word "forefather" by refiguring his own Foundling Father (and by extension the founding fathers of the nation) as "foe-father" (178, 191) and "faux-father" (184)—a slippage of meaning that signals not only his own trauma of early childhood parental abandonment but also the fraught relationship of African Americans to the national mythology of founding fathers, particularly of Lincoln. The play's key trope of the hole is similarly moved via verbal and performative Rep & Rev through various thematic refigurations. While in the Foundling Father's part, the hole comes to stand in for the absence/marginalization of African Americans from history, the trauma of individual and collective abandonment, the incomplete project of emancipation, and the melancholic reenactment of absence, it morphs in Brazil's performance into a place of "inheritance," an archaeological site for the recovery of lesser known wonders of the past, a stage for the performative resurrection of the Foundling Father, and, finally, the foundation for a new archive of history. In this manner, Parks moves key components of the national historiography through a multifaceted verbal and performative Signifyin(g) process, including the deployment of homonymic and near-homophonic puns, verbal and dramaturgical chiasmi, metonymies, metaphors, allegories, hyperboles—tropes, which according to Gates, "luxuriate in the chaos of ambiguity that repetition and difference . . . yield in either an aural or a visual pun" (1988, 45). In a way, the playwright packs, aurally and visually, "all the meaning she can into her words, charging them with plutonic power" (Drukman 1995, 58), so that eventually they must explode into new significations. "In thu beginning there were some of them voids here and then: KERBANG-KERBLAMMO! And now it all belongs tuh us," Brazil proudly announces (Parks 1995a, 185). With his performative excavations he has indeed succeeded in converting his father's traumatic void into a site of presence, plenitude, and potential. He has also blasted our conventional and commodified understanding of history apart.

The America Play stands, I suggest, as an allegory for Parks's historiopoetic praxis. It vividly illustrates the transformation of a hole into a whole through the deployment of three interrelated historiopoetic techniques: digging, Rep & Rev-ing, and faking. It also demonstrates most clearly the playwright's faith in the performative force of her work. In the self-reflective citation and performative revision of established discourses and mnemonic practices, she lays bare the constructed and iterative nature of historiography and enables her figures to participate in the process of historical scripting, to speak and act their way into history. In this sense, Parks effectively demonstrates with *The America Play* that theater can indeed make history.

Yet, even as *The America Play* powerfully illustrates how a performative archaeology can refigure a traumatic history in a salutary manner, Parks does not set up the play's overall reparative movement as a master narrative for dealing with Black history, nor as a recipe for formulating posttraumatic Black identities. Her poetics as well as politics are complex. "The relationship between possessor and possessed is, like ownership, multidirectional," Parks cautions her readers (1995f, 3). Her plays, including *The America Play*, also articulate her awareness that the possibilities for a reparative historiography are intrinsically entangled with various vicissitudes and accidents that might hinder and thwart her figures' attempts at autopoiesis. While Brazil in *The America Play* succeeds in getting "some benefits" (180) out of history, his father decidedly does not. Likewise, while Aretha Saxon takes charge of her own historical record, Sergeant Smith, with whom Parks ends *Imperceptible Mutabilities*, succeeds only partially.[35] According to her credo that "there is no such thing as THE Black Experience; . . . there are many experiences of being Black" (1995d, 21), the playwright refuses to settle on a single historical narrative or possibility for her dramatic figures. Her narratives and identities continue to be in flux. Not surprisingly, she tends to revisit certain themes and figures in later plays, to figure them differently, as evident, for instance, in her renewed engagement with the Lincoln myth in *Topdog/Underdog*.[36]

I want to conclude this chapter with a brief reading of this 2002 Pulitzer Prize–winning play, which according to some scholars represents a caesura in Parks's dramatic oeuvre as well as in her engagement with history. With *Topdog/Underdog*, Parks begins to embrace a more realist dramaturgy that foregrounds character and plot development. In 1995, in her seminal essay "From Elements of Style," Parks states that traditional dramatic structures, such as realism, could not accommodate the figures she envisions, that the kind of work she sets out to do required nonlinear, experimental forms of playwriting (1995e, 8). Her shift to realism might thus be mistaken for a return to a more conventional understanding of drama as a form of mimesis rather than poiesis. Yet, so I suggest, Parks's deployment of realism does not entail the forfeit of historiopoiesis. Although it appears to be more pronounced in the earlier, experimental plays, historiopoiesis continues to assert its force even in such seemingly closed theatrical forms as realism and naturalism.

HUSTLING REALISM

Topdog/Underdog features two fully developed, realist characters—the African American brothers Lincoln and Booth—who act in psychologically motivated ways and struggle with classic issues of realist drama, such as everyday socioeconomic struggles, dreams of upward mobility, and attendant conflicts over one's sense of dignity, thwarted dreams, and betrayals. In naturalist fashion, the play, moreover, foregrounds the protagonists' failure to refigure past and present socioeconomic conditions that continue to constrain them. In accordance with the historical script that their given names index, Booth ends up shooting Lincoln. Such a fatalistic denouement has prompted several critics to conclude that in stark contrast to *The America Play*, *Topdog/Underdog* fails to refigure history for African Americans. "Linc [sic] and Booth are condemned to relive a representation of history they do not know how to remake," Verna Foster writes (2005, 35). Myka Tucker-Abramson concurs that in this second Lincoln play "the site of history [is] stripped of its potentially transformative or liberating character" (2007, 85). Jochen Achilles similarly holds that Parks "clearly privileges predetermination over freedom. The performative scenarios in this play are prisons and traps rather than instruments of viable self-invention" (2010, 122). To be sure, as in her previous plays, Parks underscores the extent to which characters are trapped in a history not of their own making. She also raises important questions with regard to the persisting economic and psychic hold of the traumatic past over contemporary identities. Yet, as I argue in this concluding section, even as the playwright's dramaturgy gives way to realist characters and a naturalist plot development, it continues to be informed by her historiopoetic method. In addition to its astute analysis of the status quo (the way things are and have been), *Topdog/Underdog* (and, in a sense, also *Father Comes Home from the Wars* and *White Noise*) continues to remain invested in exploring performative possibilities for change.

In addition to her choice of realist themes, characters, and dialogue, the impression that Parks has forfeited the performative agenda of her earlier plays rests, above all, on the claustrophobic setting, which, according to naturalist milieu theory, determines both character and plot. Una Chaudhuri comments on Parks's mise-en-scène for this play, "instead of the openness and diffused spatiality that so powerfully conveyed the searching nature of her earlier dramaturgy, this stage is not just a room, but an archetypal room, a room with a vengeance. It is tiny, windowless, with only one door (only one way in or out). A very emblem of limits and boundaries" (2002, 289). According to Chaudhuri, this kind of setting suggests that for there to be a top dog, there must be an underdog—and there can only be one of each kind. But as Parks reminds us, we should never approach her plays with regard to content alone but always consider the politics of form.[37] Given that *Topdog/Underdog*, like its companion piece *The America Play*, abounds with metaphors of performance and play as well as with highly theatrical scenes of playacting, staging, rehearsing, impersonating (including another presidential impersonation), and a three-card monte game, the play's pronounced foregrounding of scenarios of performance and performativity and the ways these interact with the constraints of realist/naturalist form certainly merit closer analysis.

To begin with, in *Topdog/Underdog* we once again encounter two protagonists who attempt to refigure an arduous past and oppressive present through the liberal fusion of fact and fiction to "forge"—in Kevin Young's dual understanding of the term as faking and creating (2012, 24)—narratives that can enable them to act in the present. Flipping through a "raggedy" family photo album (Parks 2001c, 13), Lincoln (Link) seeks to revise a difficult childhood marked by poverty and parental abandonment into a "practical past" of picture-book suburban bliss, "selling lemonade on thu corner, thuh treehouse out back, summers spent lying in thu grass and looking at thu stars" (65). His younger brother, Booth, tries to brighten up the brothers' "seedily furnished rooming house room" (7) in a similarly performative manner by creatively repurposing two milk crates as a "sorta modular unit" (13). And there is Link's occupation as another Abraham Lincoln impersonator trying to make a living out of the nightly enactment of the president's murder. These kinds of performance clearly establish the two brothers as heirs to Parks's genealogy of historiopoetic performers attempting to forge workable identities from a history that has orphaned them.

The most prominent ludic activity and central performance metaphor of the play is the three-card monte game, an icon of conman-ship and hustling. Both brothers consider it their ticket to economic success and social status. Throughout the play, Booth, who has been making a living as a creative shoplifter, is eager to acquire his brother's expert card skills and to team up with him in a family con venture. To Lincoln and Booth, this kind of hustling offers a viable alternative to an economic system that continues to relegate Black men to the status of underdog. Link's job at the amusement park pointedly illustrates the systemic racism and precarity of employment that many African Americans face in a neoliberal economy. As a Black man, Link is forced to "wear a little makeup and accept less" (29) than his white predecessor on the job. His demeaning, low-salary employment is persistently threatened by plans to replace him with a dummy. The stark poverty of the brothers' cramped and "seedily furnished" (7) room provides a powerful visual metaphor for their economic situation and prospects. Not surprisingly, the two brothers sense in the shadow economy of street hustling the opportunity denied to them in daily life. Hustling holds forth the promise not only of thriving economically but also of asserting their acumen and virility in the public space, of gaining social status within their community—of coming out as top dog. The persistent patter of the three-card monte game, which runs as leitmotif through the play, gives audible expression to this yearning. As Booth says, "We could be a team, man. Rake in the money! . . . Pockets bulging, plenty of cash! And the ladies would be thrilling! You could afford to get laid! Grace would be all over me again" (20).

With regard to its performative nature, hustling is closely related to faking. Like the faker (e.g., Brazil and Aretha), the hustler attempts to alter our perception of what *is* through word and action. But in marked contrast to the faker, the hustler also insists on maintaining clear demarcations between fact and fiction. He insists on knowing "the real deal" (22) from the make-believe, even as he thrives on manipulating this difference for his audiences. As Link admonishes his younger brother while teaching him the monte game, "You dont know what is you dont know what aint, you dont know shit" (73). Hustling consists not in the blurring of differences (a "diamond-esque" ring presented as "just as good as the real thing") but rather in the deliberate presentation of "what aint" for "what is"—that is, in an act of deception. The hustler accepts the boundaries of a given reality, operating within them, while the faker, in the tradition of the fabulator, by blurring the categories of real and fake, pushes against these boundaries, attempting to widen our understanding of what counts as "fact" and "real."

Hustling hinges on the aggressive and underhanded manipulation of reality, primarily for monetary gain. It opens up, as Jason Bush has shown in his reading of *Topdog/Underdog*, an alternative form of masculinity, one marked by the performance of coolness and the flaunting of illegitimately earned money "as a source of pride and anti-authoritarianism" (2007, 78). This image of the hustler as the "cool cat" or "top dog," who through his performance skills freely avails himself of economic and sexual opportunities, is deeply attractive to both Booth and Link. But while Booth has a very romanticized notion of hustling as a sort of "fair" game, in which there is a genuine chance of winning for everyone involved ("Sometimes we will win sometimes they will win. They fast they win, we faster we win," 2001c, 22), Link knows it for a deceptive craft in which there is no winning. He is keenly aware of its price and limitations, its detrimental impact on the community, and the evanescence of its gains. Dividing the world into dealers and marks, "players" and "played," hustling refuses to recognize ties of kinship or empathy: "We took a father for the money he was gonna get his kids a new bike with and he cried in the street while we vanished. We took a mothers welfare check" (55). By the end of the play, Link will have hustled his own brother. Above all, as Link is painfully aware, even the best hustler eventually gets taken in by the system he is trying to trick and escape. At first, Link loses his partner, Lonny, to the violence inherent to the economy of hustling. Then he learns firsthand that in the end the system catches up with the hustler. His legitimate employment at the amusement park might give him the illusion of a fresh start ("Sit down. With benefits," 54), but the nature of his whiteface impersonation and the precarity of employment also reveal how ultimately the system hustles the hustler. As Booth remarks, "Dressing up like some crackerass white man, some dead president and letting people shoot at you sounds like a hustle to me. . . . You play Honest Abe. You aint going back but you going all the way back. Back to way back then when folks was slaves and shit" (22).

Booth, by comparison, might dream of hustling, but his idealistic faith in the transformative power of play—offering a genuine chance to both players and played—marks him as a descendant of Parks's large family of fakers. Throughout the play, Booth proves to be quite alert to the performative power of things and words, their capacity to shape perception and impact reality. For example, when he proposes that the brothers obtain a telephone, he does so not for its use value but for the cultural capital it represents. Being able to share a phone number with prospective dates, he reasons, signals that one has a home as well as cash to pay the bills, and, above all, "no wife or wife approximation on the premises" (32). Likewise, when Booth steals new suits for himself and his brother and Lincoln wonders out loud when and where he would ever wear such a fashionable outfit, Booth responds, "Just wear it around. Itll make you feel good and when you feel good yll meet someone nice" (30). Booth's faith in the performative is probably most pronounced when he changes his name to 3-Card in an attempt to refashion himself, his fumbling attempts at card throwing notwithstanding, as a skilled hustler. In short, even though based on a bluff, Booth believes that his acts of faking and make-believe will eventually have real effects and transform their lives in substantial and sustainable ways.

In pitting these two brothers against each other, Parks also seems to pit two different strategies for staking out a living, for forging an identity in the face of a crushing historical legacy of systemic economic and social discrimination, against each other: hustling and faking. In the final scene, the hustler/realist seems to triumph over the faker/dreamer as Lincoln successfully hustles his brother for his maternal inheritance. Unwilling to give it up, Booth shoots Lincoln. Such a denouement might easily be read as deterministic, as the playwright's abdication of faith in the force of performance. Neither the faker nor the hustler succeeds in refiguring the dominant historical script. On the performative level, however, the play refuses to be contained by a binary reading of hustling vs. faking. Rather, *Topdog/Underdog* makes a point of blurring and confounding these categories throughout the play. The faker strives to become a hustler, and the hustler is eventually taken aback by the performative force of faking.

Despite their realistic veneer, Link and Booth cannot easily be pinned down as hustler or faker, as advocates of either the real or the performative. Throughout the play, Parks, in fact, intertwines the two, muddling the distinctions between them. Michael LeMahieu (2012) makes an interesting case for considering Booth as a hustler in his own right, performing the little brother to Link's patronizing top dog to get his brother to teach him the game. Conversely, Link's sense of self becomes increasingly entangled with the role he performs. Despite his repeated assertion of the hustler's credo of knowing the "real deal" (2001c, 22) and his preserving a clear sense of self during his Lincoln performance ("Fake beard. Top hat. Dont make me into no Lincoln. I was Lincoln on my own before any of that," 30), he finds it more and more difficult to draw a clear line between the "real" and the "fake," between who he thinks he is and who he appears to be. He begins to wear his Lincoln costume on the way home and to fall asleep in it. His Lincoln impersonation feels the most genuine at the moment it is reflected through several levels of fake mediations. Wearing a cheap top hat and frock coat that are made to look historical, along with a false wart, fringe beard, and whiteface make-up, Link observes his faux assassin approaching him in the upside-down reflection of a dented metal fuse box on the wall opposite him. It is at this moment of heightened awareness of the various layers of surrogation and mediation that Link admits, "And for a minute, with him [the assassin] hanging back there behind me, its real. Me looking at him upside down, and him looking at me looking like Lincoln" (50). Clearly, whatever constitutes the "real" for Lincoln at this moment is already part and parcel of interlinked processes of representation, is brought about through a series of performances; the real and the performative are intrinsically entangled in Lincoln's sense of self. With regard to the play's two primary performative tropes—the Lincoln impersonation and the card game, which also hinges on the play with essence and appearance—*Topdog/Underdog* thus offers, in the words of Jon Dietrick, "a complex meditation on the nature of the real" (2007, 64). In this manner, Parks effectively undercuts the naturalist logic that something must be either real or representation, either true or false, which severely "limits the way we may think about who we are" (Dietrick 2007, 57).

Arguably, it is the insistence that "the fake" needs to be clearly distinguishable from "the real" that brings about the dramatic catastrophe. It arises when Link insists, very much in the spirit of the hustler's credo, on verifying Booth's claim of a maternal inheritance. As Lincoln brings down the knife to cut open the stocking that supposedly holds his savings, Booth shoots him. Despite repeated and drastic setbacks, Booth, unlike his brother, has up to the end held on to the idealistic notion that change is possible, that an economic or romantic opportunity will eventually arise and allow him to realize his sense of self. This faith is symbolized not by his girlfriend, "Amazing Grace" (for whom he waits in vain), but by his mother's parting gift. When she leaves her family, she hands Booth a rolled-up nylon stocking, which allegedly contains five hundred-dollar bills. Lincoln had been given the same amount of money by his absconding father but blew the bequest immediately, while Booth has held on to what he calls "my inheritance" (2001c, 17), never once resorting to it in moments of financial duress, never once even verifying the contents of the stocking. To Link's provocative banter, "How you know? She coulda been jiving you, bro" (106), he firmly responds "She was for real" (106). To Booth, it does not matter whether the inheritance is actual or merely imagined; what matters is the reality of the performative gesture that created a nurturing link to the past, to his mother, to his sense of family and community, which he now so desperately seeks to revive with his brother. The tightly knotted maternal stocking symbolizes his faith that his idea of the past will make a difference in the present and future: "I been saving it" (105). The final scene's insistence on the clear discernibility of "what is" from "what aint," however, reinforces the sense of a rigged game in which there is no winning. Link comments on the brothers' limited choices within a white hegemonic order: "It may look like you got a chance but the only time you pick right is when thuh man lets you. And when its thuh real deal, when its thuh real fucking deal, bro, and thuh moneys on thuh line, that's when thuh man wont want you picking right" (106–7).

In light of such a deterministic ending, what possibilities for autopoiesis might *Topdog/Underdog* hold forth? None, if we focus entirely on the logic of a naturalist plot. There are no surprises here. Booth will shoot Lincoln, as predicted by their given names and as foreshadowed in a Chekhovian manner in the opening scene, when a surprised Booth pulls a gun on his older brother. If we pay attention, however, to the multiple forms of play at work, to their various material, sensuous, sonic, and performative dimensions, and also to the virtuosity of the players at play (both the characters and the actors), several possibilities begin to open up.

To begin with, in interspersing a naturalist plot line and realist character development with highly theatrical scenes that repeatedly foreground how bodies rehearse, stage, and revise identities through word and action, Parks alerts us to the hustle of realism, a mode of representation that—not unlike the three-card monte game—denies its constitutive difference from reality, claiming to present us with "a slice of life," even as the assertion of this difference is at the heart of its artistic practice.[38] While the program notes, along with the mise-en-scène, ostensibly invite our full absorption into and identification with an unfolding drama about "family wounds and healing,"[39] the play's opening scene should alert us that there is nothing "real" about what is to unfold, that the realist setup (stage set, speech, characters) might very well be a theatrical sham for our empathy and, yes, also money. "Watch me close watch me close now: who-see-thu-red-card-who-see-thuh-red-card?" (7), Booth intones at the start of the play in a seemingly fumbling attempt to master the game. A little later, Link reminds the audience that "thuh perspective from thuh sidelines is thuh perspective of a customer" (71) and that any spectator/customer is also always a potential "mark." Given the repeated and heavy emphasis on the mechanics of an ongoing game of make-believe—reinforced by the persistent patter of the cards throughout the play—the question arises, whether the playwright herself might be throwing some cards for us.

If we can manage to step back from the identificatory spell of realism and switch our focus in the manner of a Brechtian spectator from character and plot development to performance, theater, and play, we might be more likely to see how Parks's drama plays with the categories of "what is" and "what aint," shuffling them about in her own theatrical three-card monte game. Note, for instance, how Link, despite his knowledge that even the best player eventually gets played, cherishes the moment of the play: "Hustling. Shit, I was good. I was great. Hell I was the be all and end all" (55). We know that he is "deft, dangerous, [and] electric" (56) because we have the opportunity to watch him perform, to witness "thuh moves and thuh grooves, thuh talk and thuh walk, thuh patter and thuh pitter pat, thuh flap and thuh rap" (75). Virtuoso performances such as this one—along with numerous others, including the brothers' parodic imitation of happy-family routines, their transformative use of clothes and props, and their joint rehearsal of the presidential murder—invite us to give ourselves fully to the thrill and sensuality of the performance. They not only reinforce a sense of theatricality that breaks with any pretenses of "slice-of-life" realism, they also suggest that the play's naturalism cuts, in Chaudhuri's words, "only skin deep" (2002, 289). Within the play, Chaudhuri claims, "lurks a vast metaphoric potentiality, both poetic and political" (289).

Hustling might be based on differentiating "thu Player from thuh Played" (Parks 2001c, 106), but what draws the played to the player in the first place is the moment of possibility that flashes up in the performance itself. We must not lose sight of the players in their play, regardless of whether that play entails faking or hustling: the virtuosity of their verbal and physical performances (their "goodlooking walk and dynamite talk," 75), their skill at handling objects, manipulating situations, and changing identities, and, above all, the "marvel of [their] live bodies on stage" (Parks 1995e, 6) and the myriad possibilities they promise. "We know what happens to Lincoln and Booth in actual history," Parks comments, "but what are the other possibilities on stage?" (quoted in DesRochers 2014, 107). Booth, along with Lincoln, as well as the other players in Parks's rich cast of fakers, embody this sense of possibility. As Parks insists, in her theatrical practice she aims to tell it not just "like it is" or "as it was" but "as it could be" (1995d, 21). We should, therefore, take Lincoln's injunction that "there aint no winning" (2001c, 106) with a grain of salt—the gain is in the reality of the performance, the way it reshuffles established categories and puts seemingly hard and fast signifiers, time-honored tropes and narratives of history up for grabs again.

A SIDELONG GLANCE AT HISTORY
Unreliable Narration and the Silhouette
as Blickmaschine *in Kara Walker*

"This work is based on a purposeful misreading of historical texts like *Gone with the Wind*," Walker comments on her 1994 debut installation, *Gone: An Historical Romance of a Civil War as It Occurred b'tween the Dusky Thighs of One Young Negress and Her Heart*.[1] Casually erasing the distinction between what is typically considered "historical" and what is considered "fictional," Walker delineates with this seemingly offhand remark her program for approaching the past. First, in designating Margaret Mitchell's historical romance of the antebellum plantation South and the Civil War as historical, she puts it on par with scholarly historiographies of slavery. Even as such a glib redesignation of a clearly fictional work mocks readers' ardent faith in the truthfulness of fiction, it also acknowledges the affective force of works such as Mitchell's (particularly in its 1939 Hollywood film adaptation) or Harriet Beecher Stowe's sentimental novel *Uncle Tom's Cabin* (1852) and the formative influence they have had on contemporary understandings of slavery. Second, having thus established the complex collusion of fact and fiction in our access to the past, Walker then sets out to misread the history these works represent. Reading well-known narratives, established themes and motifs, as well as received iconographies of slavery (scholarly and popular, dominant and counterhegemonic, white and Black) against the grain, she effectively defamiliarizes and destabilizes what has come to stand as familiar and accepted. Moreover, taking what she calls a "side-long glance" (quoted in Saltz 1996, 82) at history as we believe we know it, she excavates the wondrous histories of her viewers' collective and personal imagination when it comes to representations of race and of Blackness in particular. At the same time—and this, then, is the third step in Walker's approach to history—her playful digs at reified verbal and visual narratives of slavery also attempt to shape and refigure the intrinsic collusion of fact and fiction in our approach to the past in such ways that new subject positions may emerge. As scholar-writer Touré explains quite to the point, "This black woman has taken a knife to history and recast it in her own vision" (2011, 35).

This chapter is concerned with Walker's creative misreadings of and sidelong glances at received canonical and popular narratives of history. In particular, I will focus on two principal strategies: Walker's revival of the eighteenth-century medium of the cut-paper silhouette and her deployment of a figure she refers to as the "Negress" as the homodiegetic and highly unreliable narrator of her visual narratives. In a first section, I examine the complex role the Negress plays as artist/author/ protagonist in Walker's verbal and visual Signifyin(g) on the genre of the slave narrative. I aim to show how, with the help of this figure, Walker effectively destabilizes the genre's alleged authoritativeness in providing authentic, (auto)biographical accounts of slavery and exposes the covert contract between author, sponsors, and readers that undergirds representations of the Black subject. Performing the role of the picara—the quintessential unreliable narrator who by taking on a number of unstable roles exposes the ideologies of her time—Walker's figure of the Negress exceeds the mediations that produce and contain her. In this manner, she also refunctions (in a Brechtian sense) the genre's various, intrinsic levels of mediations as means for assuming authorship of the past.[2]

Among the broad spectrum of roles enacted by the Negress in Walker's oeuvre—including survivor, victim, witness, accomplice, rebel, leader—is that of a cutter of profiles, a silhouettist.[3] In a second section, I turn to Walker's (and the Negress's) use of the silhouette as a crucial tool in her historiopoetic project. I here focus on the ways in which the artist exposes the visual medium of the silhouette as a *Blick-maschine*—a scopic apparatus that invites a particular look or gaze, not merely representing but actively shaping and producing modes of seeing and knowing, and that turns out to be deeply implicated in the production of racialized subjects. In Walker's hands, the silhouette then serves as both the medium and object of inquiry, bringing into focus the historical role this art form has played in the collusion of fact and fiction that has informed perceptions of Blackness from the late eighteenth century onward. At the same time, the silhouette also becomes a potent means for intervening in this long history of constructions of Blackness. In several of Walker's artworks, we find the Negress with a knife, scissors, or chisel in hand, ready to destroy and alter the narratives and images into which she finds herself interpellated. The art of cutting, I suggest in a final section of this chapter, also proves to be a powerful historiopoetic technique for fabulating Blackness differently. Approaching Walker's provocative "pictorial histories"[4] with sets of questions and theories from the fields of both literary studies and visual studies, I aim to bring into focus two different yet interrelated ways in which the artist sets out to excavate and refigure the complex entanglement of narrative and visual mediations of the Black body in contemporary understandings of slavery and its various legacies: her use of the silhouette and of the autodiegetic narration of the slave narrative.

ANAMORPHIC OPTICS

Introduced in the title of her New York debut piece *Gone: An Historical Romance of a Civil War as It Occurred b'tween the Dusky Thighs of One Young Negress and Her Heart* (1994), the Negress has recurred throughout the artist's silhouette work and has also emerged as a distinctive voice in some of her writings and interviews. Modeled after the autodiegetic narrators of the antebellum slave narratives, who, having successfully escaped the South, detail in retrospect the travails of their bondage and perils of their flight to freedom, the Negress functions simultaneously as a sort of authorial alter ego, as narrator, and as character. In this complex semiotic function, she purports to guide the reader/viewer from the vantage point of the survivor and witness through the troubled factual and fictional terrain of American slavery. "I often compare my method of working to that of a well-meaning freed woman in a Northern State," Walker comments, "who is attempting to delineate the horrors of Southern slavery but with next to no resources, other than some paper and a pen knife and some people she would like to kill" (quoted in Armstrong 1997, 106). Clearly, Walker cautions us not to trust this narrator, for in addition to a strong revenge motif, the Negress professes to an intense interest in meddling with the past— "not always with malice but definitely with intent" (Als 2011, n.p.). The desire to meddle with our knowledge of the past is evident in various aspects of her visual slave narratives: the use of provocative titles, the playful Signifyin(g) on genre conventions, the instability of the narrative voice, and, above all, the use of the silhouette form.

The cut-paper silhouette is crucial to the Negress's—and Walker's— project of purposefully misreading historical texts, of meddling with the past and recasting it in her own vision. As she repeatedly performs the role of a silhouettist, she captures everything in profile, casting what Walker calls a "side-long glance" at a person or event: "It's the little look and it's full of suspicion, potential ill-will, or desire. It's a look unreliable women give" (quoted in Saltz 1996, 82). Although this sidelong glance at first seems to distort what it seeks to render (Walker's silhouette installations have frequently been described as grotesque and carnivalesque), it also reveals upon refocusing how the viewer's perception of what counts and does not count as "historical" is always already informed by contemporary presuppositions, desires, and anxieties as well as by established histories of looking and knowing.

Slavoj Žižek's notion of "looking awry" is useful in conceptualizing the anamorphic optics of the Negress's visual slave narratives with regard to her use of both the silhouette and unreliable narration. In anamorphosis, an object appears blurred when looked at frontally but takes on a clear shape when looked at from an angle. According to Žižek, this look "from aside" is also the look of interest, "a look supported, permeated, and 'distorted' by a desire" (1989, 34). Importantly, the object focused by the look of desire is posited by desire itself (Žižek calls it the Lacanian *objet petit a*); it does not exist apart from the look that produces it. This does not mean that it is merely phantasmagoric; rather, as semblance it triggers concrete, material effects, "a whole chain of consequences which regulate our 'material,' 'effective' life and deeds" (34). On this score then, the invested and distorting glance from the side can at times give the clearest shape to those immaterial yet highly consequential "facts" that determine what and how we see—or choose not to see.

In what follows, I want to make Žižek's explication of the work of anamorphosis, his concept of looking awry, productive for reading both Walker's silhouette work and her intertextual and intermedial Signifyin(g) on the genre of the slave narrative.[5] The artist's sidelong glance at the popular medium of antebellum genteel culture (the silhouette) and at the preferred genre of the abolitionist movement (the slave narrative) reveals how both have served to collude mimetic pretense and phantasmagoric projection in constructing their subjects. At the same time, the figure of the Negress herself serves as a screen for racializing projections of the Black female body. Not surprisingly then, as the artist tells us, the birth of the figure of the Negress went hand-in-hand with her discovery of the medium of the silhouette[6]—both invite the anamorphic look of desire and anxiety. The silhouette then functions as a highly ambivalent medium of historiography in the hands of a highly ambivalent narrator—together, they frustrate viewers' desire for clarity, for confirmation of established modes of seeing and knowing the past, while also bringing into focus through an anamorphic optics these desires and their accompanying anxieties of seeing and knowing differently.

NARRATIVES OF A NEGRESS: SLAVE NARRATIVE AND UNRELIABLE NARRATION

Walker likes to compare her silhouette installations to the slave narratives of the antebellum period.[7] The self-written or dictated biographical narratives of formerly enslaved African Americans bearing witness to their experience of slavery and flight to freedom were quite popular in the period from 1830 to 1865 and extremely relevant to the abolitionist movement.[8] Walker is drawn to the genre for several reasons. On a personal level, she finds in it a suitable means for rendering her experience of having suddenly been "thrust into history" (quoted in Saltz 1996, 86) when her family moved from Stockton, California, to Stone Mountain, Georgia—a suburb of the greater Atlanta metropolitan area, notorious for its memorial to the Confederacy and for being home to the reestablishment of the Ku Klux Klan in 1915. Confronted there with various blatant and latent forms of racism, Walker compares her move to the South to having "been sold into slavery" (quoted in Armstrong

1997, 104) and her later evolution as an artist, her move from Atlanta to the Rhode Island School of Design in New England, to a movement from slavery "to freedom" (quoted in Alberro 1996, n.p.).

Beyond such immediate personal uses, the genre also allows Walker to bring into focus broader concerns regarding African American history and memory culture. The slave narratives, as Henry Louis Gates Jr. reminds us, present contemporary readers with "veritable repositories of the ontological and epistemological concerns of human beings enslaved in antebellum America" (1985a, vi). At stake in their production were not only questions of authenticity but the struggle of gaining access to representation and, through representation, to the status of the human being. Walker addresses this nexus of race and representation, the intersection of the assertion of being with modes of knowing in her provocative silhouette installations. Her visual slave narratives therefore transcend the merely personal/biographical. As with the original slave narratives, "the individual 'I' of the black author" serves to focus "the collective 'I' of the race" (Gates 1985b, xxv). But even as Walker, in citing the genre conventions of slave narratives, underscores this link between the personal and the collective, she also profoundly troubles a homogenous notion of Black identity that the genre historically sought to evoke. In her refiguration neither the individual nor the community emerge as fully legible or clearly definable subjects. Rather, as her silhouette narratives make quite clear, both are products of various layers of projection and mediation. Like the silhouette, the slave narrative functions in Walker's hands both as a historicist means to access the history of New World slavery and as a provocative anamorphic lens for bringing into focus the various levels of mediation that African Americans continue to be subjected to visually and textually in their long struggle for emancipation. Walker's playful Signifyin(g) on the genre conventions of the slave narrative and her use of unreliable narration substantially refocus our reading/viewing habits of race. They share this function with the silhouette as *Blickmaschine*—the topic of the second part of this chapter.

A form of autobiographical writing (the earliest in African American literature), the slave narrative was at once an enabling and delimiting medium for bearing testimony to the traumatic experience of slavery. While it allowed former slaves to assume a voice, to fashion a self through writing, and to claim, through authorship, the human rights denied to them under slavery, it also required them to speak in a recognizably "Black" voice that corresponded to the reading habits and expectations of a white middle-class audience and to the political expediencies of the abolitionist movement, which largely sponsored the publication and dissemination of their narratives. Prevailing concerns over the authenticity and objectivity of the narrative voice, along with a desire to read the slave narratives as the indictment of an institution rather than as the recollections of an individual, severely restricted the narrators' possibilities for an imaginative engagement with the past, for rendering their experiences in a unique narrative meaningful to their particular biography. "As a result, the slave narrative is most often a non-memorial description fitted to a pre-formed mold," James Olney comments, "a mold with regular depressions here and equally regular prominences there—virtually obligatory figures, scenes, turns of phrases, observances and authentications—that carry over from narrative to narrative and give to them as a group the species character that we designate by the phrase 'slave narrative'" (1985, 151). John Sekora similarly points to the various levels of institutional, political, conceptual, and genre framing imposed on the former slave's narrative to mainstream it for white audiences and make it fit for abolitionist propaganda: "Not black recollection, but white interrogation brings order to the narration" (1987, 509). According to Sekora, one can therefore hardly speak of the creation of a self through narrative. Olney agrees: "The lives in the narratives are never, or almost never, there for themselves and for their own intrinsic, unique interest but nearly always in their capacity as illustrations of what slavery is really like. Thus in one sense the narrative lives of the ex-slaves are as much possessed and used by the abolitionists as their actual lives had been by slaveholders" (1985, 154).

Walker is acutely aware of the slave narrative's double dynamic, which, on the one hand, counters the prevalent prejudice against enslaved African Americans and provides "a higher than high uplift of the oppressed people" (quoted in Saltz 1996, 82) and, on the other hand, subjects their voices to a delimiting, even silencing, white paternalism. Going back to the slave narrative and other forms of abolitionist fiction, such as the sentimental novel, she deconstructs the discursive mechanisms of projecting a Black subject for white consumption and exposes the ongoing mediations of "this black body . . . jiggling around and representing everything but itself" (quoted in Alberro 1996, n.p.; ellipsis in the original). Two techniques feature prominently in this endeavor: Signifyin(g) with playful and parodic titles on relevant motifs and conventions of the slave narrative and introducing with the figure of "Miss K. Walker, A Free Negress of Noteworthy Talent" (Saltz 1996, 82) a highly unreliable narrator to her visual slave narratives. These techniques enable Walker to underline the ways in which the subject of the slave narrative is situated on the cusp between autobiography and public desire, determined by both fact and fiction. In addition, they also allow her to harness the performative force of her playful and critical interrogations of the genre to engender a persona who, while produced by these mediations, succeeds in transcending them.

Following her introduction in Walker's inaugural piece, *Gone* (1994), the Negress—also variously referred to as "Miss K. Walker," "Kara Elizabeth Walker," or "K. E. B. Walker"—quickly became a regular figure in the artist's silhouette installations, prominently featured in titles such as *The Battle of Atlanta: Being the Narrative of a Negress in the Flames of Desire—A Reconstruction* (1995); *Being the True Account of the Life of N—A Self Made Slave Mistress* (1996); *Presenting Negro Scenes Drawn Upon My Passage Through the South and Reconfigured for the Benefit of Enlightened Audiences Wherever Such May Be Found, by Myself, Missus K. E. B. Walker, Colored* (1997); *Freedom: A Fable by Kara Elizabeth Walker—A Curious Interpretation of the Wit of a Negress in Troubled Times. With Illustrations* (1997); *Slavery! Slavery! Presenting a GRAND and LIFELIKE Panoramic Journey into Picturesque Southern Slavery or "Life at 'Ol' Virginny's Hole' (sketches from Plantation Life)" See the Peculiar Institution as never before! All cut from black paper by the able hand of Kara Elizabeth Walker, an Emancipated Negress and a leader in her Cause* (1997); and *For the Benefit of All the Races of Mankind (Mos' Specifically the Master One, Boss), An Exhibition of Artifacts, Remnants, Effluvia EXCAVATED from the Black Heart of a Negress* (2002).[9] With some of these titles, Walker signifies, in more or less subtle ways, on the titles of nineteenth-century slave narratives. In particular, she playfully iterates certain standard motifs that convey the slave narrative's prevalent concern with authorial status and narrative authenticity. Phrases such as "being the true account of the life of N" (*Being the True Account*) or "by Myself, Missus K. E. B. Walker, Colored" (*Presenting Negro Scenes*) echo the myriad assertions of authorship in the original slave narratives, as evident in such well-known titles as

The Interesting Narratives of the Life of Olaudah Equiano, or Gustavus Vassa, the African, Written by Himself (1789) and Harriet Jacobs's *Incidents in the Life of a Slave Girl. Written by Herself* (1861). Such declarations of authorship not only helped to assuage the white audiences' concerns with authenticity, they also highlighted the author's acquisition of literacy. As Gates and Olney have shown, literacy—and, more concretely, the ability to state one's name in writing—was considered to be key to an enslaved person's coming into legibility as a human subject. Besides ascertaining the narrator's existence as an actual person and with it the factualness of his or her account, a much more essential performative task was accomplished by such written assertions of the self: "prior to the claim of truthfulness is the simple, existential claim: 'I exist.' . . . Only then can the narrative begin" (Olney 1985, 155). It is hence the written proclamation of one's self that confers not only epistemological but ontological meaning to the self; in a sort of speech act, it brings the self into being.

Walker pays homage to this early mode of autopoiesis in African American literature but also questions it and adapts it for her own purposes. The lengthy title *Slavery! Slavery! Presenting a GRAND and LIFELIKE Panoramic Journey into Picturesque Southern Slavery or "Life at 'Ol' Virginny's Hole' (sketches from Plantation Life)" See the Peculiar Institution as never before! All cut from black paper by the able hand of Kara Elizabeth Walker, an Emancipated Negress and a leader in her Cause* (1997) provides a fitting example. In the careful parsing of the concluding phrase, "All cut from black paper by the able hand of Kara Elizabeth Walker, an Emancipated Negress and a leader in her Cause," the autodiegetic narrator establishes with the assertion of her craftsmanship ("able hands") her visual literacy and, with that, her subjectivity as a person ("Kara Elizabeth Walker"), on the basis of which she then lays claim to emancipation ("an Emancipated Negress"). The interdependent trinity of literacy, identity, and freedom, which features so prominently in the original slave narratives, not only enables Walker's visual narrative to commence ("See the Peculiar Institution as never before!"), it also empowers the author-narrator to lay claim to leadership status, fashioning herself as heiress to such public figures as Harriet Tubman or Frederick Douglass. At the same time, she also deftly undermines our traditional understanding of leadership on behalf of a collective with whom one identifies when she designates herself as "a leader in her [own] Cause." The question to what extent Walker's Negress proves to be a reliable leader to her people, let alone a reliable narrator to her audience, will be taken up shortly.

In addition to riffing on concerns over authenticity and authorship, Walker's lengthy titles, in their pronounced theatricality and sensationalism, also poke fun at the very notion of autopoiesis, at the former slave's ardent faith in fashioning a discernable, unique, authentic, and "free" self on the basis of literacy and authorship. Note how the title *Slavery! Slavery!* promises at one and the same time high drama and *vraisemblance* ("GRAND and LIFELIKE"), both the epic, comprehensive scale of the panorama ("Panoramic Journey") and the rough, episodic outline of the sketch ("sketches from Plantation Life"). It avers to let us "see" the peculiar institution "as never before" while also pledging that the vision will be picturesque—that is, agreeable to our senses. The oxymoronic pairings in this particular title underscore the extent to which the former slaves' (auto)biographies were fundamentally shaped for an audience that might very well be "enlightened" (as suggested by Walker's title *Presenting Negro Scenes for the Benefit of Enlightened Audiences*) but was certainly also consumerist, voyeuristic, and pornographically inclined, fascinated by ever new twists of degradation and suffering.[10] In some of her other titles, Walker tackles this prurience head on, for instance, when she promises to reconstruct the 1864 Battle of Atlanta as *The Narrative of a Negress in the Flames of Desire* (1995) or to render, as in *Gone* (1994), the Civil War "as It Occurred b'tween the Dusky Thighs of One Young Negress and Her Heart." In the original slave narratives, such politics of desire were, of course, typically masked behind emphases of truthfulness and objectivity, but occasionally they would be brought into view in the provocative pairing of neutral and descriptive terms, such as "account," "sketches," "incidents in the life of," with stimulating attributes such as "thrilling" or "interesting."[11] Of the many antebellum slave narratives recorded and preserved, one title in particular comes presciently close to Walker's hyperbolic refigurations—albeit without Walker's acerbic irony: William Anderson's *Life and Narrative of William J. Anderson, Twenty-four Years a Slave; Sold Eight Times! In Jail Sixty Times!! Whipped Three Hundred Times!!! or The Dark Deeds of American Slavery Revealed. Containing Scriptural Views of the Origin of the Black and of the White Man. Also, a Simple and Easy Plan to Abolish Slavery in the United States. Together with an Account of the Services of Colored Men in the Revolutionary War—Day and Date, and Interesting Facts* (1857). The sensationalism of Anderson's title underlines the extent to which the original slave narratives fictionalized and commodified their subjects for the consumption of white audiences. As these narratives sought to bear testimony to the lived experience of an actual person, they also took into account the exigencies of (white) middle-class taste and desire, the literary field, and political expedience. The slave narratives' claim to autopoiesis is thus inherently entangled with the market's demand for reification and consumption. Because they had to target a specific and rather homogenous audience (white middle class) and because they had to advance the political interests of the abolitionist sponsors who enabled and promoted these publications, the author-narrators of the slave narrative were hardly free in fashioning their own life stories.[12] Walker's hyperbolic and histrionic Signifyin(g) on the titles of slave narratives points up the ways that these writings of the self are prescribed by an unwritten pact between author, institutional setting, and audience.

Walker too is keenly attuned to the ways in which she, as a female artist of color operating within a predominantly white art world, is heir to this particular legacy. In a public talk at the California College of Arts and Crafts in 2019, she opens the conversation by performing the role of the author-narrator of her own life story, an artist who escaped from the racist culture in Georgia to the supposedly liberal climate of a New England arts school. As Walker relates parts of her life story, she filters them through the lenses of the historical romance and the slave narrative, which she credits with having begotten the autobiographical character she now performs.[13] "What I discovered was that possessing a black body through which history and fiction coexist was the stuff performance was made of, and I performed a number of parts in a series of vignettes too sordid to relate here to you, my dear audience" (quoted in Lott 2000, 70). So, just as the protagonists of these older genres had to serve as conduits of desire and emotion between authors and readers, she too now offers her character up as "the blank space into which people projected their fantasies" (71), ready to perform the roles inscribed on her.

Walker's figure of the Negress is situated precisely at this intersection of authorial and spectatorial desire. Sharing her name "Kara Elizabeth Walker" (or "K. E. B. Walker") with the artist, she provides a complex interface between artist and narrator-protagonist. This narrator is, in contrast to the original slave narrator, from the start conceived as a performative entity. Hers is not a coherent self, striving for self-articulation, legibility, and recognition. Neither is it a self that performs on occasion to survive (as was the case for numerous fugitives, such as Harriet Jacobs and Ellen and William Craft). For the Negress, performance is not, to invoke Sojourner Truth's memorable phrase, the shadow she sells "to support the substance";[14] rather, it *is* the substance. She exists solely in and through performance; she is performance as such.

Walker explains that the figure was inspired by the fictional character of Lydia Brown in Thomas Dixon's 1905 novel, *The Clansman: An Historical Romance of the Ku Klux Klan,* later adapted for the screenplay of D. W. Griffith's movie *Birth of a Nation* (1915). In both works, the character fulfills the sole function of embodying the racist cliché of the Jezebel figure, a "tawny vixen" seeking to manipulate the white statesman through her sexual wiles. Walker sees the function of Brown and similar figures in popular fictions of the time as that of a "receptacle— she's a black hole, a space defined by things sucked into her. . . . She is simultaneously sub-human and super-human" (quoted in Shaw 2004, 19). Her figure of the Negress is a product of and heir to this genealogy of racist performances projected by the white imaginary. She is the "tall young tawny vixen, / a good Negress, / a comely wench / . . . a scheming, chicken stealing, hoop-skirt haulin', mistress-balling monster of the American imagination" (quoted in Lott 2000, 70). Notably, Walker not only sets out to expose the various roles the Black (female) body is forced to play in the white imaginary, she also provocatively asks, "What about the possibility that I might reflect those fantasies back into the projector's unsuspecting eyes, and cause them to want to face the shame of (our) collective psyche?" (71).

This is where unreliable narration comes into play. Before the concept of unreliable narration is developed in more detail, a brief consideration of the relevance of narratological concepts, such as narrative, homodiegetic narrator, and unreliable narration, for the analysis of a visual medium such as the silhouette may be useful. From a Lessingian perspective, which insists on a clear demarcation between the possibilities of the pictorial and poetic arts,[15] such a transmedial approach would indeed appear ill suited for an analysis of Walker's works. Then again, Walker herself uses the term "narrative" freely in reference to her silhouette installations and silhouette-based video and film work.[16] Her spatial arrangements of silhouettes, moreover, clearly evince several key elements generally considered to be constitutive of narrative, among them temporality of events, experientiality, and representationality.[17] In accordance with "the convention of 'reading' spatial juxtapositions as an index of chronological sequence" (Wolf 2010, 433), Walker's vignettes unfold in a temporal sequence—mostly linearly (according to Western reading habits from left to right), across the space of the wall of a gallery or the page of the catalogue reproduction, with the edge of the wall or page constituting the end of the story, but occasionally also cyclically, as in her cyclorama pieces *The Battle of Atlanta* and *Slavery! Slavery!* Representational rather than abstract in nature, Walker's images also render more or less recognizable events and actions, often connecting individual vignettes through lines and minor visual details (such as a trail of feces in *The End of Uncle Tom*) or the direction of a character's gaze; this creates the impression of a dynamic unfolding of events (rather than sequence of static images). Last but not least, the presence of clearly delineated (even though stereotypical) characters engaged in various actions encourages viewers to decipher these visual figurations as representations of the characters' experience, for instance, by linking up apparently related images, by inferring causal relations (plot) and likely further developments, and, in general, by constructing a temporal sequence of events (story). Walker's titles supply further stimuli for such narrative constructions. In short, because her silhouette installations clearly elicit narrative scripts in the reader, they have narrativity.[18] It therefore seems productive to analyze these scripts in terms of narratological concepts, such as narrative situation and un/reliability.

Having announced herself as author-narrator in the title of the artworks, the Negress reappears as one of the characters, often as the protagonist, in the visual stories she relates. She thus qualifies in Genettian terms as a homodiegetic, and frequently even autodiegetic, narrator. And as with any narrator, we can gauge his or her reliability with the help of various text-external, paratextual, or text-internal clues. In Walker's case, paratextual title phrases such as "Being the Narrative of a Negress in the Flames of Desire" (*Battle of Atlanta*) or text-external announcements such as "This Female Artist Is Wont To Illustrate / Lascivious Subjects / [Miscegenation Is Key Among Them]"[19] alert us to the utterly subjective and frequently erotically charged nature of the

Negress's account. In a similar manner, the provocative title *No mere words can Adequately reflect the Remorse this Negress feels at having been Cast into such a lowly state by her former Masters and so it is with a Humble heart that she brings about their physical Ruin and earthly Demise* (1999) cautions us not to take its declarations of remorse and humility at face value. While the first half of the title mockingly iterates the expected performance of humility on the part of the colonial/ enslaved subject,[20] the second part bluntly exposes the menace that underwrites such colonial mimicry.

Likewise, on the text-internal level we behold a startling discrepancy between the form and content of the artist-narrator's visual utterances: the undeniable elegance of the silhouette lines frequently clashes with the violent and grotesque subject matter they render. Similarly, the pronounced impassiveness displayed by many of the female figures in scenes of sexual violation (e.g., *Battle of Atlanta*) as well as the glee and high spirits marking some of the brutal actions of the child figures (such as the small child with a tambourine leaving a trail of feces in *The End of Uncle Tom* or two kids running off with the amputated leg and hand of their master in *Battle of Atlanta*) raise further doubts about the narrator's reliability. Last but not least, the Negress's stories of slavery and civil war appear to be rather incommensurable with the reader/viewer's text-external frames of reference, particularly with regard to our general knowledge of history and genre conventions. Clearly, the Negress's rendering of *The Battle of Atlanta* has little to do with established historiographies of the event, not even with popular visual renditions of it, such as in the cyclorama at the Atlanta History Center, just as her rendition of *The End of Uncle Tom and the Grand Allegorical Tableau of Little Eva in Heaven* (1995) bears only rudimentary resemblance to its antetext, Harriet Beecher Stowe's sentimental novel *Uncle Tom's Cabin* (1852). According to narratologist Ansgar Nünning, the reader tends to resolve such obvious discrepancies between "the narrator's view of the fictional world and the divergent state of affairs which the reader can grasp" (1997, 87) by attributing them to the narrator's unreliability.

On narratological grounds, then, the Negress's narratives qualify as unreliable ones. But unreliable in what sense exactly? Narratological scholarship tends to be preoccupied with the unreliability of the narrator in relation to the reader's standards of knowledge and morality.[21] Ansgar Nünning, for instance, explains the discrepant awareness between reader and narrator as a sort of dramatic irony in which the reader simply knows "more" or "better" than the narrator. It is the reader then who functions as the normative site of values against which the thoughts and actions of the narrator are judged. On the basis of our own limited perspective, which we tend to mistake for the universal one, we decide whether a narrator is simply fallible and foolish (not getting the full picture) or, worse, untrustworthy and deceitful.[22] In Walker's case, however, this dramatic irony cuts the other way: it is the narrator who exposes the fallibility and conceit of the reader's standards and expectations. The essential question to ask concerning the Negress's unreliability is not, as in classic narrative theory, whether the narrator according to the reader's standards is a fool or a liar, but rather to what extent the narrator's perception of events troubles our own habits of looking at the history of slavery and its various histories of articulation.

This question was brought to the fore during the initial public outcry over Walker's provocative tableaux of slavery. In 1997, just after Walker had been awarded the prestigious MacArthur fellowship, artist Betye Saar, a veteran of fighting racist clichés in the field of the visual arts, famously attacked Walker for "being young and foolish" in perpetuating negative images of Black people (quoted in Bowles 1997, 4) and started a letter campaign to elicit support for banning Walker's works from museums. Art critic Juliette Bowles followed up by reprimanding the artist for failing to rise to "the challenge of producing art that is 'great' in the opinion of most knowledgeable African American art lovers" (quoted in Sanneh et al. 1998, 48). Walker responded to this criticism by insisting that any such dictates of respectability and racial obligation on part of the reader/viewer must be challenged because they delimit what can be said, seen, and imagined.[23] Her seemingly familiar and yet utterly surprising and unsettling historiographies serve as an anamorphic lens for precisely such normative expectations. What appears distorted when looked at straight, comes into focus when looked at awry. Walker's unreliable narratives set out to reveal to us not slavery as we believe to know it but, as Walker puts it, as "An Historical Drama by the (subversive) hand of *a mediated black body set on betraying her confines*, misinterpreting appropriated morsels of a lived reality, and delighting in the uncomfortable repositioning of taboo, pride, decency, and power" (48; emphasis added). In this regard, she does indeed succeed in reflect-

FIGURE 2. Kara Walker. 1998. *Virginia's Lynch Mob*, Cut paper on wall. Installation dimensions variable; approx. 10 × 37 ft. (2.8 × 11.2m). © Kara Walker, courtesy of Sikkema Jenkins & Co., New York. Installation view: *Kara Walker*, Forum for Contemporary Art, St. Louis, MO, 1998. Photo: David Kingsbury.

ing the beholders' "fantasies back into the projector's unsuspecting eyes" (quoted in Lott 2000, 71).

Let us take a closer look at the Negress as an unreliable, even untrustworthy, narrator set on betraying her *and* her readers' confines. As suggested by many of the works' titles, the narrator "K. E. B. Walker" positions herself as recounting her tales of slavery from the vantage point of emancipation and often with a clear pedagogical and social agenda in mind: "for the benefit of mankind" and as a "leader in her cause," as she puts it in some of her titles. One might thus surmise that her interest in the past is motivated by a desire to enlighten her audiences for the sake of advancing her race—a role traditionally assigned to the Black artist from W. E. B. Du Bois to Betye Saar. To be sure, the Negress frequently depicts herself accordingly in text and image. In *Virginia's Lynch Mob* (1998), we behold her as a sort of superwoman, unfettered by the shackles

FIGURE 3. Kara Walker. 1998. *Untitled (Girl with Bucket)*. Cut paper on wall.
80 × 55 in. (2 × 1.4 m). © Kara Walker, courtesy of Sikkema Jenkins & Co., New York.

of the past, who is boldly pointing the way upward as a motley crowd marches and runs behind her (fig. 2). In *The Battle of Atlanta*, we see her, Harriet Tubman–like, picking up a rifle, and in the 1998 vignette *Untitled (Girl with Bucket)*, a younger version of her is marching on, undaunted, with a flag raised high in her hands (fig. 3). But then again, we also often find her as a rather inadequate leader. In *The Battle of Atlanta* she gets distracted by her sexual desire for a white soldier, and in *Virginia's Lynch Mob* she seems to abandon rather than lead her people.[24] Quite frequently, we also behold her sidling up to the very powers she purports to undermine, as in *Being the true account of the life of the Negress* (1996) and *Emancipation Approximation* (1999–2000).

Robert Reid-Pharr argues that the Negress is not so much a Tubman-like figure "confidently leading her people to the promised land" as she is a "black girl lost" (2002, 28). She is lost, however, not in any conventional understanding of having been violently displaced from her African roots or of having come from a damaged family but rather because of her intense awareness that the historical role she is expected to perform (leadership) is already freighted by various layers of mediation. Given the flimsiness of American cultural memory and the sparsity of the archive that might "give her access to her own black past" (33), so Reid-Pharr maintains, Walker's Black girl understands "that all of her tools are faulty, that both *Incidents in the Life of a Slave Girl* and *Mandingo* are products of their times"; hence, "she must come to recognize, however vaguely, that though she acts as guide she is indeed lost" (35). As should be evident from my argument so far, I agree with Reid-Pharr's perceptive reading of Walker's "black girl alter ego" (33), particularly with his assessment of the challenges she encounters in her endeavor to engage the past. And yet, I do not see her as quite so lost, nor does she strike me as a "newly emerging subject who barely knows herself" (35). Rather, I read the Negress as a confident and self-aware picara figure who, tossed into a landscape of myths, mediations, and desires, learns to chart her course situation by situation. Or as Reid-Pharr states, "lacking clear direction, she works with the information she has at hand, even as it is infinitely apparent that this information is deeply flawed, sullied some might say. Thus when we catch her—always in profile—we are never able to adequately understand exactly what her intentions are" (35).

The picaresque mode, as Charles Nichols has shown, is not unusual for the slave narrative: "Like the Spanish 'rogue,' the slave narrators tell their life story in retrospect, after having triumphed over the brutalizing circumstances of their youth" (1985, 283). In the endeavor to unmask an inhuman economic system, the picaro/picara narrator combines the presentation of realist detail with which to illustrate his or her "experience as a victim, a commodity, a rootless, alienated soul without hope or future" (283) with an emphasis on the various modes of deception and guile necessary for the survival in and escape from the corrupt society in which these narrators find themselves. A concern for verisimilitude thus goes hand in hand with an emphasis on role-playing and performance. "The slave's stratagems for survival, his ingenuity in playing out the roles his situation demanded is the leitmotif of the narratives" (285). Linda Brent, the narrator-protagonist of Harriet Jacobs's *Incidents in the Life of a Slave Girl* (1861), for instance, performs the antebellum white middle-class discourse of "true womanhood"[25] when trying to justify to her white female readers her stratagem of taking a lover to protect herself from the relentless sexual persecution of her former owner, only then to sharply undercut this discourse by pointing out its inherent double standard: "There may be sophistry in all this; but the condition of a slave confuses all principles of morality, and, in fact, renders the practice of them impossible" (Jacobs 2010, 80). William Wells Brown's comic sketch *The Escape: or, A Leap of Freedom*, excerpts of which he performed during his lectures on the abolitionist circuit between 1857 and 1858, playfully underscores in the character of Cato the creative ways in which the enslaved effected their escape by mimicking their masters' expectations (e.g., playing the buffoon or obedient servant), imitating their trade, and donning their clothes.

Walker's Negress is heir to this picaresque tradition. She too performs a variety of roles according to the circumstances at hand. In contrast to her literary progenitors, however, she performs these roles without manifest intent or motivation. Even as her "narratives," "scenes," "interpretations," and "panoramic journeys" promise to render legible the narrator-protagonist's various performances under slavery as somehow essential to a larger cause, the sheer number of performances and ambiguity of their visual implementation radically undermine any such legibility. They emerge as just that: pure performance. In *Slavery! Slavery!* (fig. 4), for instance, we find her copulating with a white boy on a roof-

FIGURE 4. Kara Walker. 1997. *Slavery! Slavery! Presenting a GRAND and LIFELIKE Panoramic Journey into Picturesque Southern Slavery or "Life at 'Ol' Virginny's Hole' (sketches from Plantation Life)" See the Peculiar Institution as never before! All cut from black paper by the able hand of Kara Elizabeth Walker, an Emancipated Negress and leader in her Cause*, detail. Cut paper on wall. © Kara Walker, courtesy of Sikkema Jenkins & Co., New York. Installation dimensions variable; approx. 12 × 85 ft. (3.7 × 25.9 meters). Installation view: *Kara Walker: My Complement, My Enemy, My Oppressor, My Love*, Hammer Museum, Los Angeles, CA, 2008. Photo: Joshua White.

top (fig. 5), while another version of her, with a baby tied to her back, bites into an apple and pulls a cart loaded with hay and some people hiding in it. In the same visual narrative, she reappears in the figure of a fountain sculpture, standing atop a crouching monkey, one leg raised high in the air as she spouts various bodily fluids from her mouth, ears, nipples, and vagina, while a white man prostrates himself before her (fig. 6). To be sure, each of these vignettes suggests possible story lines about resistance and complicity, endurance and fugitivity, as well as the commodification of Black femininity in the racialized economy of plantation slavery. But each of these narrative possibilities remains ambiguous since neither the context nor the scenarios in the other vignettes in the installation support it. For instance, it is quite plausible to read the sexual act on the rooftop both as one of mutual, cross-racial desire and ecstasy and as one of rape (fig. 5). The bodily shapes of both figures seem aligned in visual harmony; the erect nipples of the female breasts indicate arousal and perhaps pleasure. But then again, the female is perched precariously at the edge of the roof and her extended arm drops a

watermelon slice into the depth, as if she has been forcefully and involuntarily interrupted while eating—the stark nakedness of both bodies, however, indicates that some time has passed between eating and copulating. The recurring motif of the bitten fruit (apple and watermelon slice), moreover, signals the acquisition of forbidden knowledge and links the sexual act on the rooftop to the fugitive act of pulling a cart with hidden runaways. But then again, because the installation takes the shape of a cyclorama, it is unclear whether the woman with the cart is taking her human cargo away from slavery or further into it. Finally, with regard to the Negress's appearance in what Walker calls the "all-giving black girl fountain" (quoted in Hobbs 2001, 31), her attitude suggests both reification and agency. Even as her body yields the fluids of nourishment (milk), reproduction, and hard physical labor (blood) that sustain the plantation economy, her hand daintily waves a cotton flower toward the white man prostrated in front of her. Since it seems unlikely that the flower serves as a balancing weight, it is tempting to read it as a symbol of titillation and seduction rather than enslavement. One wonders who ultimately is in control in this relationship: might the fountain act be an elaborate performance designed to mock the master?

These ambivalences of interpretation refocus contemporary viewers' understanding of slavery in important ways. In terms of content, the Negress's performances of a variety of roles in an array of situations—subversive, complicit, victimized, observant, curious, devious, rebellious—highlight known aspects of the sexual economy of slavery

(*opposite, top*) FIGURE 5. Kara Walker. 1997. *Slavery! Slavery! Presenting a GRAND and LIFELIKE Panoramic Journey into Picturesque Southern Slavery or "Life at 'Ol' Virginny's Hole' (sketches from Plantation Life)" See the Peculiar Institution as never before! All cut from black paper by the able hand of Kara Elizabeth Walker, an Emancipated Negress and leader in her Cause*, detail. Cut paper on wall. 12 × 85 ft. (3.7 × 25.9 meters). © Kara Walker, courtesy of Sikkema Jenkins & Co., New York. Installation view: *Kara Walker: My Complement, My Enemy, My Oppressor, My Love*, Walker Art Center, Minneapolis, MN, 2007. Photo: Dave Sweeney.

(*opposite, bottom*) FIGURE 6. Kara Walker. 1997. *Slavery! Slavery! Presenting a GRAND and LIFELIKE Panoramic Journey into Picturesque Southern Slavery or "Life at 'Ol' Virginny's Hole' (sketches from Plantation Life)" See the Peculiar Institution as never before! All cut from black paper by the able hand of Kara Elizabeth Walker, an Emancipated Negress and leader in her Cause*, detail. Cut paper on wall 12 × 85 ft. (3.7 × 25.9 meters). © Kara Walker, courtesy of Sikkema Jenkins & Co., New York. Installation view: *Kara Walker: My Complement, My Enemy, My Oppressor, My Love*, Walker Art Center, Minneapolis, MN, 2007. Photo: Dave Sweeney.

(such as rape and miscegenation) as well as aspects routinely tabooed in canonical accounts (such as concubinage and pleasure). On the one hand, they serve the classic picaresque function in slave narratives of destroying the idyllic plantation myth of Southern romance and exposing "the rude and violent behavior of the master class and the inhumanity of the plantation system" (Nichols 1985, 287). On the other hand, the ambiguity of many of these images also suggests that there were many subject positions and roles performed by the enslaved within the power structures of slavery and that, at times, no clear moral demarcations could be drawn. In terms of form, even as the Negress's diverse performances offer a broad spectrum of subject positions, most of these performative vignettes ultimately remain elusive, gratuitous, and opaque. Inviting a sort of hyper-legibility, they resist being reduced to one overarching meaning and/or narrative, and thus also effectively destabilize the silhouettes' legibility, especially their readability for clearly demarcated subject positions. Rather than serving a coherent goal (whether narrative-wise, political, or ethical), the performances in Walker's tableaux remain just that—pure, autonomous performances. Constructing a narrative out of the various performative events rendered in Walker's silhouette installations ultimately requires a confrontation with one's own imagination. "My narrative surely says as much about me and my history, as it does about Walker and hers," art historian Anne Wagner concedes (2003, 101).

Walker frequently signals her silhouettes' investment in exposing the look of desire by including a surrogate beholder in the visual narrative itself. *Slavery! Slavery!*, for instance, in a parodic riff on Eastman Johnson's 1859 pastoral painting, *Negro Life in the South*, foregrounds the voyeurism of the (white) observer. Considered to be one of his masterpieces, Johnson's oil painting renders a rather idyllic portrait of slavery, showing the inhabitants of the slave quarters frolicking in dance, music, and pastoral flirtations. The beholder's gaze at the pastoral scene is echoed and amplified by the gaze of a figure within the painting—the white mistress, who is entering the scene from the far right to join the festivities as a discreet spectator. According to David Wall, Johnson's popular nineteenth-century genre painting demonstrates "the full range of the white social imaginary as it looks at, embraces, and constructs the black body" (2010, 294). Walker targets this white social imaginary when she cites the basic elements of Johnson's composition in her sil-

FIGURE 7. Kara Walker. 1997. *World's Exposition.* Cut paper on wall. Installation dimensions variable; approx. 10 × 16 ft. (3 × 4.8). © Kara Walker, courtesy of Sikkema Jenkins & Co., New York.

houette installation *Slavery! Slavery!* (fig. 5). Here the voyeuristic mistress appears center stage, in Diderotian fashion, attempting to espy a slice of "authentic" black life through the keyhole of the gate separating the big house from the slave quarters. In Johnson's painting, the mistress's straightforward gaze from the side articulates the perspective of power, of control over representation. In Walker, by contrast, the view through the keyhole skews the beholder's gaze to bring into focus the anamorphic optics of desire. What seems naïvely idyllic in Johnson is here underwritten by the menace of mimicry that destabilizes power; articulations of the onlooker's desire (dancing, frolicking, courting) are shadowed by articulations of anxiety (violence, rebellion, even suggestions of cannibalism). Looking awry at entrenched visions of slavery, Walker thus reveals their investment, first and foremost, in "an idea of the black body" (H. Young 2010, 4) rather than actual black lives.[26]

With the silhouette installation *World's Exposition* (1997), Walker thematizes such entrenched stereotypical perceptions of Blackness specifically with regard to the role of the female artist of color in the white imagination (fig. 7). In this tableau, we see the Negress perform a number of racialized roles for an audience of white male onlookers. She enacts the subhuman, hanging naked by a monkey's tail from the branch of a tree as she paints its foliage and defecates with abandon.[27] As the eroticized Other, she performs Josephine Baker–like—seminude and banana-skirted—an exotic dance with the falling feces. And she appears in the role of the African primitive, featuring a grass skirt, ear hoops, and elongated head and suckling an infant on her bare breasts. Three onlookers with distinctive Caucasian facial features react differently to the painter's artistry: one eagerly accumulating her feces in a towering heap, a second holding his knee and crying out with pain (did someone step on his foot—literally or metaphorically so?), and a third staring at the painter's behind while fondling or strangling a small Black boy. Meanwhile, a fourth Negress, clad in Victorian dress and artist's smock, is chiseling away at the third onlooker. Hers, however, is an act not of creation but of destruction. The male figure's head is nearly cut from his body, and the artist has already managed to break off an arm—which, holding a quilt, is flying toward the African primitive, as if to offer her, who is also armless, a replacement of sorts and with it the possibility of recreating herself artistically. Alas, at the same time, the African's infant is threatened by another flying object: the broken-off head of the sculptor's hammer is about to smash into the little boy's head. This complex allegory of acts of artistic performance renders in a grotesque manner the various racist and sexist expectations and objectifications the black female artist might be subjected to by audiences and critics. But it also asserts the creative power of the Black female artist to bring worlds into being (painting and writing), to mock existing worlds (defecating), and to undo them with her artistry (cutting and carving).[28] Importantly, just as the artist-narrator sees herself scripted by the libidinal fantasies of her onlookers, she also seizes these fantasies as the very ground for a performative enactment and refashioning of the self.

In conclusion then, Walker's Negress is hard at work at "retraining her audiences," as Reid-Pharr puts it (2002, 28). Her picaresque silhouette narratives prompt us to take a fresh look at the history of American slavery, to discern the various layers of mediation through which it has

FIGURE 8. Kara Walker. 1996. *Brown Follies (Negress Notes)*, detail. Watercolor on paper. One from a suite of 24; 21 parts: 9 × 6 in. (22.9 × 15.5 cm); 3 parts: 6 × 9 in. (15.2 × 22.9 cm). © Kara Walker, courtesy of Sikkema Jenkins & Co., New York.

been articulated over the past four hundred years, including the mediations of popular fantasies as well as collective and individual phobias and desires that contemporary audiences bring to them. An untitled image from Walker's 1996–97 series *Negress Notes (Brown Follies)*—not a silhouette but a watercolor—provides a pointed, compact allegory of the artist's project of retraining her audiences by exposing and undercutting habitual modes of seeing and provoking new ones (fig. 8). In this image, the Negress as a little Black girl is intently peering through a spyglass as she sits backward astride the back of an Uncle Tom figure, who is crouching on his hands and knees. The image's use of dual movements and temporalities is striking. When read in classic Western tradition from left to right, discrepant movements become apparent: the girl peering intently to the right, supposedly into the future as her carrier moves—depending on the direction we attribute to his crawl—either away from this future, back into the past, or backward into the future, guided by the girl's vision. In other words, at stake in this image is precisely the dynamic friction between past and future as brought together in the present encounter of the two figures. Given the stereotypical features and debased position of the male figure (signified by being on all fours), we might read it as an image of the past—perhaps as representative of what Alain Locke termed the mythology of the "Old Negro"[29]—one that much of African American literature and visual arts has set out to overcome. Yet, notably, the crude gouache strokes outlining the girl's figure and, above all, her pronounced, unruly braids mark this representative of a new generation just as much a product of racial caricature and stereotype as her ancestor-companion—not a "New Negro" as envisioned by Locke, Du Bois, and others, but a Topsy-like figure, or what Arlene Keizer calls a "nouveau pickanniny" (2008, 1663). Herself a product of the "fiction that has come out of history" (Walker quoted in Saltz 1996, 82), of racializing and racist projections, the Black girl nonetheless asserts her control over this history, playfully directing it according to her whims and needs, keeping a firm yet slightly askew eye on whatever she sees in the past and/or future.

THE SILHOUETTE AS A *BLICKMASCHINE*

The Negress's unreliable narration and picaresque self-fashioning are tightly linked to her use of the silhouette. In her hands, the intricate shapes and delicate curlicues of this genteel lady's art of the antebellum period turn out to reveal various performances "too sordid to relate" (quoted in Lott 2000, 70). They also manifest surprising—and sometimes shocking—new modes of approaching the past of slavery. This part of the chapter aims to further the discussion by taking a closer look at Walker's use of the silhouette. Three interrelated aspects in particular are of interest. First, Walker deploys this art form as an anamorphic lens for bringing into focus the history of the medium, along with the manifold ways in which it has contributed, from the late eighteenth century onward, to the consolidation of racial formations. Second, in deploying the silhouette, she also exposes the *Schattenriss* (shade, silhouette) as an effective medium for visually channeling desires and anxieties concerning alterity and thus as a fundamental mechanism of processes of racialization. Third, I will consider the artist's refunctioning of this laden medium for a historiopoetic approach to the past. These three points come together in a larger thesis: Walker both exposes and uses

the silhouette qua silhouette as a *Blickmaschine*, a visual/scopic apparatus that engenders a particular look/gaze, not merely representing but
actively shaping and producing modes of seeing and modes of knowing.[30]

Walker's visual essay *After the Deluge* (2007), which accompanied her
exhibition *Kara Walker at the Met: After the Deluge*, provides a productive basis for developing this thesis. In 2006, on the occasion of the first
anniversary of the flooding of New Orleans and the destruction of several of its neighborhoods in the wake of Hurricane Katrina, the Metropolitan Museum of Art in New York City invited Walker to curate a
show that combined artworks from the Met archives with some of her
own works. In "Murky," a preface to the essay, Walker explains that her
selections were driven by the objective of understanding "the subconscious narratives at work" in visual representations of disaster and of
drawing attention to the ways that a Black subject in the present continues to function as "a container for specific pathologies from the past
and is continually growing and feeding off these maladies" (9). With her
provocative juxtaposition of canonical artifacts with some of her own
visual and textual work, Walker takes what art historian Krista Thompson calls a "sidelong glance" at the archive of the Met (as well as the Boston Museum of Fine Arts, from which two artworks were on loan) to
bring into focus the ways in which some of these revered masterpieces
have contributed to the reification of notions of Blackness and have thus
collaborated in the long history of slavery.[31] With this intervention into
the institutionalized production of knowledge of the past, Walker joins
a longer tradition of museumist and museological interventions by artists since the late 1970s. In particular, she follows in the wake of Fred
Wilson's groundbreaking curatorial work, *Mining the Museum* (1992–
93), at the Maryland Historical Society in Baltimore, which radically
challenged the ways that the white institutional grammar of museums
has impacted perceptions of race and racial relations.[32]

Krista Thompson identifies the sidelong glance as a central technique
in African diasporic art. In common usage, the term refers to forms of
observation in which the looker is not seen to be looking; it presents
a "furtive, sagacious, critical and yet desirous way of looking" (2012,
26). Historically, the sidelong glance frequently articulates the gaze of
the oppressed at power; it is the "watchful and attentive perspective" of
those who are "simultaneously cast out of and intrinsic to the economies
of vision in the West" (11–12). In the field of the visual arts, Thompson

finds it deployed by artists and art historians of the African diaspora to highlight "histories of seeing and representation that sometimes go unseen or uninterrogated" (26). It constitutes a reoriented "perspective that is vigilant of what representation does, what it affords and affects" (28). The sidelong glance thus provides a powerful strategy for reading canonical cultures of visuality against the grain, probing their impact on perceptions of race, destabilizing and deconstructing established art histories, and drawing up an African diasporic art history. To demonstrate how this sidelong vision operates in Walker's creative curatorial work, I too am taking a sideways approach by focusing on the image that opens Walker's visual essay: *The Magic Lantern*, a black paper cutout by renowned nineteenth-century silhouettist Auguste Édouart (fig. 9).

Walker's selection of Édouart's silhouette of a magic lantern show references her own uses of the silhouette as *Blickmaschine* in complex ways. On a most basic level, it foregrounds her deployment of the silhouette as a historicist medium for mimicking the genteel art of the antebellum period—a period that serves as the setting for much of her work on slavery. From the late eighteenth to the mid-nineteenth century, when silhouettes were replaced by daguerreotypes, they were widely popular as a decorative art form and a means of bourgeois self-fashioning. More affordable than oil paintings and easily procured from itinerant profilists, silhouettes enabled middle-class families to have their portraits rendered quickly and inexpensively. The skill of paper cutting could also be easily acquired by amateurs, particularly with the help of tracing machines. In the United States, it was soon considered a ladies' art, one that specialized in producing decorative remembrances and polite conversation pieces. Not surprisingly then, the delicate paper cutouts—or "shades," as they were also called at the time—would adorn the walls and albums of many a middle-class household in North America and Europe during this period.[33] Although the intricate curlicues and delicate details of the paper cutout might seem inappropriate for addressing the ghastly peculiarities of the institution of slavery, Walker uses them in her own work to target a genteel leisure culture that was firmly rooted in the slave economy, even as it sought to erase all traces of this economic base in its visual culture. Furthermore, the pronounced mediality of Édouart's *Magic Lantern* (its visual focus on the pleasures and socioeconomics of a shadow show) beckons to Walker's own use of

FIGURE 9. Auguste Édouart. ca. 1835. *The Magic Lantern*. Cut paper on wash. 9½ × 13⅜ in. (24.2 × 33.9 cm). Metropolitan Museum of Art, New York City, Bequest of Mary Martin, 1938.

the silhouette as an anamorphic lens for exposing the silhouette as a central mechanism for processes of racialization. Prominently placed at the opening of an essay on how Western art channels racial pathology, Édouart's fine papercut thus serves as a sort of epigraph for Walker's sidelong glance at the archive of Western visual culture, signaling to the reader how to read the silhouette as a *Blickmaschine*.

Auguste Édouart (1788–1861), a French-born silhouette artist who practiced mostly in England, Scotland, and the United States, was one of the most influential profilists of his time and crucial to the revival of the medium in the antebellum period.[34] While called on to cut the likeness of many a famous person (among them Daniel Webster, Martin van Buren, Edwin Forrest, Catherine Maria Sedgwick, and Lydia Maria Child),[35] he is best known for his domestic scenes. *The Magic Lantern* (ca. 1839–49),[36] for instance, renders the private screening of a "gallantie show" in an affluent household.[37] Drawn in brown watercolors, it depicts a large parlor, covered with a plush carpet and other luxurious fabrics, such as the heavy drapery framing the projection of a horse chase in a Wild West setting. Ten human figures, along with the figure of a dog, three chairs, and a projection apparatus, are pasted as black paper cutouts onto this gouache. The assembly of human figures arranged directly in front of the projection screen and taking up the entire right-hand half of the picture suggests a family: the parents on the far right, standing arm in arm, upright and composed, clad in elegant Victorian dress; to their left, three children, a nanny, and a dog— all portrayed in various states of excitement, with the three children reaching toward the screen, apparently eager to enter its phantasmagoric reality. Slightly off-center, to the left, a projectionist is operating the *laterna magica*. Seated behind him in the background on the far left, near a fireplace, is an elderly lady (perhaps the children's grandmother) in a ruffled dress and bonnet, her left hand holding a fan and her feet propped on a low stool. At a considerable distance from her in the foreground so as to indicate their lack of kinship, but on the same forward plane as the father figure so as to indicate a connection between the two men, is another seated figure, an elderly gentleman holding a sort of portfolio on his knees and stretching out a wooden leg. This figure is the only one in the room not absorbed in the projection on screen; as he glances down at the contents of this portfolio, his thoughts seem to be preoccupied with other matters. The triangular, pictorial relation between the standing father figure on the far right, the seated elderly lady in the background, and the seated elderly gentleman in the foreground of the far left frames all the other figures in the room including the projectionist, indicating some kind of power or authority over the family's welfare and prospects, perhaps of the sort that is anchored in relations of inheritance (elderly lady) or relations of business (gentleman with portfolio). The leisurely enjoyment of the magic lantern show appears to be a mere distraction from weightier family affairs.

The essential detail of Édouart's silhouette painting, however, is the tenth figure on the far left: a young man standing at the open door between the elderly lady and the gentleman. His hands on the door and its knob, his slightly forward-bent posture, and his lifted foot suggest that he has only just now opened the door and done so rather cautiously, so as not to interrupt the family's pleasure but perhaps so as to surreptitiously enjoy it himself. His placement on the very threshold of the parlor (neither inside nor outside), along with the considerable distance between his position on the picture's far left and the paterfamilias on the far right, indicate his subservient position in the family hierarchy. Clearly not part of the intimate family/business triangle, he nonetheless seems to be crucial to it. Is he a servant? His clothes, actions, and posture imply as much. He is, furthermore, also set apart from the people inside the room by his distinctive facial features (rounded nose, full upper lip) and hair (short and wavy)—visual clues that invite a racial reading.

Reading the figure on the threshold as a Black house servant is particularly tempting for several reasons. It explicitly links the genteel, middle-class art of the silhouette, via the gallantee show, to a racialized economy (note that the popularity of shadow shows coincided not only with the height of silhouette fashion but also with the high phase of slavery). It also opens up another narrative possibility concerning the figure's relationship to the gentleman with the wooden leg in the left-hand foreground as well as the projected Wild West fantasy on the far right. The seemingly gratuitous wooden leg turns the gentleman into a sort of Captain Ahab character, a seafaring man involved in various lucrative, perhaps even fanatical maritime enterprises, such as whaling—or perhaps even slave trading.[38] His businesslike demeanor might well be related to concrete economic interests that the family might stand to benefit from—interests that enable the life of idleness and leisure, which allows them to enjoy a gallantee show in the first place. The figure's possible connection to the slave economy seems particularly germane when paired with the projection of a Wild West adventure; it evokes ideological notions of Manifest Destiny as well as its related economic, political, and legal dimensions (such as the Kansas-Nebraska Act of 1854 and other legislation). The narrative and pictorial lines connecting the attendant on the threshold to the wooden-legged entrepreneur and magic lantern show suggest that at play in this family parlor are not only the entertaining projection of a popular fantasy of the Wild West but the concrete role of slavery in the family's as well as the nation's economic and geopolitical future. The refined and popular visual culture of the nineteenth century (the silhouettes and magic lantern shows of the first half of the century, along with the daguerreotypes and photographs succeeding them in the second half) turn out to be deeply implicated in a racialized economy.

There is yet another history at stake in Édouart's silhouette gouache— the latent, invisible history of form that Walker persistently seeks to expose and refigure in her own silhouette works. Note that my reading of *The Magic Lantern* hinges entirely on positing the figure on the threshold as Black. But with all figures cut in black paper, how do we know who is Black and who is white in this room? The silhouette, as Walker reminds us, is but "a hole in a piece of paper"; it is a "blank space that you could project your desires into" (quoted in Sheets 2002, 128). Artist Eva Rothschild similarly describes the silhouette as "the object without information . . . . We can agree on the edges of the black hole but its interior is something we have to complete on our own" (quoted in Ackermann and Friedel 2001, 7).[39] Reading a silhouette is thus by necessity an act of projection; even as it purports to trace the precise contours of an object or person, it remains open to speculation. Since portrait silhouettes were typically cut from blackened paper,[40] an extrapolation of a figure's racial identity is by default based on anything but skin color. Instead, it is inferred—not unlike the operations of racial profiling, the history of which is deeply implicated in the drawing of silhouettes—from facial features, hairstyles, postures, costumes, spatial placements, etc. But how reliable are such visual clues? Do they indeed render incontestable evidence of the sitter's racial identity? What constitutes racial identity to begin with? And even when clues to racial identity are agreed on, how do we know whether a silhouettist renders them faithfully, smudges them deliberately, or creates misleading ones? The ambiguity of the silhouette with regard to racial identity begs the question of the extent to which race has all along been a heuristic construct of the beholder. Undeniably, racial attributions are always inflected by a viewer's cultural background, social prejudice, and his or her desire for one particular narrative rather than another. Édouart's silent figure on the threshold (just like Walker's figures) aptly brings into focus these and other related questions about race, visuality, and scopic desire. In *The Magic Lantern*, the figure thus stands not only in a narratological but also in a symbolic relation to the eponymous "gallantie show" of the silhouette gouache. Not unlike the projection screen on the right-hand side of the image, it too serves as a surface for phantasmagoric projections. The centrally placed projection apparatus, the *laterna magica*, might then well be read as an allegory for the mechanics and pleasures of racializing projections—or, put differently, as a *Blickmaschine*.

Whether Édouart was aware of his silhouette gouache's powerful ironic edge regarding the collusion of fact and fiction in visual projections of race, we do not know; Kara Walker certainly is. Just as Édouart's threshold figure seems to cast a sidelong glance (seeing yet unseen, avoiding being seen) at the magic lantern show in the family parlor, so the curator and art historian Kara Walker, with her prominent citing of Édouart's work at the start of her visual essay, *After the Deluge*, encourages us to cast a wary eye on the canonical artworks included in the essay and exhibition, such as John Singleton Copley's *Watson and the Shark* (1778), J. M. W. Turner's *Slave Ship* (1840),[41] John Warner Barber's wood engravings *A History of the Amistad Captives* (1840), John Carlin's *After a Long Cruise* (1857), Winslow Homer's *Dressing for the Carnival* (1877) and *The Gulf Stream* (1899), along with various street scenes by William P. Chappel from the 1870s. All these works bespeak what Toni Morrison calls the "Africanist presence" in the white imagination (Morrison 1993, 5). On a typewritten index card from her own *American Primitive* series (2001), placed adjacent to Édouart's piece, Walker cautions her viewers: "Perhaps Now is the time to / do / away with / pictures of / things / which / engage / our / pleasure / centers, / before/ trying to / destroy / them" (Walker 2007, 5). Read alongside Édouart's *Magic Lantern*, which thematizes the work of projection on both the diegetic and non-diegetic levels, the index card clearly alerts us to take into account the various libidinal investments that undergird representations of race in this particular assemblage of Western artworks. Walker asks her readers/viewers to look at the images awry so as to bring into focus the racial imagination at work in these representations and to take a sidelong glance at the ways they have been implicated in the construction, containment, and reification of Black identities.

Her own silhouette works provocatively puncture the sequence of canonical artworks included in her essay (and exhibition), commenting on them and amplifying our refocused perspective. Following Édouart's silhouette and her own index card, Walker, for instance, continues her investigation with a full-page display of Bill Haber's widely circulated AP photograph of an African American woman braving the toxic—and yet also startlingly beautiful—oily waters of New Orleans as she floats a brown duffle bag in one hand and a string of water bottles in the other. This image is juxtaposed with a two-page spread of Turner's masterpiece *The Slave Ship* (originally titled *Slavers Throwing overboard the Dead and Dying—Typhoon Coming on*), in which we also behold Black bodies struggling through oddly aestheticized (with the sinking sun) deadly waters; next is Walker's own silhouette *Untitled* (1996), in which we encounter a little Black girl, with braids and frayed skirt, clubbing a horse that is already prostrate on the ground, an action set against the background image of a Mississippi steamer. In a not-so-subtle visual rephrasing of the idiomatic phrase "to beat a dead horse," Walker connects the brutality of slavery to the ongoing disregard for Black bodies in our contemporary world and provocatively underlines how a history of aestheticizing Black suffering is repeated once again in the coverage of death and survival in the city of New Orleans. In another silhouette, *Big House*, from Walker's *American Primitives* series (2001), the artist pastes onto a gouache representation of the iconic tree-lined driveway to Oak Alley Plantation in Louisiana (popularized by the movie *Interview with a Vampire*, 1994) the silhouettes of one female figure (racialized as Black) devouring another prostrate female figure (racialized as white). In this image, critic Michael Bibler observes, "Walker plays with the myth of the predatory black, the myth that the inhuman savagery of this Africanist presence threatens to destroy white society like a vampire"; it is precisely this lingering myth that fueled the "racist hysteria" in Algiers Point in New Orleans (2010, 510), where a group of white residents formed a vigilante troop to bar at gunpoint African Americans, fleeing from the flooded neighborhoods, from entering this part of town. This mythology also informed a good part of the media coverage of Hurricane Katrina, effectively contributing to reframing a social catastrophe in terms of urban warfare, which, in turn, led to the mobilization of military intervention rather than civic support for New Orleans.[42]

Walker's deployment of silhouettes throughout the exhibition evinces a somewhat different archaeological approach to "mining the museum" than the approach Fred Wilson espoused in 1992. Wilson's project in targeting the politics of collection at the Maryland Historical Society was essentially one of recovery. His confrontational juxtaposition of intricate colonial silverware with iron shackles, elegant parlor room chairs with a whipping post, and his highlighting barely visible dark figures in portraits of white people targeted the museum's repressed racial history. It sought to make visible the brutal and exploitative racial formation that sustained colonial and early republican material cultures, to point up the elision of Black and Indigenous histories in the construction of Maryland state history, to excavate information about the few Black presences in the collection, and to retrieve hitherto unknown objects from the museum's archives.[43] Walker, by contrast, seeks to uncover a somewhat different history: the repressed or subconscious history of American "racial pathology," as she remarks in the index card that serves as a sort of motto for her exhibition.

Given the abundance of crude, hyperbolic stereotypes in *Big House* and other silhouettes, I propose to read Walker's approach to these racial pathologies in the manner of an Artaudian theater of cruelty. Like Antonin Artaud, Walker insists that latent disorders might best be done away with by being embraced fully. Accordingly, she "dredges the muddy bottom of the mind for stereotypes and archetypes" (Walker quoted in Armstrong 1997, 104) and, again like Artaud, excavates them from our collective psyche, projects and amplifies them in a stylized manner so that they might at long last be recognized, acknowledged, and purged. The somewhat ambiguous phrasing on her opening index card "to do away with pictures of things that engage our pleasure centers before trying to destroy them" suggests such momentary dwelling in excess ("to do away with") as a basis for final release ("destroy"). Artaud similarly describes his theater of cruelty, which he famously compares to the plague, as a "total exorcism." It "takes images that are dormant, a latent disorder, and suddenly extends them into the most extreme gestures"; it fights "a battle of symbols" (1994, 27). Like the plague, Artaud concludes, this kind of theater is resolved by "death or cure" (31). Walker, likewise, expresses her hope that the "murky, toxic waters" of racial pathologies that she engages with in her images might eventually "become the amniotic fluid of a potentially difficult birth, flushing out of a coherent and stubborn body long-held fears and suspicions" (2007, 9).

As a medium, the silhouette has been deeply implicated in the history of pathological projections that Walker seeks to expose in her visual essay, *After the Deluge*. The eighteenth-century art of silhouette cutting stands in a straight genealogical line with contemporary practices of racial profiling.[44] This genealogy begins with Johan Caspar Lavater's physiognomic studies of the late eighteenth century, which postulate that the true character of a person can best be extrapolated from the person's *Schattenriss*, or "shade."[45] To capture the anatomical correctness of his sitters' profiles, Lavater employed complex tracing devices and developed a special chair for holding his clients still during the sitting. As he and other advocates of physiognomy (and later, phrenology) believed, the exactly rendered profile of a person would reveal a person's moral and spiritual character, or, as Lavater states in his *Essays on Physiognomy*, the shade would render "the truest representation that can be given of man" (quoted in Shaw 2004, 20).

The art of shade-drawing lends itself more easily, however, to typecasting and stereotyping than to accurate portraiture. As a form of typecasting, it has continued to assert its racializing powers from the late eighteenth century onward, for example, in the crude pencil profiles accompanying the bills of sale for slaves,[46] the generic lithographs of slaves used on broadsheets advertising for the return of runaways, or Josiah Wedgwood's well-known profile of the kneeling slave, *Am I Not a Man and Brother* (1787), which became iconic for the abolitionist movement. Furthermore, the silhouette's successors—the daguerreotype (introduced in 1839) and other forms of photography—were to become deeply implicated in the scientific racism of the late nineteenth century and the first half of the twentieth century. Among the more infamous cases are the daguerreotypes of African slaves on a South Carolina plantation taken in 1850 by Joseph T. Zealy of Richmond on behalf of Harvard biologist Louis Agassiz. They were to provide the visual evidence for Agassiz's theory of polygenesis, the idea that the various human races are in fact separate species.[47] The art of profiling—taking a person's likeness through shadow-tracing, silhouettes, or photographs—has from the start thus been accompanied by the centuries-old practice of moral and racial profiling:[48] the suspecting or targeting of a person based on racial stereotypes and biases, which continues to impact Black lives daily in the United States of America and elsewhere. Walker is quite aware of this weighty—even though largely invisible—history of the silhouette form. Her controversial use of crude racial stereotypes is designed to expose this history but also to compel the beholder to recognize and reflect on his or her own participation in it. As Walker remarks, concerning her intention to expose and undermine the legacy of Lavater that continues to haunt this form, "The silhouette speaks a kind of truth. It traces an exact profile, so in a way I would like to set up a situation in which the viewer calls up a stereotypic response to the work that I, black artist/leader, will 'tell it like it is.' But the 'like-it-is,' the truth of the piece, is a clear Rorschach test" (quoted in Armstrong 1997, 106).

Walker's sidelong glance at the history of the silhouette is important for yet another reason: its indebtedness to a long history of artists' sidelong uses of the medium. Even at the time of its closest alignment with racial profiling in the late eighteenth and nineteenth centuries, the silhouette has been subject to manipulation, particularly in the hands of artists of African descent. Gwendolyn DuBois Shaw, for instance, relates the story of the African American Moses Williams (1777–ca. 1825), a slave to the renowned, Philadelphia-based artist and museum owner Charles Willson Peale. Williams was trained at an early age in the use of the physiognotrace, a silhouette-making machine, which he operated at Peale's museum (continuing even after his manumission at the age of twenty-seven). Producing up to eight thousand profiles a year, Williams contributed significantly to both the Peale family's substantial silhouette output and its economic gain. Among these profiles is one entitled *Moses Williams, Cutter of Profiles* (ca. 1804). The silhouette testifies in its title to the fact that African Americans have worked in the profession of profilists; it also reveals how African Americans have creatively appropriated the medium and intervened in processes of mechanical reproduction for their own purposes. Studying the deviations of the actual scissor cuts from the mechanical traces imprinted on the paper by the tracing machine, Shaw concludes that Williams's profile has been manipulated so as to provide "a decidedly anglicized" portrait of its sitter (2005, 37): "the 'cutter' altered the length of the hair by extending it nearly one centimeter from the original trace line, causing it to lie closer to the head. In concert with a stylized lock curling over the forehead, the altered hair follows a smoother, more flowing line" (37). Given these significant alterations, Shaw surmises that the portrait was most likely cut not by Peale's son Raphaelle (to whom it has been attributed) but probably by Moses Williams himself. This radically changes the way we read the portrait: Moses Williams emerges not as someone whose likeness has been taken by a white artist, a member of a prominent slave-owning family, but as someone taking charge of his own representation in the public sphere. His artistic scissor-cutting skills allow him to intervene in the reductive blueprint imposed on him by a mechanical operation and to fashion his own identity from it. Seen in this light, the function of the portrait's caption, "Moses Williams, Cutter of Profiles," changes from classifying an object of study to rendering an autobiographic signature and with that to proclaiming a self and asserting a professional identity. Even if Shaw's attribution of this portrait to Moses Williams himself should prove to be incorrect, its caption nonetheless bears testimony to the fact that African Americans have not only been objects of profiling but have also appropriated the art form for their own purposes, turning it into a tool for making a living and, possibly, for intervening in canonical representations of Blackness and whiteness.

A second relevant example of how African American artists have used techniques of cutting to expose and intervene in the racial assumptions of Western visual culture is offered by Carrie Mae Weems's *Here I Saw What Happened and I Cried* (1995–96). In this installation, Weems refunctions photographic images of African Americans taken during slavery, among them the notorious Zealy daguerreotypes.[49] Subjecting these enslaved individuals—Delia, Drana, Renty, and Jack—to the brutal gaze of scientific racism on behalf of establishing racial typologies and systems of classification, the images Zealy created for Agassiz "further commodified an already commodified body, reducing it to a miniaturized, two-dimensional object with a scientific value tantamount to the life-size, three-dimensional figures of the slaves themselves" (H. Young 2010, 45). Weems intervenes in these mechanical reproductions on behalf of a supremacist ideology through several formal manipulations of the images. Most notable are the white inscriptions across the sitters' bodies: "You became a Scientific Profile" (Delia), "A Negroid Type" (Renty), "An Anthropological Debate" (Jack), and "& A Photographic Subject" (Drana). These phrases make explicit the underlying racist assumption of the early photographic eye of the daguerreotype. In addition, Weems enlarges the images, cuts them for circular frames, pastes them on black mats, and infuses them with a warm, red tint. She also bookends the series with mirror images of an indigo-tinted reproduction of Léon Poirier and Georges Specht's 1925 iconic portrait of Nobosodrou, wife of the Mangbetu king Touba. In this manner, Weems modifies the harsh context and intentions of the Zealy sitting. These portraits now appear as personal keepsakes, viewed from the perspective of an African woman who bears witness to the suffering of the portraits' subjects and mourns for them: "From here I saw what happened . . . and I cried." With these radical formal interventions, Weems effectively transforms these images from pseudoscientific evidence of racial difference into testimonials of racist structures of economic and visual exploitation; more than that, she retrieves the subjects from underneath the racializing projections imposed on them, commemorating them in portraits of ancestors.[50]

Walker can be seen as an heir to Williams's and Weems's interventions into mechanical ways of seeing and the existing archive of representations of Blackness. Like Williams, she manipulates the devices that enable stereotypical ways of reproducing Blackness. I use the term "stereotype" both in the original sense of a fixed printing plate that can be used over and over again and in the modern sense of a fixed mental image that expresses oversimplified opinions, preconceived judgments and attitudes. Walker has repeatedly commented on the structural kinship she sees between silhouettes and stereotypes. She considers them negative spaces of representation that thrive on the ambivalence of mimetic pretense and phantasmagoric projection. Both of them, moreover, present us with seemingly arrested or frozen forms of knowledge.[51] In *Working Drawing* (1992)—a doodle, really, on a piece of scrap paper—she visually works out her strategy as a silhouettist for attacking mechanical reproductions of an abstract notion of Blackness. Next to a swarm of arrows attacking the circled words "mammy," "vixen," and "buck," Walker has scribbled the note, "Aiming for all these (stereo)typical targets and hitting them off to the side / to accentuate the negative space left by the archetypes' holes (silhouettes)."[52] In a series of minute manipulations, her silhouettes manage to blur the beholder's familiar and habitual encounter with stereotypes, rendering them out of focus so that the beholder is forced to look again, to look awry, and thereby to focus her own desires and anxieties in looking.

Walker also embraces more drastic and incisive techniques of intervention. Like Weems, she uses techniques of cutting to excavate the repressed racial history of art forms and expose the tacit racial assumptions of Western visual culture as well as to intervene in these histories of representations. This is made most explicit in her appropriation of Winslow Homer's painting *The Gulf Stream* for *After the Deluge*—probably her most conspicuous and radical intervention into the archive of Western visual culture. Homer's renowned painting portrays a Black man on a battered fishing boat (mast and rudder broken), facing his imminent demise by shark attack and/or an approaching storm. There is a schooner passing on the horizon, but the man seems oblivious to it and quite resigned to his doom. The oil painting is placed center stage in Walker's essay, just as it was probably also prominently displayed at the actual exhibition at The Met. At the end of her essay, Walker, however, repeats and revises Homer's masterpiece. In a bold act of visual

Signifyin(g), she enlarges the image of the painting's protagonist and then quite literally cuts the rest of the painting to size. Gone is the schooner, but also the predatory sharks and the brewing storm; what remains is the portrait of Black man, reclining at ease on a sunlit raft, leisurely gazing out on a calm blue sea. An image of abandonment (the passing schooner), extreme vulnerability (the predatory sharks), and visual containment (the man is tightly framed by the hurricane and the sharks) is, by a sleight of hand—or rather, adroit use of a pair of scissors—transformed into an image of tranquility, safety, and self-sufficiency. In an act of visual Signifyin(g) par excellence, Walker has simply cut out a threatening history.

Importantly, this is not to be understood as a naïve act of revisionism or even denial. Because the original Homer is still present in the gallery and an accurate reproduction is included in the essay, any visitor or reader will easily recognize the image for what it is: a manipulated version of the original, a repetition with a signal revision. The meaning of this bold act of Signifyin(g) emerges precisely in the ironic semantic interplay of the original and its creative interpretation. I here draw on Linda Hutcheon's notion of "irony," which, moving beyond the classic notion of irony as an antiphrastic statement, describes the meaning-making process entailed by this rhetorical operation as the constant flipping back and forth between two opposing meanings, between a statement and its seeming negation. Irony is produced in "a kind of rapid perceptual and hermeneutic *movement between*" two meanings (Hutcheon 1994, 60; italics in original); it generates "meaning in addition to and different from what is stated, together with an attitude toward both the said and the unsaid" (11). Walker's juxtaposition of a canonical image of Blackness with her own interpretation of it invites the beholder to consider the two in relation to each other. On the one hand, her radical refiguration of Homer's classic constantly refers us back to its source, prompting us to take a sidelong glance at the representation of the Black body as well as the ways that this representation is underwritten by a longer history of representations of Blackness. Homer's painting alludes to John Singleton Copley's 1778 *Watson and the Shark* as well as J. M. W. Turner's 1840 *Slave Ship*, both of which are also included in the exhibition and accompanying essay. On the other hand, the source image propels us forward to its adaptation again, asking us to consider how changes in visual representation impact perception, how poetic-visual techniques—such as framing, perspective, and shading—actively construct (rather than merely portray) subjects and the horizons of expectation in which they act, and how art thus has the capacity to open up possibilities for thinking about subject positions in past and present. Above all, as Hutcheon reminds us, irony has an edge and "can also make you edgy, nervous about how to fix meaning securely and how to determine motivation" (38). It removes the secure sense that words and images are fixed, that they simply mean what they say and portray, and that these meanings cannot be changed. Walker's historiopoetic intervention proves otherwise. With her radical cut(s) into representations of Blackness canonized by institutions such as The Met, she releases the Black body from a history of visual and semantic containment. The "murky, toxic waters" of racial pathologies, which run through the various images collected in Walker's *After the Deluge* visual essay, have indeed become "the amniotic fluid of a potentially new and difficult birth" (9).

Walker's various interventions into visual culture (like those by Williams and Weems) demonstrate the extent to which, as Krista Thompson and Huey Copeland state, "the visual *matters* to the rewiring of slavery's imaginary" because "it is in the specular realm that subjects emerge, that racialization functions, and through which the materiality of those signifiers upon which the meaning of slavery has come to rest might be recast" (2011, 10, italics in original). Highly aware of the various levels of mediation involved in depicting the Black body and in speaking with a Black voice, Walker deploys these mediations to intervene in received images and narratives of history—not, however, to set the record "straight" (for "straightness" always already masks its own biases and claims to power)—but to render it askew and cut it to size with the help of an X-ACTO knife or a pair of scissors. This artist does not merely record what happened or might have happened; she deploys the intrinsic collusion of fact and fiction in our understanding of the past to stake out an opening in the discourse of slavery that might allow for the articulation of new subject positions. This production of fresh meanings of and attitudes toward the past along with possibilities for the future is at the heart of Walker's (as well as Parks's and many other contemporary artists') historiopoetic praxis.

STEREOTYPES AND THEATRICALITY
(Re)Staging Black Venus

PUSHING BUTTONS

The works of Kara Walker and Suzan-Lori Parks have tended to polarize audiences into admirers and detractors. As Walker, following a provocative debut with the silhouette installation *Gone: An Historical Romance of a Civil War as It Occurred b'tween the Dusky Thighs of One Young Negress and Her Heart* (1994), began to garner accolades and fame, several critics protested her controversial interpretations of Black history, insisting that the artist was making her "reputation and large sums of money off of [her] own people's suffering" and catering to the tastes of a predominantly white art word (Bowles 1997, 3).[1] When Parks ventured in March 1996 with her play *Venus* a rather unconventional take on the historic figure of Saartjie Baartman[2]—a Khoikhoi woman put on public display in London and Paris in the 1810s as the "Hottentot Venus"—she similarly received both public acclaim (including an Obie Award for playwriting) and harsh criticism. Foremost among Parks's critics was scholar Jean Young, who objected that the playwright's playful approach "diminish[ed] the tragedy" of Baartman's life and "reifie[d] the perverse imperial mindset" that exposed her to the racial-izing gaze of the European public in the first place (1997, 700).

In both cases, it was the artists' deployment of racial stereotypes that became a bone of contention. While a number of critics appreciated it as a valiant attempt of antiracist, parodic Signifyin(g) in the service of liberating representations of African Americans in a "profound act of artistic exorcism" (Gates quoted in Bowles 1997, 5), others insisted that the use of stereotypes merely reiterated "the travesty of objectifi-cation of 'Otherness'" (J. Young 1997, 700). According to Jean Young, "Saartjie Baartman becomes twice victimized" in Parks's play: "first by nineteenth-century Victorian society, and, again, by the play *Venus* and its chorus of critics" (701). Artist Howardena Pindell likewise considers Walker's rehearsal of stereotypes a form of "visual terrorism" against people of color (quoted in Bowles 1997, 12). Pindell's colleague Betye Saar, known for refiguring negative images of Blackness into images of empowerment, as in her landmark piece *The Liberation of Aunt Jemima* (1972), similarly concludes, "Kara is selling us down the river" (4).[3] In short, while some appreciate the works of Parks, Walker, and other contemporaries for their humor and playfulness,[4] others dismiss the artists as "young and foolish" (Saar quoted in Bowles 1997, 4) and their artworks as detrimental to Black people.

In the mid-1990s then, Walker and Parks heated up an ongoing con-troversy over the reiteration and function of racializing stereotypes in contemporary art.[5] While agreeing on the enduring legacy of racist iconographies, opinions largely split over whether these images should be suppressed and countered with affirmative images of Blackness or acknowledged and engaged—and, if so, in what ways. Some critics maintain that the violent nature of these negative images cannot simply be undercut by irony and playfulness, that it persists beyond the best of intentions. They also believe that in reiterating stereotypes, young art-ists are disrespectful to a generation of African Americans who ded-icated their lives to battling such racist images. As artist and scholar Michael D. Harris writes with regard to Kara Walker and Michael Ray Charles, "I think that these artists who are dealing with stereotypical imagery have not fully grasped the complexity and pain that some of these things can inflict upon people in the community who remem-ber things longer, who are older than they, and who do feel some pain"

(Sims, Dalton, and Harris 1997, 28).[6] Other critics, however, point out that the insistence on the creation of affirmative images not only "strengthens the negative stereotypes in both the white and black imagination" (Diawara 1999, 7) but is itself caught up in the reification of Blackness, in establishing a counter-representational regime, in this case, one of Black nationalism.[7] For Manthia Diawara, the only way of depriving these negative images of their power is by "embracing" them, by revealing them as objects of desire (15). Stuart Hall similarly insists on the affective purchase of stereotypes on the "inner landscape[s]" of both white and Black viewers (1996, 17). "If you want to begin to *change* the relationship of the viewer to the image," he concludes, "you have to intervene in exactly that powerful exchange between the image and its psychic meaning, the depths of the fantasy, the collective and social fantasies with which we invest images" (1997b, 21).

Diawara's and Hall's observations on the affective dimension of stereotypes underline the extent to which a stereotype functions not only as an epistemological tool, as a way of producing and freezing knowledge, but also as a complex interplay of anxiety and desire, fear of and fetish for the imagined Other. The stereotype, Homi K. Bhabha explains, is not simply "a false image which becomes the scapegoat of discriminatory practices" but rather "a much more ambivalent text of projection and introjection, metaphoric and metonymic strategies, displacement, overdetermination, guilt, aggressivity, the masking and splitting of 'official' and phantasmatic knowledges to construct the positionalities and oppositionalities of racist discourses" (1994, 88). In this regard then, the stereotype is undergirded by multilayered and powerful intersubjective dynamics that engage the beholder in an ongoing process of identification and disidentification. This complex intersubjective dimension of the stereotype can help explain the heightened emotive language used by some of the critics in their reaction to Parks's and Walker's oeuvres—for the language of stereotypes is also the language of affect.

According to Gregory Seigworth and Melissa Gregg's definition of the term, "affect is the name we give to those forces—visceral forces, beneath, alongside, or generally *other than* conscious knowing, vital forces insisting beyond emotion," which are "found in the intensities that pass body to body" (2010, 1, italics in original). These visceral forces can be minute and barely noticeable; they can also be quite powerful, leaving us stunned and paralyzed but possibly also driving us "toward movement, toward thought and extension" (1). As Seigworth and Gregg insist, there is no "pure" state of affect; affect is always messy and complex because it "arises in the midst of in-between-ness: in the capacities to act and be acted upon" (1). In this regard, the authors consider affect to be "in many ways synonymous with *force* or *forces of encounter*" (2). To be affected, Seigworth and Gregg explain, also means to be "'effectuated,' moved, put into motion by other entities, humans or nonhumans" (11; quoting Bruno Latour 2004, 205).

Considered from this angle, Hall's notion of going "inside the image itself" (1997b, 21) can be read as an artistic strategy that purposefully effects a charged encounter between subject and object in order to trigger a discharge of affect—the outcome of which is far from predictable. Ideally, it might expose the epistemological and psychic powers of the stereotype, undermine its seeming fixity of representation, and open up again the play of difference, which, according to Hall, can generate new forms of knowledge and new subjectivities. But the affective charge of the encounter with the phantasmagorical body of the stereotype might also exhaust itself in a myriad of other reactions: discomfort, embarrassment, shame, indifference, silliness, and, yes, also impudence and vulgarity. This is the risk the artist takes in tapping the affective hold of the stereotype.[8] In fact, I contend that it is very much the broad range of audience reactions that many contemporary restagings of racializing stereotypes bring into focus.

In this chapter, I discuss Parks's and Walker's works as purposeful attempts to tap the psychic hold and affective claims that stereotypes originating in the past of slavery continue to have today; to tease out the complex intersection of desire and phobia, fantasy and anxiety, humor and shame that mark contemporary audiences' relationship to these overdetermined visual signs. The goal of these provocative restagings of racializing stereotypes, so I argue, is to move spectators: to provoke them, demand attention, elicit a response. Juliette Bowles points out that "Walker pushes a lot of buttons all at once" (1997, 14). Referring to the premiere of Parks's *Venus* at the Yale Repertory Theatre in March 1996, Shawn-Marie Garrett similarly writes, "it was impossible to guess who would walk out after 15 minutes and who would rise at the end to give a standing ovation, and this is nearly always the case with Parks's productions" (2000, 133–34). In the case of *Venus,* in fact, a good third of the audience felt provoked to walk out of the premiere.[9] But what does it mean to stay and encounter the performance? What does it mean to submit to having one's buttons pushed by these contemporary artworks on the traumatic histories and legacies of slavery? As Josephine Lee remarks in *Performing Asian America* (1998), although restaging stereotypes inevitably invokes their ugly, racist histories, "they can nonetheless reveal in their performance the inner dynamics of this history, which already suggests the potential for its disruption" (96). I therefore consider the performance of stereotypes in contemporary works on slavery, particularly in the works of Parks and Walker, an effective historiopoetic strategy for disrupting habitual processes of perception and flipping established scripts of knowledge production, if only to open up again, in Hall's words, "the practice of representation itself" (1997b, 21).

This chapter focuses on two case studies: the above-mentioned 1996 production of Parks's play *Venus* at the Yale Repertory Theater (subsequently moved to the New York Public Theater) and Kara Walker's 2014 installation *A Subtlety, or the Marvelous Sugar Baby* at the Domino Sugar Refinery in Williamsburg, Brooklyn. Both works examine one of the most charged images of slavery, the Black female body. As Hortense Spillers points out, the Black woman, having served throughout American history as "signifying property *plus*" (1987b, 65, italics in original), presents at once the key lexical and yet most ambiguous figure in the "American grammar" (68), the symbolic order underwriting the cultural syntax of the United States of America. The Black woman describes "the locus of confounded identities, a meeting ground of investments and privations in the national treasury of rhetorical wealth" (65). With *Venus* and *Sugar Baby*, Parks and Walker target this "national treasury" of rhetorical and phantasmagoric investments in the Black female body and the various articulations it finds in the twentieth and twenty-first century head-on. "Going inside" the stereotype, as Hall proposes, they peel back the various mythological layers imposed on black women's bodies in Western visual and performance cultures at least from the eighteenth century onward, particularly in her role as sexual Other, or "Black Venus."[10] In the process, the play and installation not only examine prevalent fantasies but also break with established taboos concerning the role of women in the libidinal economy of slavery. For the spectator/beholder—both Black and white—Parks's and Walker's rigorous archaeological approach to seemingly fixed knowledges of and deep-rooted feelings toward the past can be extremely confrontational since it reveals how deeply embedded in the collective psyche these racializing stereotypes are, how profoundly they continue to impact contemporary identities. As Walker remarks, "the impassioned connections that many people have with these images suggest the continued currency of an exaggerated Black body in American culture that refuses to be buried and is clearly intact enough to warrant further investigation" (quoted in Sanneh et al. 1998, 49).

I aim to bring the affective, confrontational dimension of Parks's and Walker's engagement with stereotypes into focus through the concept of theatricality. A notoriously slippery term, "theatricality" has been used to describe a great variety of instances of performance, both on and off stage.[11] Three interrelated uses of the term, however, are useful in analyzing the affective quality of recent cultural productions addressing the legacy of slavery: (1) as the foregrounding of a communicative situation between performer and spectator; (2) as the self-reflective metaquality of a particular performance that foregrounds its own presentational qualities, its specific mediality (theater as live performance) over its representational qualities (theater as mimesis); and (3) as the resistance of the performing object.

Regarding the first meaning of theatricality, various scholars have treated the stage-audience relationship as the constitutive dimension of theater and performance.[12] Willmar Sauter, for instance, defines theatricality as "the communicative process between the performer's exhibitory, encoded, and embodied actions and the emotional and intellectual reactions of the spectator" (2000, 69). Michael Fried, ironically one of theatricality's harshest critics, elaborates the affective dimension of this communicative process further. In his 1967 essay "Art and Objecthood," he vehemently disapproves of what he considers to be a theatrical impulse in modern conceptual artworks. In creating "a kind of *stage* presence," these works trigger for him the experience "of an object in a *situation*"—one that, virtually by definition, *includes the beholder*" (153). For Fried, a fervent advocate of the notion of the artwork's absolute autonomy (and hence its inherent negation of the beholder), "the literalist espousal of objecthood amounts to nothing less than a plea for a new genre of theater, and theater is now the negation of art" (153). In his vehement attack on the object-subject relation, he nevertheless puts forth a perceptive definition of theatricality: "It is a function not just of the obtrusiveness and, often, even of the aggressiveness of literalist work, but of the special complicity that that work extorts from its beholder" (155). Put differently, Fried conceptualizes the complicity of the beholder/spectator as a crucial part—if not the focus—of the communicative process between a theatrical artwork/performance and its spectator. This concept of theatricality helps us understand in more complex ways what critics have quick-handedly referred to as the "in-your-face" quality of Walker's and Parks's works (Kuspit 2004; Touré 2011, 37). It foregrounds the relational dimension between art object and beholder and its attending affective charges: the myriad possibilities for anger, disgust, shame, insouciance, desire, and laughter.[13] At the same time, in addition to enabling the play of the affective force of the stereotype, theatricality also functions to mediate it; for the "beholder knows himself to stand in an indeterminate, open-ended—and unexacting—relation as *subject* to the impassive object on the wall or floor" (Fried 1998, 155). In other words, the theatrical performance of stereotypes also has the potential to trigger a cognitive engagement with those affective forces.

In Parks's and Walker's artworks this self-awareness—which I believe is anything but unexacting, but rather demanding and unsettling—is enhanced through the artists' skillful foregrounding of the mediality of the performance itself; the second definition of theatricality used here. As noted in chapter 2, Parks's signature dramaturgy of Rep & Rev draws attention to the materiality as well as the performativity of language, its capacity for perpetual resignification. Similarly, Richard Foreman's idiosyncratic mise-en-scène and production style in the 1996 production of *Venus* serves to highlight to audiences in a Brechtian manner the constructed nature and processual character of the performance. With *Sugar Baby*, a massive sculpture coated in refined sugar, Walker, too, foregrounds the materiality of the object, provoking the viewers' interactions with the body of the sculpture. Sugar, hence, serves as the medium through which audiences are asked not only to engage the fraught past of plantation labor but also their own reactions to contemporary articulations of this past. Given these works' pronounced, self-reflective emphasis on mediality, there is no mistaking their references to slavery as mimetic or their presentation of racist stereotypes as laying claim to be being realistic. Rather, so I suggest, theirs is a highly theatrical act of signifying on the epistemic and affective legacies of slavery, a reiteration with signal differences.

There is yet a third notion of theatricality that comes into play with Parks's and Walker's works: the "essential theatricality of blackness" that is "able to mess up or mess with the beholder" (Moten 2003, 234, 235). In a remarkable refiguration of Fried's notion of theatricality, Moten contemplates the "specific objecthood that joins blackness and black performance" (234). He refers to the commodification of Blackness that has historically cojoined "person" and "object" while also requiring the ongoing performance of objecthood. In this case, the object is the performer as well as the performance of the object. The crucial question that Moten raises is in what ways the object-performer might, through performance, articulate objection to her ongoing objectification. How can racial performance be deployed to critique and undermine "the visual pathology of racial categorizations" (234)? Moten's elaboration of theatricality points us to the possibilities of reading performances of race against the grain, of gauging the resistance of the performing object, of the ways that stereotypes can be deployed to disrupt the economy of desire between object and beholder.

In the remainder of this chapter, I will examine the intricate interplay of these three notions of theatricality (complicity of the spectator, self-reflective mediality, and resistance of the object) in close readings of the Foreman production of Parks's *Venus* and Walker's *Sugar Baby* installation. I begin with some preliminary remarks on the affective force of the emblematic icon of the enslaved and violated Black woman in visual and performative renderings of slavery and the complex issues involved in the attempt to represent her.

BLACK VENUS

"Variously named Harriot, Phibba, Sara, Joanna, Rachel, Linda, and Sally, she is found everywhere in the Atlantic world. The barracoon, the hollow of the slave ship, the pest-house, the brothel, the cage, the surgeon's laboratory, the prison, the cane field, the kitchen, the master's bedroom—turn out to be exactly the same place and in all of them she is called Venus" (Hartman 2008, 1). In the opening to her essay "Venus in Two Acts," Hartman points out the ubiquitous presence of images of the violated Black woman in the archives of slavery, setting up the figure of Venus as "emblematic for the enslaved" (1). As Hartman and other scholars have noted, recovering the actual lives of Black women from the sediments of representation and examining the legacies of their emblematic status presents historians and artists alike with its own set of challenges. First, Hartman asks, how can we tell the story of Venus "without committing further violence in [one's] own act of narration," without duplicating the violence of words that have buried her in the archives to begin with (2)? Spillers adds that the Black female body has been "so loaded with mythical prepossession that there is no easy way for the agents buried beneath them to come clean" (1987b, 65). And Arlene Keizer (2008) points to a set of cultural taboos and discursive restrictions regarding female sexuality that have further complicated the task of representing Black women in slavery. The question of archaeological recovery is thus profoundly and intricately intertwined with questions of representation, as is the history of the Black female body with the history of its various articulations; the two aspects cannot be separated neatly. In their provocative, ludic work with stereotypes, Parks and Walker target this entanglement of the archive and its articulations, or of what Walker calls the collusion of fact and fiction in our access to history.

Like no other figure from the racialized cast of colonialism and slavery, the figure of the Black Venus brings into focus the continuing epistemological and libidinal hold of a number of historically grown ideas, preconceptions, and mythologies about Black people in general and Black women in particular on the white imagination as well as the trauma and shame that African American people associate with them. Sander Gilman has shown how in the nineteenth century women of color, particularly Saartjie Baartman in her role as "The Hottentot Venus," were eagerly set up by a confluence of pseudoscientific discourses, imperial interests, and popular fantasies as the quintessential racial and sexual Other to European perceptions of middle-class metropolitan whiteness.[14] In particular, Baartman's buttocks and genitalia came to signify excess and deviance, turning Baartman into "the central nineteenth-century icon for sexual difference between the European and the black" (Gilman 1985, 231). Kianga Ford has, furthermore, noted that Baartman's body has continued to serve as the predominant "interpretative frame" through which Black women have been read "across both temporal and geographical boundaries" (2010, 100). According to Ford, "Baartman's 'hypersexuality' and genital 'excess' are always already present as frames through which black women and their representations are read and interpreted" (105).

Such hypersexualization of the Black female body has led, in turn, to a series of taboos regarding the representation of Black female sexuality. As Keizer explains, addressing the issue of sexuality and rape was nearly impermissible in eighteenth- and nineteenth-century discussions of slavery and continued to hold a "terrifying power" in the twentieth century (2008, 1656).[15] Faced with the pervasiveness of negative stereotypes of women's sexuality, Black women felt compelled to create a "culture of dissemblance" (Hine 1989) in which, according to Darlene Clark Hine, any form of sexual expression was downplayed and even denied. Even as the figure of the abused Black woman soon emerged as one of the key "conceptual icons" (Keizer 2008, 1651) in the literary and visual neo–slave narratives of the second half of the twentieth century, making plain "the convergence of terror and pleasure in the libidinal economy of slavery" (Hartman 2008, 1), its representations continued to be circumscribed, as Keizer points out, by rules of "decorous memorializing" (2008, 1650). Typically, this meant depicting the icon of the abused female slave in the language of resistance and/or "unequivocal victimization" (1650). Faith Ringgold's *Slave Rape Series* (1970) and Octavia Butler's portrayal of the slave Alice in *Kindred* (1979) are two powerful examples of works aiming, on the one hand, to articulate protest and outrage and, on the other, to initiate, through identificatory empathy, a process of mourning in the reader/observer (Keizer 2008, 1656).

In evoking the figure of the Black Venus in their artworks, Parks and Walker respond to the legacies of both these histories of representing Black women—the overwhelming, degrading mythology that continues to influence mainstream perceptions of Black women as well as what Roderick Ferguson calls the "poetics of evasion" (2009, 187) that informs the politics of dissemblance as well as a series of other historiographic "blanks" (187) in African American memory culture. They tend to tackle existing taboos and narrative restrictions head-on in order to dissect the various constitutive layers of residual ideologies, prevalent fantasies, and mnemonic anxieties that inform contemporary perception of Black women "with all [their] concomitant contradictions" (Ford 2010, 98).

A vignette from Walker's silhouette installation *Emancipation Approximation* (2000) provides a helpful entry into this discussion (fig. 10).[16] We behold—rendered in profile, sitting erect—a white male dignitary (closely resembling George Washington, even though the title of the installation would suggest Lincoln), ostensibly bestowing his blessing of freedom on a young African American woman kneeling in front of him and looking up in a posture of supplication—a gesture familiar from popular abolitionist imagery, such as Josiah Wedgwood's antislavery medallion ("Am I Not a Man and a Brother," 1787) and the Emancipation Memorial in Washington, DC (1876). At first glance, Walker chooses to replicate the sentimental racial discourse of the early republic in the familiar iconography (paternalism) and domestic medium (the silhouette) of the time. On closer examination, however, we notice that the genteel hand extended in benediction to the young woman's head is also gently encouraging her to proceed with an act of fellatio. For this gratifying act, the dignitary chooses to recline on the back of a male African American figure bent down in the iconic Atlas pose. The silhouette of an eighteenth-century dignitary, quite possibly a founding father of the nation, thus morphs into a complex emblem conjoining the project of white Enlightenment with the sexual and physical exploitation of people of African descent. At the same time, however, the stereotypical binaries of "strong white male" versus "weak effeminate Black" are subtly inverted. For the dignitary, in his erotic pursuit, seems rather precariously perched on the Black man's shoulders, likely to topple over at any moment; and regarding his relationship to the young woman, one wonders who, ultimately, is in control of the situation. As Keizer has argued, the act of fellatio not only bestows a certain sexual power on the female but also signifies an erotic excess beyond the strictly reproductive logic of slavery's sexual economy (2008, 1669).

With this playful silhouette, Walker intervenes in discussions of the history of slavery on various levels. Rendering the sexual encounter between white man and Black woman as highly ambivalent in terms of desire and power relations, she challenges established historiographies and goes against the grain of long-standing codes of memory culture. Much to the consternation of her critics, her work in general repeatedly features female figures that seem to be compliantly yielding to sexual abuse, observing it with a detached curiosity, receiving pleasure, and, at times, even asserting their sexual agency.[17] The same can be said of Parks's play *Venus*, in which, as will become evident shortly,

FIGURE 10. Kara Walker. 2000. *Emancipation Approximation, Scene #6*. Silkscreen. 44 × 34 in. (111.8 × 86.4 cm). © Kara Walker, courtesy of Sikkema Jenkins & Co., New York.

the playwright emphatically departs from the established historiographies that render Saartjie Baartman as a victim and national hero by presenting her as a woman complicit in her own oppression, as experiencing intimacy and pleasure, perhaps even love, with one of her owners. Both Parks's and Walker's works thus index the "tangled moral quagmire" (Cameron 1997, 11) that also characterized the power system of slavery, in which demarcations between dominance and intimacy were sometimes anything but clear-cut. To be sure, as Spillers (1987b) and Hartman (1997) caution us, to conceive of pleasure or even agency under conditions of nonfreedom is quite problematic. And yet to foreclose the possibility of posing such questions seems equally problematic because it delimits our access to and understanding of the archive. As Treva B. Lindsey and Jessica Marie Johnson (2014) maintain, the recurrent emphasis on subjugation, exploitation, and dehumanization does not capture the whole spectrum of women's sexual lives under slavery. Parks and Walker, by contrast, sketch out the varied and messy terrain of subject relations and pose uncomfortable questions about consent, complicity, agency, and pleasure in the libidinal economy of slavery. As Keizer suggests, "sexual and familial relationships between masters and slaves" may be "the most significant, haunting, and relevant affective legacy of American slavery" (2008, 1664). Not surprisingly, then, Walker's and Parks's unconventional portraits of these relationships have frequently triggered shock and outrage among their spectators. In tackling the "unfamiliar, the invisible, the unspeakable, and the contested" (Ferguson 2009, 185),[18] the two artists seek to gauge the continuing affective force of this legacy as well as to widen the conceptual lens for approaching the archive.

At the same time, Walker's vignette *Emancipation Approximation* also troubles the very possibility of reading the archive in a simple and straightforward manner. Hovering above the interracial couple, we find two winged putti in a tight amorous clasp. The camp aesthetics of their cherubic embrace—their silhouette bodies shape a heart between them—queers both the very notion of a romantic interracial encounter and the possibility of an objective narrative. The putti's allegorical evocation of childlike innocence and romantic purity can hardly be transferred to the libidinal power game played out by the black-and-white ménage à trois below them. Rather, the vignette's visual excess alerts us to the ways in which perceptions (and representations) of interracial encounters are hardly disinterested to begin with. They are conditioned and mediated by prevailing iconographies (such as the Black Venus) and their attendant discourses (such as paternalism and sentimentality) as well as by the viewer/reader's desire for different narrative possibilities. Confronted with the abuse and murder of two young African girls on board of the slaver *Recovery*, Hartman concedes that she feels tempted to supplement the archival evidence of violence with a story of romance, friendship, and witnessing to counter the overwhelming "libidinal investment in violence" manifest in the archive and to provide a "glimpse of beauty" and "possibility" in its place (2008, 5, 8). "I admit that I wanted to console myself and to escape the slave hold with a vision of something other than the bodies of two girls settling on the floor of the Atlantic," she writes (9). Hartman responds to the fundamental problem posited by the archive of slavery (how to tell the story of violence without replicating its grammar in the act of narration?) by developing the method of "critical fabulation" (11)—a self-reflective, subjunctive mode of narration that enables her to strain against the limits of the archive and envision the humanity of the enslaved outside a grammar of violence while simultaneously marking the impossibility of doing so.[19] Although neither Walker nor Parks share in the recuperative impulse that marks Hartman's endeavor, the visual excess in Walker's silhouette as well as the theatrical excess of Parks's play evince a similar self-critical impulse. The visual excess of the winged embrace in *The Emancipation Approximation* simultaneously invites and undercuts the attempt to read the encounter between the three central figures in sentimental or romantic terms. This ironic movement, correlating two contrary meanings, draws attention to issues of narrative mediation, to "layers of attenuated meanings, made an excess in time, over time" (Spillers 1987b, 65). Walker is interested not only in the layers sedimented by the racial formation of slavery but also in those added by contemporary readers and spectators, scholarly and otherwise. Underneath these layers, awaiting the archaeologist perceptive to such historiopoetic mediations, so she would agree with Spillers, are the "marvels of [her] own inventiveness" (65).

In what follows, I discuss how Parks and Walker, through the deployment of visual hyperboles and/or theatrical excess (such as the amorous putti), expose and undercut habitual visual practices and narrative desires to alert us to the mediated nature of the ways in which archives are produced, accessed, read, and refigured. As noted in the preceding chapters, the two artists are not so much concerned with correcting the facts on the ground, with filling in gaps, and expanding the archive as they are with exposing the anxieties and desires through which these facts have been established in the first place, along with those that fuel and mediate the stories through which we continue to narrate them visually and verbally. Put differently, when Walker and Parks, along with other contemporary artists—for instance, Renee Cox, Renée Green, Carla Williams, and Carrie Mae Weems, to name only a few[20]— retrieve "The Hottentot Venus" from the cast of racializing stereotypes that has served to bolster up notions of white supremacy and sexual normativity, it is not to recover the actual woman/women behind the stereotype but rather to probe the meanings and longevity of what Ford fittingly calls "the symbolic Venus" (2010, 99).

VENUS: THE BUSINESS OF LOOKING AND SHOWING

In 1815, shortly after Saartjie Baartman arrived in Paris, a satirical cartoon appeared in the metropolis, "Le Curieux en exstase, ou les cordons de souliers" (The curious in ecstasy, or the shoelaces) (fig. 11). It depicts three fully clothed men (two wearing kilts, probably Scottish soldiers)[21] and a woman in a white Empire dress gawking at a woman standing in the nude, with only a beaded loincloth for protection, on a soapbox that bears the engraving "La Belle Hottentote." The satire clearly aims to ridicule the sexual fascination of the early nineteenth-century European public with the live display of African women. As the spectators seem enraptured with the exposed body—seeking to touch it, leaning forward to get a closer look at it, using optical aids to focus more closely, exclaiming "Qu'elle étrange beauté," "Oh! godem quel rosbif," "Ah! que la nature est drole"—a dog mocks their libidinal ecstasy, in its turn seeking to take a peek and sniff beneath the Scotsman's loincloth. The animalistic nature that contemporaries such as anatomist Georges Cuvier notoriously sought to ascribe to women of color, particularly to Baartman, is here transferred to the "civilized" onlooker. Likewise, the male spectator's body becomes subtly but unmistakably sexualized, not only by the analogy between the kilt and the loincloth but also through the men's assorted accouterments of daggers, swords, and umbrellas girded prosthesis-like to their loins, suggesting that their supposedly disinter-

CHAPTER 4

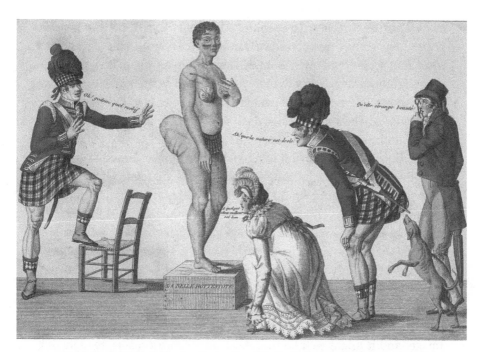

FIGURE 11. Louis François Charon. September 1815. *Le Curieux en exstase, ou les cordons de souliers*. Hand-colored etching. 8¾ × 11⅝ in. (22.2 × 29.5 cm). © The Trustees of the British Museum.

ested, anthropological interest could hardly be divorced from prurient sexual desire. Hypersexuality, stereotypically ascribed to Black women, is here clearly marked as white male. Last but not least, the French woman is shown bending down, apparently to tie her shoelaces, while looking up beneath the Belle Hottentote's loincloth and exclaiming: "A quelque chose malheur est bon" (Sometimes a misfortune turns out to have its advantages). Whether she is referring to the mishap of the loosened shoelace or to the displayed woman's exposed position remains unclear. In any case, the genteel lady is not below stooping to her own voyeuristic desires and prurient fantasies.

What strikes me most in this image—besides the obvious satire on nineteenth-century Europeans' sexualized investment in otherness—is the way the unknown artist has rendered the central object of desire, "La Belle Hottentote." She stands erect, with a noble posture, apparently ignoring her "ecstatic" audience, looking out directly at the beholder of the cartoon—as if to rise above the absurd spectacle of banal desire played out around her. In breaking the "fourth wall" of the diegetic frame, she invites our consideration as a product of staging and its attendant scopic dynamics. Notably, the exhibited woman is sketched in only slightly darker shades than her onlookers. The unknown cartoonist chose to mark her otherness primarily with the help of her positioning on a pedestal, the application of dark smears of facial make-up, and the lack of clothing. Racial difference emerges thus not as ontological but as the product of spectacular staging and performance as well as perception. Furthermore, the onlookers' exclamations are rendered as written lines that visually reinforce the direction of their gazes, holding the African woman in place, circumscribing her. When in the midst of this economy of looking, the subject center stage gazes straight at us, with her left hand raised in a gesture pointing to herself, she also seems to address us with a caution: "Me? Do not mistake this display as giving insight into my subjectivity. What you are beholding is merely a spectacular staging of all these people's fantasies and desires, including your own."

Perhaps mine is very much a twenty-first-century reading of this image, and it might well be that most nineteenth-century readers did not pick up on the cartoon's critique of colonial scopic regimes but merely chuckled over its bawdy sexual humor. Yet, I find in this 1815 cartoon's foregrounding of visual and libidinal dynamics in the construction of otherness striking parallels to late twentieth- and early twenty-first-century artworks in which, as Ford observes, the "Hottentot Venus functions as a visual signpost that points toward the rampant indulgence in the fantasy of the extreme other" (2010, 100). In chapter 2, I elaborated on the various ways in which Parks undertakes with her play *Venus* an archaeology of the various discourses (anthropological, medical, juridical, commercial, popular cultural) that produced "The Hottentot Venus" as a knowable subject in the first place. In this chapter, I want to focus on Parks's staging of the various scopic mechanisms that interpellated Baartman's body into a racializing visual regime as well as on the various ways that the play's pronounced theatricality exposes and undercuts the continuing legacy of such a representational regime.

In the "Overture" to Parks's *Venus*, we find the eponymous protagonist prominently displayed on a small platform, slowly revolving 360 degrees, as the Negro Resurrectionist announces her presence to the audience: "The Venus Hottentot!" (1). The cast of actors mills about her, voicing their fascination with the exhibited woman's body: "Good

God. Golly. Lookie-Lookie-Look-at-her. / Ooh-la-la. What-a-find. Hubba-hubba-hubba" (6). The general excitement hardly abates when the spectacle's emcee announces, "I regret to inform you that thu Venus Hottentot iz dead" (3). Few of the spectators on stage seem deterred by the fact that the Venus they behold is a mere surrogate and the show they witness a re-enactment rather than "the real thing." They quite eagerly accept the invitation to "take yr peek" (5) at the substitute. From the start, the play thus operates on two levels: it attempts to excavate the historical discourses and scopic mechanisms that fabricated the symbolic body of the Black Venus in the first place, but it also makes clear that these discourses and mechanisms persist independent of their historical referent; the Hottentot show continues well past its original historical moment in the early nineteenth century. Baartman's dead body becomes the very stage for an ongoing spectacularization of Black women.

The public's rampant voyeurism and fetishization of the Venus is reiterated throughout the play in various settings: by paying clients in Mother-Showman's freak show, courtroom inquirers into the Venus's labor status, scientific observers at the anatomical theater, and, finally, the outraged mob outside her prison cell. In these various scenes, Parks zooms in on the protagonist's constant exposure to the gawking, grop-ing, and poking crowd. The dramaturgy reinforces this scopic econ-omy by including what the playwright calls "spells"—that is, wordless moments of "elongated and heightened" pause in which figures "expe-rience their pure true simple state" (Parks 1995e, 16). The architectural set-up on the page—

The Venus
The Baron Docteur
The Venus
The Baron Docteur
The Venus
The Baron Docteur
The Venus (1997, 80)

—translates on the stage as prolonged moments of looking at each other. A version of such scopic exchange recurs throughout the play—in fact, there is no scene in which the Venus is not exposed to someone's gaze.[22]

A photograph from the 1996 production of *Venus* at the Yale Repertory reveals how Richard Foreman's carnivalesque staging techniques reinforce Parks's dramaturgical emphasis on the Venus as first and foremost a visual signpost for spectators' fantasies (fig. 12). The arrangement of figures and the dynamics between them are in many ways reminiscent of the 1815 cartoon. Only this time, the onstage spectators use pointers, fingers, and umbrellas to fix the Venus's body in place, while they are gazing out at the audience offstage, inviting it to share their particular notion of the Black woman's body, as if to say, "Here, see? Can you see? This is how we fathom the Venus Hottentot!" Pulled in several directions by the demands of her beholders, the Venus looks rather helplessly offstage. Compared to the 1815 cartoon, Foreman's production appears to be more blatant and aggressive in underlining the scopic mechanisms that quite literally seem to twist and torment the Black female body center stage. The multiracial cast of onstage spectators, moreover, suggests that, having internalized the colonizing gaze, nonwhite subjects are also liberally partaking in the Venus spectacle.

The play's opening dialogue, moreover, underlines that the pleasure derived from the spectacle of the Venus is motivated by a complex interweaving of erotic, moral, and racial imaginaries. In their various exclamations, the voyeuristic crowd combines the attribution of absolute physical difference for the purpose of securing clear racial demarcations ("Wild Female Jungle Creature. Of singular anatomy. Physiqued / in such a backward rounded way that she outshapes / all others," 5) with the concurrent sexual fetishization of this difference ("I'll stick / my hand inside her / cage and have a feel / (if no one is looking,)" 6). This dualism of differentiation and fetishization, phobia and pleasure is, as Homi K. Bhabha (1994) and Sander L. Gilman (1985) have pointed out, one of the key techniques of processes of racial stereotyping.

The play's overture then already demonstrates the various visual mechanisms of exhibition, scrutiny, consumption, assessment, and classification at work in turning Saartjie Baartman from a historical subject into a phantasmagoric and even mythical object of collective desire and anxiety as well as fixed object of knowledge. This process is reinforced by the citation of various historical documents throughout the play: diaries, court records, advertisement bills, ballads, a parody of a popular French burlesque of the time.[23] Together these sources demonstrate the extent to which the "Hottentot Venus" captured the imagi-

FIGURE 12. *Venus* by Suzan-Lori Parks, dir. Richard Foreman. 1996. Yale Repertory. Photo © T. Charles Erickson.

nation of the metropolis in the early nineteenth century and also the uses to which blatant objectifications of Black women's bodies were put in the service of shoring up imperial ideology and white heteronormative middle-class identity.[24] The announcement at the start of the play that "Exposure iz what killed her" (3) thus resonates with a disconcerting double entendre, suggesting that Baartman perished not only from physical illness but also from relentless exposure to public scrutiny and consumption. The exposure of Baartman's body notoriously continued well beyond her death with the dissection of her corpse in 1816, the dissemination of the autopsy report in 1817, and the display of her skeleton, brains, and genitalia at the Musée de l'Homme in Paris well into the second half of the twentieth century.[25]

Foregrounding its very mediality as theater, *Venus*—particularly in Richard Foreman's 1996 production—moreover brings into focus the role of spectacle and theater in producing the racialized body and shaping racial histories. Foreman's mise-en-scène takes its cue from the popular freak shows and vaudeville acts of the nineteenth century. The play is staged as a carnivalesque sideshow that unremittingly assaults its audience with boisterous talk, flashy lights, abrasive sounds, general bustling about, and rapid scene transitions. Throughout the performance, the wires of theatrical production are clearly visible, thus highlighting the mechanisms at work in producing and performing "The Hottentot Venus."[26] The funhouse atmosphere aggressively hails its spectators with frequent apostrophes as clients of a show: "THE ONLY LIVING CREATURE OF HER KIND IN THE WORLD / AND ONLY ONE STEP AWAY FROM YOU RIGHT NOW / COME SEE THE HOT MISS HOTTENTOT / STEP IN STEP IN" (7). Since, thanks to the impresario's earlier announcement of the death of Venus, it is quite clear that what is being staged here is not the original but its surrogate, not history but its revenant, the invitation seems addressed equally to the audience onstage as well as offstage. As paying theater patrons, we also step into the show. In this manner, the production creates and thematizes a close bond between stage and audience.

This close relationship is mirrored by the production's ongoing modeling of performer-spectator relations on stage: the Venus is being gawked at by the Chorus (of Spectators, Anatomists, the Court), which is being scrutinized by the Baron Docteur, who in turn is being watched by the Venus herself, while they all, including the audience, remain under the constant gaze of the show's impresario, the Negro Resurrectionist—posing the question of who ultimately is being staged for whom. Such theatrical doubling, inversion, and mirroring of spectatorship makes it impossible to ignore one's own complicity as a participant in the contemporary spectacularization of the "Venus Hottentot." When the Venus revolves in the nude on stage, she signifies not only on a colonial history of scopic regimes and libidinal desires but also on its enduring legacies in contemporary culture, in which, as bell hooks suggests in "Eating the Other" (1992), a visual, sexual, or culinary fetish for otherness frequently serves to consolidate the dominant white order. Lest contemporary audiences fail to recognize their own complicity in the spectacle of the Venus, Parks drives home the point during the intermission by turning the tables and staging the audience. As the actor playing Baron Docteur—modeled on the French anatomist Georges Cuvier—invites the audience to take a break, he continues to read out Cuvier's infamous report of the dissection of Baartman's body. The audience is now caught in a double bind, as Harry Elam and Alice Rayner observe: "To stay to hear the report is almost obscene . . . . To resist the lie of biological determinism and refuse to participate means leaving the theater. But leaving is also ignoring the fact of the textual reality that defined the meaning of her body" (1998, 277). One cannot escape participation either by staying or leaving.

In foregrounding its theatricality (its theater-ness), Parks's play becomes, in Steven Drukman's words, "a profound tract about the power of theatre and the murderous implications of showing and gazing" (1996, 5). The spectator is made intensely aware of having paid for what a member of the Chorus of Spectators calls that "special looking place" (1997, 6) that joins the pleasure of watching a play with the discomfort of partaking in a humiliating spectacle of staging otherness. As Elam and Rayner remark about Foreman's production at the New York Public Theatre, "The vulnerability, shamefulness, and the shame of her exhibition are repeatedly reenacted: . . . When Venus stands alone in profile for the audience, the paying spectators of the Public Theater, no one can escape the discomforts of the Mother Showman saying 'What a bucket / what a bum! / What a spanker! / Never seen the likes of that, I'll bet'" (1998, 271). At the same time, however, both the play's and the production's pronounced self-reflectivity persistently undercut a naïve iteration of nineteenth-century colonial visual regimes. Clearly, Parks's Venus has very little to do with the actual woman, Saartjie Baartman. In fact, she has little to do with any actual Black woman. Actress Adina Porter, portraying the Venus in the Foreman production, wore a body-suit with enormous padding, highlighting the discrepancy between her actual, living body and the body she was enacting for the spectators in such a grotesque costume.[27] The costume made clear that hers is a figure of the spectatorial imagination that makes manifest various latent and not so latent fantasies, fears, and desires. Yet, despite such Brechtian devices of *Verfremdung* (alienation) that enable spectators to recognize the object of desire as the product of phantasmagoric projection and to see through the various scopic and discursive racializing mechanisms at work, "the persistent affective power" (Catanese 2010, 59) of the spectacle of Blackness remains. As Brandi Wilkens Catanese remarks, "condemning the spectacle does not allow us to deny the power that these racial displays continue to have today" (59). Knowledge and affect thus interact in complex ways in our encounter with the history and ongoing legacy of the racial stereotype.

In addition to laying bare the mechanisms of staging and looking, *Venus* is a play about showing and performing. Parks calls it "a play about show business—the business of showing yourself" (quoted in Drukman 1996, 4). Indeed, the trope of showmanship prominently features throughout the play, with various characters—the Negro Resurrectionist, the Mother-Showman, Baron Docteur—directing and emceeing various productions of "The Hottentot Venus" for audiences on and off stage. The protagonist's very name, "The Venus," is a stage name. In the beginning, the character is simply referred to as "The Girl," emerging in mythological fashion as the Venus only after a bath given to her by the Mother-Showman. Moreover, despite her bondage to a series of owner-showmen, Parks's Venus character is keenly attuned to the business of being put on display, determined to put on the best show she can and to "make a mint" (1997, 75). When business is slow, she suggests to the Mother-Showman that she could "spruce up" their act (51) by reciting some poetry. In the anatomical theater of Paris, she charms the Chorus of the 8 Anatomists by showing off her French-language skills. And with the anatomist Baron Docteur, she negotiates the terms of her sexual/medical submission: "100 a week . . . . New clothes and good meals" (88). Although the Venus's repeated question "Do I have a choice?" (17, 87) accentuates her awareness of the limits of her agency (symbolically, she fails to negotiate her own room), her subjectivity is not contained by victimhood. Instead, Parks presents her as a complex figure, a performer, who is keenly attuned to her own commodification but nonetheless seeks to benefit from it, a bonded woman complicit with and resistant to the power structures that objectify her. Her feelings for her owner and lover Baron Docteur are similarly complex, motivated by a mixture of compromise and romance: "He is not thuh most thrilling lay Ive had / but his gold makes up thuh difference and hhhh / I love him" (135). She fully embraces the performance of her role as his anatomical "discovery," determined to shine on his side. Diva-like she fantasizes about having her buttocks perfumed and sprinkled with gold dust and leading a celebrity life in the limelight of society: "The Docteur will introduce me to Napoléon himself: Oh, yes yr Royal Highness the Negro question does keep me up at night oh yes it does. / . . . Society will seek me out: Where's Venus? Right here!" (135). Parks notes, "I didn't want to make her a victim. . . . So I tried to give her little things—she can count and she can wheel and deal, and later, when things are a bit better for her . . . how she enjoys showing herself off, how she's so thrilled with herself" (quoted in Chaudhuri 2014, 56–57). In this regard then, the Venus emerges not only as "a passive icon of difference constituted entirely by the gaze of the audience" (Catanese 2010, 52) but also as a figure of complex agency who cannot be separated from her desire to perform.

Overall, Parks/Foreman's Venus emerges, like Walker's figure of the Negress (discussed in chapter 3), as a figure of opacity rather than legibility. As a performer, the Venus persistently slips through the cracks of the commodified narratives spectators, readers, and historiographers habitually bring to Baartman's history. In his opening pitch of the Venus show, the Negro Resurrectionist sharply sums up the limited repertoire available for emplotting her story:

> Tail end of our tale for there must be an end
> is that Venus, Black Goddess, was shameless, she sinned or else
> completely unknowing of r godfearin ways she stood
> totally naked in her iron cage.
> She gaind fortune and fame by not wearin a scrap
> hidin only the privates lippin down from her lap.
> When Death met her Death deathd her and left her to rot
> *au naturel* end for our hot Hottentot. (1997, 8–9).

The Venus as Goddess and the Venus as sinner; the Venus as unwitting victim and as willing participant in and beneficiary of an exploitative scheme. While the African-woman-as-prostitute narrative has fueled Western colonialism and its legacies since the early nineteenth century, the victim-turned-hero narrative has proved to be at the heart of various nationalist desires for counterhistories in the late twentieth century.[28]

How can we retrieve the actual Baartman from such narrative sedimentation? We can't, Parks seems to suggest, and her play certainly does not attempt to do so. As Catanese (2010) points out, the few pieces of "historical" information we glean from Parks's play comprise the mythos of the Hottentot and not the biography of Baartman: her "discovery" by the Man's Brother in South Africa, her journey to England and vain hopes for streets paved in gold, her abusive display in a side show, the courtroom investigation into her labor status, her "rescue" by the Docteur and ensuing classification by French anatomists, sickness, premature death, and autopsy.[29] When provided with a soliloquy—conventionally the part of a play in which characters articulate their "true" feelings and innermost thoughts—Venus does not speak to us. In the scene with the promising title "The Venus Hottentot Tells the Story of Her Life," she merely recycles the bits and pieces of plot we have already been given and does so in the most fragmented and distracted fashion ("Where wuz I," 159), undermining any lingering hope for the "real story." In short, our knowledge of the Venus's life amounts to nothing more than a handful of prefabricated narrative segments. In another soliloquy, "A Brief History of Chocolate," by contrast, her lengthy figurative, even mythological, account of the colonial desire for cacao indicates some awareness of mechanisms of exploitation that she has been subjected to, but in the end she asserts her "pleasure" (156) in consuming chocolate and having, in turn, her "chocolatized" body devoured by others.[30] This Venus then does and does not fit the established mold of narrative/historiographic expectations. She is a victim but also a chance survivor; she is complicit in her exploitation, and yet her love for Baron Docteur as well as for the stage can neither be reduced to mere complicity nor commodified as pure resistance. The Venus is and is not all this and more. In her performative excess she challenges not only the audience's role as spectators but also as historiographers, as interrogators of the historical record. Given Parks's playful repetition and revision (Rep & Rev) of fragments of habitual readings of "The Hottentot Venus," Sara Warner's assessment of Parks's approach to history strikes me as quite to the point: "A hagiography this play is not. Parks is interested in freeing Baartman not from the imperialist gaze but from the burden of representation itself. Baartman does not belong to all of us, she seems to say—she belongs to none of us" (2008, 197).

The burden of representation is, to an extent, also at stake in another theatrical strategy deployed by Parks and foregrounded in the Foreman production. Repeatedly, Parks's Venus looks back at those who seek to contain, discipline, and consume her—onstage and offstage. In the courtroom scene, she proudly parades, even struts, in front of her interrogators: "To hide yr shame is evil. / I show mine. Would you like to see?" (1997, 76). Moments such as this, in which the Venus deliberately poses her body for lawyers, doctors, clients, and, by extension, the contemporary audience to gaze at, present some of the most disconcerting moments in the play. Elam and Rayner comment on how the protagonist's pose conjoins complicity and resistance: "The pose is . . . a sign of consciousness and knowledge. The object of surveillance knows the power that belongs to the focal point of the gaze; she accepts awareness of being watched and develops that awareness into a decisive pose or attitude that holds the spectator in its power" (1998, 278). In posing, the colonized subject refracts the gaze of spectatorial desire, effectively turning her observers into the observed.

Building on this observation, I want to highlight the pose as a striking instance of theatricality. As a highly artificial *re*-presentation and embodiment of spectatorial desire, it thrives on and underscores the interpersonal relation between object/performer and beholder/spectator. Fried's and Moten's notions of theatricality prove useful in further teasing out the moment of agency in such performances of the pose. When the Venus strikes the pose of "The Hottentot Venus," when she thrusts out her "gold-dusted" buttocks to perform the stereotype already inscribed on her, she also foregrounds in a Friedian sense her theatrical objecthood, her existence for and in the imagination of the beholder. Drawing the spectator into a situation, she undercuts the possibility for spectatorial self-absorption. As a posing object, the Venus can no longer be absorbed at a mere glance; her meaning is no longer manifest in an instant. Rather, it commands the sustained attention of the beholder, an acknowledgment of the relationality of their situation, as well as an awareness of her materiality as object of desire. As Fried states, in the moment of the pose, the performing object is no longer simply in the same space with the beholder but "in his *way*" (1998, 154, italics in original). This is the point at which, for the high modernist critic, art loses its aesthetic value and degenerates into theater. According to Fried, "true" art does not require a beholder but exists in and by itself; to require an audience, as theater does, means to forsake the status as art.[31]

Fred Moten, by contrast, sees in this moment of pronounced theatricality the assertion of objection and the opening of possibility. In his nuanced and complex reading of artist Adrian Piper's performances of objecthood, he conceptualizes the aesthetic and ethical possibilities of a theatricality that Fried did not and could not envisage, the theatricality that emerges when "object, person, commodity, artist, and artwork converge" (2003, 239), as has typically been the case in performances of Blackness. Reflecting on her *Untitled Performance for Max's Kansas City* (1970),[32] Piper reports that the moment she purposefully presented herself in her performances to (white) art connoisseurs as "silent, secret, passive, seemingly ready to be absorbed into their consciousness as an art object" (quoted in Moten 2003, 239–40; Piper 1999, 27), she became unabsorbable. "My objecthood became my subjecthood," Piper writes (240; 27). Her *"voluntary* objectlike passivity" (240; 27) aggressively undercut any possibility of (self)absorption for the beholder but underlined, Moten points out, the "presentness of the object in all of its internal difference, in all of its interiority" (239). I see the Venus's pose as strikingly similar to Piper's pose: holding and refracting the gaze of the beholder, "subjection as beholding is cut by sharp objection" (239). In this regard, the Venus also presents us with a powerful example of what Uri McMillan calls an "embodied avatar," a strategic performance of objecthood that challenges and "disrupts presumptive knowledge of black subjectivity" (2015, 9). For Moten such resistance of the object is at the heart of the Black radical performance tradition. The manifest posing of objecthood compels the beholder into a different attitude toward the object-performer. It forces beholders to move out of themselves, to encounter and acknowledge the interiority of the object (2003, 236). As Moten explains with a view to Piper's work, "to be for the beholder is to be able to mess up or mess with the beholder. It is the potential of being catalytic. Beholding is *always* the entrance into a scene, into the context of the other, of the object" (235). The outcome of this encounter between self and other, beholder and object-performer is entirely open, comprising all the possibilities of the affective encounter mentioned earlier in this chapter.

In Parks's *Venus* then, the beholding of the theatrical Venus pose is a matter not only of its recognition as "a representation of a representation" (Elam and Rayner 1998, 279) but also of the possibility for change that can be triggered in the affective encounter between performing object and beholding subject in the course of a theatrical event. "Please visit," the Venus proclaims at the "tail end of the tale" (1997, 161). With this she indicates that she has no desire to remove herself from the stage any time soon. Hers is an invitation to a prolonged affective encounter with the stereotyped object that in its theatrical posing objects to the process of visual and narrative subjection. The look of shame (*"Dont look at me* / dont look," 158), articulated earlier in her encounter with the Negro Resurrectionist, is transformed into a look of challenge to her visitors. Her final words— the concluding lines of the play—significantly raise the bar of affect for these anticipated further encounters: "*Kiss* me *Kiss* me *Kiss* me *Kiss*" (162). Thus, while representational exposure may have contributed to the death of the actual historical Baartman, her ghostly theatrical revenant runs no such risk; her performativity and narrative opacity exceeds and resists legibility and thus also containment and control.

Given its pronounced theatricalities, *Venus* is indeed, as Elam and Rayner claim, "a test *of* the audience, not *for* the audience" (1998, 278). More than that, it is, as artist-critic Michele Wallace perceptively remarks, at once "archaeological and devilishly playful" (1996, 31). As it playfully digs up the history of exposing, abusing, and consuming the Black female body, it also excavates its burden of representation, taking digs at the various narratives and iconographies through which this body has been rendered. This archaeological procedure includes staging the complicity of the spectators in the various discursive and scopic mechanisms that have come to define the Black female body and to expose their latent and not so latent desires and expectations. It also entails the affective encounter with representation itself, offering up a genuine possibility for reopening its practice and reenabling the play of difference that can produce "new kinds of knowledges" and explore "new kinds of subjectivities" (Hall 1997b, 22).

THE MARVELOUS SUGAR BABY: OBJECTHOOD AS THEATRICAL EVENT

The location is the abandoned and run-down Domino Refinery in Williamsburg, Brooklyn, which from 1856 until 2004 operated as one of the main sugar refineries in North America, by 1890 producing half the sugar consumed in the United States.[33] Coated in layers of sticky molasses, the walls of the factory building quite literally drip with the history of sugar production. Art critic Kay Larson describes her impression of the space: "The stench is sweet and odorous in the same moment. To walk through the factory across its soiled concrete floor is to be almost overpowered by the cloying perfume of molasses, the smells of sweat and iron, the river-stink, the humid air" (2014, 509). In the midst of this murky mise-en-scène, Kara Walker sets up a massive sculpture with the epic title: *At the behest of Creative Time Kara E. Walker has confected: A Subtlety, or the Marvelous Sugar Baby, an Homage to the unpaid and overworked Artisans who have refined our Sweet tastes from the cane fields to the Kitchens of the New World on the Occasion of the demolition of the Domino Sugar Refining Plant* (fig. 13). Its title notwithstanding, there is nothing subtle about this 75-feet-long, 35-feet-high, and 26-feet-wide Styrofoam sculpture in the shape of a Sphinx with grotesquely exaggerated African facial features, a substantial female bosom, massive behind, and exposed vulva—all of it coated in some forty tons of white sugar. Surrounded by darkened factory walls, the monumental sculpture, also referred to as the Marvelous Sugar Baby, appears like a blazing apparition. Thanks to its central positioning on the factory floor directly underneath a skylight, the whiteness of the refined sugar coating is striking, almost blinding in the sunlight. Exhibited for nine weeks in late spring 2014 (May 10–July 6, 2014), the Sphinx-shaped figure sits with her legs tucked under her enormous buttocks, her back arched in feline pose, arms extended in front of her, and her head raised high in a regal manner. She is surrounded by a retinue of small boy figurines made of dark brown, unprocessed sugar and modeled after Black collectibles (fig. 14). Appearing to attend to their sugar queen, they tote cane, pieces of molasses, sometimes their own broken limbs. The general impression, despite the overwhelming miasma of industrial decay, is of a royal court with the New World

---

(*opposite, top*) FIGURE 13. Kara Walker. 2014. *A Subtlety, or the Marvelous Sugar Baby, an Homage to the unpaid and overworked Artisans who have refined our Sweet tastes from the cane fields to the Kitchens of the New World on the Occasion of the demolition of the Domino Sugar Refining Plant.* Polystyrene foam, sugar. Approx. 35½ × 26 × 75½ ft. (10.8 × 7.9 × 23 m). © Kara Walker, courtesy of Sikkema Jenkins & Co., New York. Installation view: Domino Sugar Refinery, a project of Creative Time, Brooklyn, NY, 2014. Photo: Jason Wyche.

(*opposite, bottom*) FIGURE 14. Foreground: Kara Walker. 2014. *African Boy Attendant Curio with Molasses and Brown Sugar, from "The Marvelous Sugar Baby" Installation at the old Domino Sugar Factory Warehouse.* Cast pigmented polyester resin with polyurethane coating with molasses and brown sugar, or cast sugar with metal armature. Front basket: 59.75 × 33 × 36 in. (151.8 × 83.8 × 91.4 cm). Back basket: 59 × 25 × 33 in. (149.9 × 63.5 × 83.8 cm). © Kara Walker, courtesy of Sikkema Jenkins & Co., New York. Installation view: Domino Sugar Refinery, a project of Creative Time, Brooklyn, NY, 2014. Photo: Jason Wyche.

Sphinx, as Walker calls her, granting an audience, waiting for her visitors to approach (Walker 2014, n.p.).[34]

Given the pregnant context of the exhibition, the careful staging and expressive posture of its central figure, it should be evident that the Marvelous Sugar Baby is more than simply a sculpture or art object. She is both a visual allegory and a performer in a highly theatrical event, signifying on the economic and representational histories of sugar plantation slavery and implicating the spectator in its legacies. Fried's definition of theatricality comes in handy again. Sugar Baby is, at first glance, all objecthood. The very title proclaims it as such: *A Subtlety.* Inspired by the elaborate confectionary works that graced aristocratic tables in medieval and early modern times, called *sotiltees* or subtleties, this work is presented as a treat designed for consumption.[35] It requires the beholder, without whom it is incomplete; or, as Fried states: "it *has* been waiting for him. And once he is in the room the work refuses, obstinately, to let him alone—which is to say, it refuses to stop confronting him" (1998, 163–64). Due to its size, the spectator-visitor is required to walk around the sculpture to behold it in its entirety, to appraise its magnitude, materiality, and shape, to take in its multiple, composite meanings—all of which bespeak the long and fraught history of objectifying the Black body through various forms of physical and representational exploitation. Because of such extended engagement, denying the beholder the aesthetic pleasure of immediate self-absorption, the sculpture forfeits, according to Fried's standards, its status as an autonomous art object and "degenerates" to the condition of theater. As mentioned earlier, I see this fundamental theatricality (which Fried objects to) not as a weakness but as the artwork's great performative and artistic strength.

As in the case of Parks's protagonist Venus, the charged staging of the Marvelous Sugar Baby can be considered an extended pose, drawing its beholders into a discomfiting situation. The Sphinx thrusts her body into spectators' faces, overwhelms with the sweet smell of molasses, and irritates with the iteration of racist stereotypes. The relationship of beholder and performing object is thus more complex than a mere culinary one, as Fried's reductive conception of theatre and theatricality would imply,[36] even though Walker riffs on such habitual attitudes of consumption with the title, materiality, and shape of her sculpture. This *sotiltee*, however, is clearly not meant to go down easily. Posing her provocatively sugarized, mythologized, sexualized, and racialized female body, the Marvelous Sugar Baby confronts her audience with "a set of representations that can't be fully embraced at once" (Walker quoted in Rooney 2014, n.p.). As Moten insists, there is something very powerful and potentially catalytic about an artwork that withholds legibility at a quick glance and refuses to let go of its beholders, demanding their sustained attention and challenging them with "the presentness of the object in all of its internal difference" (2003, 239). Below I will discuss the role of the beholder/the audience in the theatrical event of the sugar Sphinx in more detail. Here, taking my cue from Fried, Moten, and Walker, I want to underscore the ways in which the Marvelous Sugar Baby challenges its beholders with the overwhelming presentness of a historically produced objecthood. As a visual allegory of the nexus of New World slavery and global capitalism, the sculpture indexes the complex intersections of issues of race, class, gender, and sexuality with forced labor, industrialization, and consumption in the history of sugar production. Additionally, as a composite icon of racist stereotypes of Black womanhood, it also speaks to enduring histories of representation that likewise have their roots in the racial formation that sustained the colonial sugar economy and colluded in the production of whiteness.

To begin with the Sugar Baby's layered economic and material index: the sculpture's very title and mediality point us to the material history and legacy of the sugar economy. In medieval and early modern times, subtleties—elaborately crafted sugar sculptures in the shape of castles, ships, bouquets, animals, etc.—presented visually alluring center pieces at a banquet table. They were designed to delight the guests but also and primarily to signal the host's wealth, power, and political intent. Walker declares her intent as hostess to the *Sugar Baby* exhibition up front in the sculpture's title as paying "Homage to the unpaid and overworked Artisans who have refined our Sweet tastes from the cane fields to the Kitchens of the New World on the Occasion of the demolition of the Domino Sugar Refining Plant." The elaborate title interlinks in unequivocal terms plantation labor (cane fields) with domestic labor (kitchen) and the unpaid labor of slavery with the hazardous blue-collar labor of industrial capitalism, thus drawing a straight line from past to present. One of the oldest refineries in the United States, the Domino Sugar Refinery (formerly the American Sugar Refinery Company) was once the largest sugar factory in the world. At the height of its productivity in the 1880s, it most likely refined cane imported from Cuba—cane, which until 1886 was planted, cultivated, and harvested by slaves.[37] The Williamsburg refinery was thus one of the crucial pillars of the global trade that connected the colonial plantation economy in the Caribbean and South America with the thriving metropolitan centers in North America and Europe. Building on relevant late twentieth-century scholarship in the field of economic and cultural history (foremost Sidney Mintz's 1985 study *Sweetness and Power: The Place of Sugar in Modern History*), Walker locates with her New World Sphinx slavery at the heart of the profitable sugar economy fueling Anglo-American economic growth and geopolitical expansion from the early sixteenth to the late nineteenth century. In the spirit of Mintz, she understands the history of sugar as metonymically representing the history of capitalism as such.

Furthermore, the title's reference to the imminent demolition of the Domino Refinery (slated for conversion into genteel urban living and leisure spaces) indicates the artist's awareness that the material legacy of colonial labor extends well into today's neoliberal economy.[38] Read in conjunction with the site specificity of the installation, the title implies that "the unpaid and overworked artisans in the cane fields and kitchens of the New World" effectively enabled the production and accumulation of capital in the hands of those few who by the late twentieth century could afford to demolish industrial labor in the United States and outsource production, to transform a factory into up-scale condominiums and convert a work space into an art exhibit. Slavery, the Williamsburg sugar sculpture insists, both erected the cathedral-like spaces of industrial capitalism (the factory-refinery)[39] and continues to haunt the cathedral-like spaces of the neoliberal economy (luxury condominiums), its legacies persistently evident in contemporary structures of production, accumulation, distribution, and consumption. Walker remarks that when she first encountered the vacant Williamsburg factory, she recognized the space "as emblematic of the kind of short-sighted progress—the entrepreneurial, industrial, moneyed, ever forward, ever onward, no matter what, no matter who gets hurt—that has taken hold of the city" (quoted in Rooney 2014, n.p.). Her massive sugar Sphinx messes with such narratives of unhampered progress that effectively erase the labor sustaining it. In pointing up the subaltern labor consumed and wasted in the name of growth and expansion, Walker proposes an alternative historiography to what Édouard Glissant calls the totality of a Western "History . . . written with a capital H" (1999, 75) and brings into focus the material foundations of today's economy and culture.

In a similar vein, Walker continues Mintz's project of unveiling and demystifying "the mysteriousness that accompanied my seeing, at one and the same time, cane growing in the fields and white sugar in my cup" (1985, xxiv). Marking her sugar confection in terms of race (the stereotypical facial features connoting "Blackness") and class (the headkerchief of the laborer), she links in no uncertain terms the consumption of white sugar to the productivity of Black labor and, even more disturbingly, brings into focus the white consumption of Black labor. Sugar was, as Vincent Brown pointedly asserts, "a murderous commodity" (2008, 118). Its production hinged on the exploitation and destruction of Black lives. The labor and lives that went into the production of sugar sustained not only the wealth of the British mercantile class but from the eighteenth century onward also "the energy needs" of the British working class (118).[40] West Indian sugar, particularly in combination with East Indian tea, was quite literally feeding the English proletariat. The fact that sugar was a tainted commodity did not escape the attention of some abolitionists, who in the late eighteenth century called for a nationwide boycott of the "blood-stained" sugar from the West Indies.[41] Such early protests notwithstanding, white metropolitan consumers tended to remain oblivious to the Black labor hidden in the titillating whiteness of refined sugar and the fundamental role that it played in the daily assertion of "Englishness" performed by the drinking of tea. As late as 1989, the Jamaican-born British cultural theorist Stuart Hall felt compelled to remind an audience at an academic conference: "I am the sugar on the bottom of the English cup of tea" (1997a, 48), attempting to draw attention to the long-standing and inextricable material presence of the Caribbean at the heart of English self-identification. Walker's provocative mixing of tropes of whiteness with tropes of Blackness in the materiality and shape of the sugar Sphinx exposes these entangled economic and cultural histories. Her white sugar goddess bears pronounced African facial features. And lest her visitors miss the interdependency of white consumption and Black labor and not recognize it in the features of the Sphinx, she has surrounded her white sugar goddess with a retinue of small cane- and molasses-toting brown boy figures (fig. 14).

In addition to excavating the material histories that undergird contemporary economic structures along with ideologies of whiteness, Walker's sculpture targets a second history of exploitation: the history of producing Blackness through representational regimes and, more specifically (and like Parks's *Venus*), through visual regimes imposed on enslaved women's bodies. Sugar Baby is a composite of two distinct stereotypes of enslaved women. While the bust, with its kerchiefed head and large breasts, evokes the mythical domestic caregiver who selflessly nurtures the white middle-class family in both physical and emotional terms (the Mammy, Aunt Jemima),[42] the exposed and protruding vulva at the back of the sculpture signifies on the equally mythical, hypersexualized Black slave mistress (Jezebel, Venus), perceived as readily available to white appetites. In playing up these stereotypes, amplified by the enormous scale of the sculpture, Walker provocatively foregrounds the nexus of power, labor, and sexuality that has been a key theme throughout her oeuvre. At the same time, her work with entrenched racializing stereotypes also brings into focus the intricate ways in which the history of physical exploitation is interlinked with the history of cultural representation. "Our journey back to the founding moments of Black American identity," Robert Reid-Pharr writes, "is one that takes us not simply through the museum but also across the minstrel stage" (2002, 35). This is the journey that Walker aims to take. In combining in her sculpture the coveted whiteness of refined sugar with debasing stereotypes of Blackness, she brings to the fore the ways notions of whiteness have been culturally produced and sustained in canonical and popular visual constructions of Blackness.

Notably, this tradition, too, has its roots in the colonial sugar economy of the eighteenth and nineteenth centuries. According to art historian Kay Dian Kriz, the notion of "refinement was at the heart of British culture at a time when West Indian sugar was the most important commodity traded on the world market" (2008, 4). While British refineries labored to extract the purest form of white sugar from the crude muscovado produced in the colonies, British arts and culture also toiled to highlight in visual terms the spatial distance of the "white" metropolis from the "Black" labor economy of the colonies, to maintain clear cultural and moral boundaries between the "West Indies configured as the place where raw materials were extracted by slave labor, and the metropole were they were refined, consumed, and exchanged" (4). This contrast between "colonial rudeness" and a metropolitan "culture of refinement" (4) had to be constantly reasserted through cultural productions. Ironically, the iterative performance of economic, moral, and, above all, aesthetic distancing required keeping the Black body visually present—albeit in the abject position of submission, inferiority, crudity, debasement, and immorality. The spectacle of the "Hottentot Venus," discussed earlier, provides a powerful example of the metropolis's quest for refinement—and not only in England. As Robin Mitchell (2010) has argued with regard to Baartman's display in Paris, her body became the foil against which "French-ness"—in particular, the Frenchness of the white female body—would be defined.[43] Later examples of such imperial visual regimes include Édouard Manet's rendering of the Black servant attending to her nude mistress in his iconoclastic painting *Olympia* (1865) and David Selznick's staging of Hattie McDaniel as the stereotypical Mammy figure attending to Vivien Leigh's Scarlet O'Hara in the 1939 film adaptation of Margaret Mitchell's *Gone with the Wind*.[44] In all these instances, the laboring Black female body (marked by dark color and crude form) serves to highlight the delicacy and refinement (and the supposed superiority) of the nonlaboring white woman—regardless of whether the white woman is presented as a Southern belle or a fallen flower of the demimonde. The woman of color, by contrast, exists in these representations only through stereotypical features that serve to interpellate her body as Other in terms of class, race, and sexuality into the dominant visual regime. Aside from these markers, she is deprived of subjectivity; her biography and history are erased to allow for the projection of refined whiteness.

As Walker's Sphinx cites and restages such visual regimes of power, it also challenges them by refusing to keep Blackness and whiteness (and their associated values) neatly distinct, conjoining them instead in one and the same body. Are we beholding the white goddess of refinement in blackface, or are we encountering a Black goddess (the ancient Sphinx of the Nile) in whiteface? What constitutes whiteness and what Blackness in this case? These questions are undecidable, and this undecidability points up the relational quality of these aesthetic and racial categories. To paraphrase Frantz Fanon's incisive remark about the relational quality of processes of visual racialization: the Black woman is made Black only in relation to the white woman.[45] The Marvelous Sugar Baby powerfully foregrounds this entanglement of fantasies of Blackness with fantasies of whiteness, while also driving home the massive material and physical effects that this entanglement has produced.

Furthermore, in conjoining racial ambiguity with the tropes of hyper-sexualized femininity, Walker serves up yet another set of desires, historically codified in the visual icon of the mixed-race woman. In colonial pictorial as well as theatrical productions of the eighteenth and early nineteenth century, the figure of the *mulâtresse* occupies a prominent place. She serves as the site for the titillating interplay of rudeness and refinement in one and the same body, as Kriz (2008) compellingly shows with the example of Agostino Brunias's late-eighteenth-century paintings of the West Indies. The Italian-born painter was hired by British estate owners and the British crown to portray life in the newly acquired colonies of Dominica, Saint Vincent, and Tobago in a visually appealing manner so as to promote settlement. Many of Brunias's paintings center around the racially ambiguous woman, who fulfills a dual ideological function. *A Linen Market with a Linen Stall and Vegetable Seller in the West Indies* (ca. 1780), for example, features a central female figure along with her female attendant, who both stand out in the visual landscape of the Caribbean for their pronounced whiteness—they are clad in brilliant white clothes, one of them wearing a white headdress, and indicate their interest in the purchase of fine English linen. The alignment of the two women with fine white cloth marks island culture as a space in which a culture of refinement is possible. Brunias visually enhances this sense of attainable refinement (and thus, whiteness) by setting off the two focal figures against the darker-skinned women in the square, among them a half-naked, indigenous Carib woman toting unprocessed, dark sugarcane to market. The protagonists are thus clearly marked as "not Black." At the same time, however, the painter also blurs their racial identities by slightly modifying their "whiteness" with the codified markers of Blackness (hair texture and the native headdress, the tignon) and, above all, by visually aligning them with the market sphere and the Black labor that sustains it. Their bodies are thus also coded as commodities available for monetary exchange, not unlike the linen and sugarcane offered up for sale. That this exchange is of an explicit sexual nature is underlined in a number of Brunias's other paintings of the same period, such as *Linen Market, Dominica* (ca. 1780), in which the central female figure is blatantly appraised by the gaze of white men—surrogates for the paintings' typically white male beholders. Brunias's portraits thus simultaneously cater to two sets of desires: the acquisition and possession of whiteness and the satisfaction of libidinal fantasies of otherness. Kriz notes that "Brunias's *mulâtresses* provoke the fantasy of possessing a body that both is and is not white, bearing the marks of refined whiteness and the promise of savage sexual pleasure, so closely associated with blackness" (55).

Eighteenth-century theater culture similarly titillated audiences with performances of racial ambiguity. Thomas Southerne's hugely successful drama *Oroonoko* (first performed in 1695 and remaining popular with audiences throughout the eighteenth century), adapted from Aphra Behn's 1688 novella of the same title, strikingly transformed the character of Imoinda, beloved of African prince Oronooko, from an African woman into a European woman, the daughter of an English officer in Suriname. According to Theresa Saxon (2021), as performances of Southerne's play emphasized Imoinda's whiteness by playing up the contrast to her partner's racialized Blackness (the role of Oroonoko was typical performed in blackface), they also ambiguated the heroine's racial identity with the help of exoticized costumes as well as racially coded portraits of the actresses playing Imoinda in the popular print media of the time. In addition, Behn's well-known African prototype for the character continued to influence audience perceptions of Southerne's "white" Imoinda. Along with these intertextual traces, Imoinda's missing matrilineal heritage was similarly suggestive of racial indeterminacy. These layered allusions to Imoinda's elided Blackness, as Felicity Nussbaum points out, continue to haunt the heroine's whiteness in a sort of "spectral *presence* that links desire with fear, dread, physical defect, and monstrosity" (2003, 188, italics in original). As with Brunias's *mulâtresse*, in emphasizing the heroine's "blackened whiteness" (172), popular eighteenth-century performances of Imoinda thus conjoined for metropolitan audiences the symbolic resonances of whiteness with the appetite for the exotic, sexualized other.

Considered in the context of such long-standing histories of racial representation, the Marvelous Sugar Baby exposes not just a history of economic exploitation but also one of aesthetic and sexual consumption. Like popular colonial performances of racialized femininity, the sugar Sphinx joins Blackness and whiteness, holding out to her spectators "the promise of refinement without relinquishing the baser pleasures of the flesh" (Kriz 2008, 64). In Western culture, such sexual desire for otherness has frequently been reified by placing the body of the mixed-race woman in a metonymic relation with the trope of sugar, such as in Brunias's paintings.[46] This libidinal craving extends well beyond the colonial period, continuing to be blatantly evident in what Walker calls "the sort of Rolling Stones-y brown sugar dovetailing of sex and slavery as it reaches the American imagination" (quoted in Rooney 2014, n.p.), which has found conscious and subconscious expression in various forms of popular culture, particularly those that represent women of color. bell hooks conceptualizes this continuing layered desire for otherness (economic, emotional, sexual, and aesthetic) more broadly as a desire for what she mockingly calls "a bit of the Other" (1992, 22). "Within commodity culture," she explains, "ethnicity becomes spice, seasoning that can liven up the dull dish that is mainstream white culture" (21). The sexualization and/or exoticization of racial and ethnic difference brings to the surface "all those 'nasty' unconscious fantasies and longings about contact with the Other embedded in the secret (and not so secret) deep structure of white supremacy" (22). While contact with otherness might hold out the possibility for critical intervention in structures of racist domination (22), hooks cautions that it more often than not serves to corroborate existing power relations: "Whatever difference the Other inhabits is eradicated, *via* exchange, by a consumer cannibalism that not only displaces the Other but denies the significance of that Other's history through a process of decontextualization" (31).

The Marvelous Sugar Baby's pronounced objecthood, however, substantially hinders such decontextualization (even though it cannot prevent it). The entangled meanings of her massive mythical shape, seductive materiality, hyperbolic body features, as well as the intriguing setting and charged staging challenge spectators in such multiple ways that both the facile consumer act of what hooks calls "eating the Other" (36) and the act of Friedian self-absorption, respectively, averting the gaze altogether, become unlikely. This performer-object demands sustained attention, requiring spectators to engage with it both viscerally and cerebrally. The beholder—trying to make sense of the various historical layers of objecthood that the Sphinx confronts us with—inevitably becomes implicated in these enduring histories, compelled to consider his or her own positionality within and toward them. Like her silhouettes, Walker's sculpture reflects this long history of material, representational, and libidinal investments in otherness "back into the projector's unsuspecting eyes, and caus[ing] them to want to face the shame of (our) collective psyche" (Walker quoted in Lott 2000, 71).

AN AUDIENCE

As Walker's installation foregrounds the sugar sculpture's consumability in its title, materiality, and shape, its not-too-subtle signifying on the fraught histories of physical, aesthetic, and libidinal exploitation of the Black body suggests that this particular *sotiltee* does not go down easily, that it would at least cause what Kyla Wazana Tompkins (2012) calls "racial indigestion." There is plenty of evidence that this was the case. Video footage of the exhibition shows visitors encountering the sculpture with rapt attention and deep emotion. "It was the heaviest, literally and figuratively, artwork I'd ever seen," Stephanye Watts testifies, admitting to feeling quite overwhelmed by her encounter with this massive history of sugar (2014, n.p.). Art critic Jerry Saltz, who has followed Walker's career from the start, similarly felt "flattened" by the piece, considering it "a Melvillian symbol for the original sin of slavery and its disquieting contemporary connections to the hubris that brought us Iraq and then Abu Ghraib" (2014, n.p.). Testimonies such as these indicate that for many the event triggered a profoundly reflective as well as affective engagement with the past of plantation slavery and its various contemporary legacies. Other visitors, however, exhibited no such qualms regarding the consumability of the exhibited object. As evidenced by a swarm of Sugar Baby images posted on social media platforms such as Instagram, Facebook, and Twitter, a great number of visitors, of all races and ages, used the event to pose in front of the sculpture for photo ops. Most of these interactions appear harmlessly narcissistic; some, however, render various suggestive poses of ogling, fondling, and licking the Sphinx—poses that were in turn considered offensive and racist by other spectators, triggering vehement internet outcries and on-site interventions.[47] In fact, more than anything, it was the reactions of the audience that became the focus of heated debates about the marvelous sugar baby.

Just as with her silhouettes, Walker had set her audience up that way. In an interview with Carolina Miranda, she describes how in staging a ten-foot vagina, along with massive buttocks and breasts at a public art event, she intended to provoke the Sphinx's visitors, to draw out their "mucky and violent and messed-up and inappropriate" behavior (2014, n.p.). Critic Kay Larson observes that in the context of the dim factory interior, the extreme whiteness of the Sphinx's skin shone forth like a film screen inviting people to pose, to stage themselves in front of it (2014, 505). She correctly surmises that Walker must have taken such "movie star" aspirations into her calculations. For Walker, questions of looking are at the heart of her work: "How do people look? How are people supposed to look? Are white people looking at it in the right way? And are black audiences looking to see this piece?" (quoted in Miranda 2014, n.p.). She sets up the Sugar Baby installation as a *theatron*, a looking space that invites visitors to view a performer-object and in the process challenges them to "view . . . themselves viewing, then viewing each other viewing it" (n.p.). It serves as a sort of looking glass for contemporary audiences in which they behold their own as well as other spectators' responses to a long and layered racial history and its various legacies.[48] All the while, and much like Parks's Venus, the protagonist of Walker's show, the Marvelous Sugar Baby, looks on at the spectacle around her, the fingers of her left-hand conspicuously crossed in the sign of the figa.[49] Like the Sphinx in Greek mythology, she withholds the answer to the riddle she poses, refuses legibility, suggesting that the performance that matters most in this situation is not so much her performance of objecthood but rather the audience's myriad performances of responding to it.

Indeed, as with Parks's play *Venus*, it *is* the audience that was staged in the theatrical event of the sugar Sphinx. The sculpture was demolished after nine weeks, as was the former refinery a few weeks later. What remains is a short film about the event, provocatively titled *An Audience* (2014), in which Walker recorded the visitors' various interactions with the Marvelous Sugar Baby: their waiting in line outside the factory; their entrance into the exhibition hall and first reactions to the sculpture; their recording of their encounter through camera, tablet, and smartphone; their eager posing in front of the sphinx's bosom and buttocks; their awe and antics; and, above all, the various forms their act of looking took—"at the work, at themselves, at one another, and especially looking at their phones and cameras."[50]

Toward the end of the film, however, the camera surprisingly shifts its focus from chronicling the various performances of looking to exploring those of touching. Following a loudspeaker's invitation at the closing of the exhibition to touch the Sphinx on their way out, we now behold the beholders hesitatingly, curiously, gently, almost caressingly touching the Sphinx's body.[51] Again, like the Venus's concluding invitation to a kiss, the invitation to touch suddenly shifts the terrain of encounter, provoking a very different level of affect. Because of the extreme brevity of the moment, the closing minutes of the show, Walker's invitation to touch presents us with a mere gesture, a hint of possibility, rather than an earnest exploration. But it does underline the material, corporeal, and intersubjective dimension of the spectators' encounter with the Marvelous Sugar Baby. As scholars of the emerging field of touch theory have pointed out, tactile interactions present us with a highly charged and layered terrain of affect that entails varied histories, registers, and power differentials. Because touch is always an action of the body, for/ against the body, between bodies, it exceeds and disturbs the autonomy of the subject: "Touch makes our bodies more-than-one: one cannot touch without being touched," scholars Taina Kinnunen and Marjo Kolehmainen write (2019, 5). They also emphasize the multidimensional temporal dimension of touch. As a form of affective communication, touch carries "past, present, and future within them in non-linear and unpredictable ways;" it can thus also be the "site of both repetition and change" (17). Considered along these lines, Walker's closing emphasis on the affective possibilities (and risks) of touch underscores how the fraught past of slavery continues to touch contemporary subjects in multiple, unpredictable ways but also how these encounters can enable change.

In conclusion then, neither Walker nor Parks serve up consumer-friendly, easily digestible, or prurient versions of a troubled past, as a few critics have argued. Rather, they acknowledge the multivalent affective charge that the encounter with slavery and its various legacies continues to carry for contemporary audiences, white and Black. Their playful, parodic and satirical—frequently humorous and often confrontational—restagings of well-known narratives, entrenched themes and motifs, popular images and deep-rooted stereotypes target precisely this affective charge. Fragmenting frozen representation, upsetting revered discourses, and distorting habitual perspectives, they challenge us in multiple critical ways to rethink what we have come to perceive by training and habit as "history." Above all, they challenge the ways we feel about these established narratives and entrenched iconographies, provoking a wide range of reactions in the process: indignation, laughter, shame, embarrassment, silliness, nervousness, admiration. Walker once remarked about her art, "I didn't want a completely passive viewer. . . . I wanted to make work where the viewer wouldn't walk away; he would either giggle nervously, get pulled into history, into fiction, into something totally demeaning and possibly very beautiful" (Cameron 1997, 84). In provoking our various affective responses, both Walker's and Parks's works reveal the extent to which the history of slavery is not closed but continues to pull us back in—not, however, in any melancholic way that insists on the inextricable fusion of the present to the past. Rather, the artists' affective engagements with racist stereotypes expose and highlight the ways in which contemporary subjects continue to be complicit with the representational techniques and epistemic regimes that have helped produce and sustain the racial formation of slavery as well as with those that continue to underwrite its contemporary legacies. In messing with these established regimes, Parks and Walker mess with our understanding of history and challenge us to take a more critical approach to how knowledges of the past and of human subjects have been produced and articulated, to the ways that issues of perception and representation matter, so that the troubled past of racist regimes, which continues to affect the present, does not have to be our future.

CODA
Whither Historiopoiesis?

The primary objective of this study of selected works by Suzan-Lori Parks and Kara Walker has been to illustrate a shift in late twentieth-century engagements with the traumatic past of New World slavery, its histories and legacies—a shift away from the "melancholic historicism" (Best 2012, 460) evident in a number of cultural productions of the 1970s and 1980s and toward "the not yet formulated possibilities of the future" (Crawford 2016, 70) more typical of the 1990s and 2000s. Not loss and haunting inform Parks's and Walker's engagements with slavery but the effort to take ownership of its histories and to rearticulate them in ways that enable the fashioning of postslavery subjectivities.

Parks's and Walker's highly imaginative engagements with established narratives are marked by the deployment of a set of techniques that I have summarized with the term "historiopoiesis" to underscore two central aspects of their approach: their interest in exposing the work of form (the various devices and procedures employed in crafting verbal or visual discourses) and their stress on the performative dimension of discourse (the capacity to create and not merely reflect). Put differently, both artists tend to emphasize the poetics and performatives at work in what we have come to call history: the constructed and mediated nature of knowledges of the past and the ways knowledge can script certain identities at the expense of others, along with the possibility of creative intervention in the processes of scripting and rescripting. The purposeful collusion of fact and fiction; the ludic Signifyin(g) on entrenched images, themes, figures, and narratives of the past; the self-reflective engagement with issues of narrative construction, mediality, and materiality; and a pronounced theatricality—these are key aspects of a historiopoetic engagement with the past. These techniques often work in concert or in certain combinations with each other. In this regard, I understand historiopoiesis not as a comprehensive poetics but as a set of recurring tools for intervening in and refiguring entrenched orders of representation and knowledge.

Importantly, this study sees the shift in Parks's and Walker's poetic approach and general stance toward slavery more broadly at play in late twentieth- and early twenty-first-century African American culture, suggesting that we read the two artists' works as part of a larger generational effort. In chapter 1, I have cited examples from the works of Cheryl Dunye, Jamaica Kincaid, Keith Townsend Obadike, Renée Cox, and several others. These and other artworks operating in a similar vein have been discussed in depth and with eloquence by other scholars, often in terms similar to those identified in this study.[1] I offer them as evidence for why I believe that Parks's and Walker's historiopoetic engagement with the long history of slavery can be situated in the context of a larger cohort of artists emerging from the late 1980s onwards and well into the 2000s and sharing a similar poetic approach and political stance toward the past and its legacies. A great number of cultural productions of the turn of the millennium, ranging across diverse media (literature, visual and performing arts, digital media), turn to the past of slavery in the spirit of mining its archives for those images, figures, tropes, motifs, and narratives—whether canonical, counterhegemonic, or mass-cultural; revered, routine, or prejudiced; Black or white—that continue to give shape to perceptions of race in general and Blackness in particular. Deploying various forms of playfulness, self-reflectiveness, and theatricality, they seek to intervene in and refigure the "fictions that have come out of history" (Walker quoted in Saltz 1996, 82) to expand our understanding of slavery and to engender new ways of thinking about Black subjectivities, past and present. While slavery and its legacies clearly continue to matter in the work of these artists, they also attempt to decenter it from its preeminent place in African American identities. Their explorations are undertaken in the spirit of a broader, generational ethos—variously referred to by critics as post-soul or post-black[2]—that seeks to "trouble blackness, . . . worry blackness; . . . stir it up, touch it, feel it out, and hold it up for examination in ways that depart significantly from previous—and necessary—preoccupations with struggling for political freedom, or with an attempt to establish and sustain a coherent black identity" (Ashe 2007, 614).

Many of these millennial historiopoetic works foreground the creative and performative powers of their protagonists. Kara Walker's figure of the Negress, who features prominently as silhouettist, performer, and unreliable narrator in a number of cutouts, and Parks's ensemble of imaginative historiographers, storytellers, impersonators, fakers, and hustlers are cases in point. Thylia Moss's verse narrative *Slave Moth* (2004) and Edward P. Jones's novel *The Known World* (2003) offer further examples. With the protagonists Varl and Alice, these two texts present characters who escape the physical and psychological confines of slavery by creatively manipulating its signs and discourses. In her perceptive reading of these two works, Evie Shockley underscores the role of the imagination as "a powerful form of agency, whereby the enslaved subject can, in a sense, alter her world by perceiving it differently" (2013, 146). These texts, she concludes, "encourage us to understand artistic imagination—expressed largely as writerly, visual, and conceptual art—as a form of resistance to limiting definitions of black identity, whether the objectifying status of 'slave' imposed by (white) law during slavery, the legally and socially constructed concept of black 'inferiority' that continues to color dominant culture to this day, or the restrictive notion of 'authentic blackness' proposed by late-twentieth-century, black nationalist–inflected conceptions of race" (143). Shockley's reading of Moss's and Jones's works succinctly captures a key feature of the historiopoetic approach of a number of Black cultural productions from the 1990s to the 2000s: their foregrounding of the dual role of the imagination in unmasking the collusion of fact and fiction at the heart of established histories of slavery as well as in appropriating it for the production of new histories.

Given our current moment at the start of the second decade of the twenty-first century, which is so starkly marked by innumerable blatant and latent assertions of an emboldened white supremacy, one might very well wonder about the relevance and viability of the imagination as a powerful form of agency. In the ongoing struggle against an entrenched system of anti-Black racism, what could be the place of such imaginative, self-reflective, performative interventions into the discursive traces of slavery and their concomitant stress on the capacity for autopoiesis? In this coda, I want to offer some thoughts on how the millennial poetics and politics that this study has brought into focus have evolved at the start of the twenty-first century—that is, in a period that saw within the short span of eight years the election of both America's first Black president and, in the words of Ta-Nehisi Coates (2017), its "first white president" and the consequent re-entrenchment of a racial formation that has its roots in slavery.

The unprecedented rise in the number of people of color incarcerated since the 1990s and the concomitant denial of basic civil rights to millions of citizens, the shocking disregard for Black lives in the wake of Hurricane Katrina in 2004, as well as the persisting daily experience of extreme vulnerability by people of color on the streets of American (and European) cities, the continuously accumulating evidence of cases of lethal deployment of police force against them, the racist public remarks by politicians in office[3]—all indicate that despite enormous strides taken toward racial equality, despite neoliberal discourses of tolerance and diversity, systemic conditions for racism and violence have continued well past the election of a Black president and cheerful proclamations of the alleged arrival of a post-racial era. On this score, we might just now be witnessing the emergence of yet another "structure of feeling"—one marked by the resurgence of what Soyica Diggs Colbert, borrowing the term from a Lauryn Hill song, calls "Black rage." Black rage, Colbert insists, "acknowledges the limits of black citizenship and enables the cultivation of black political collectivity by uniting individuals through a shared feeling" (2016a, 337). It has found potent expression in the protest actions organized by the Black Lives Matter movement, in the critical framework of Afro-pessimist theory, as well as in a number of cultural productions, including Hill's song "Black Rage" (2014); Ta-Nehisi Coates's epistolary essay, *Between the World and Me* (2015); Claudia Rankine's award-winning volume of poetry, *Citizens: An American Lyric* (2015); and Ava DuVernay's documentary *13th* (2016), to name just a few examples that underscore how present-day

Black citizenship continues to be delimited by the legacies of slavery. In line with a prominent tendency in contemporary African American thought, slavery functions here not only as the primary point of reference in explaining entrenched structures of racism in present-day institutions and discourses but also as "the metonymy for understanding blackness" (Patterson 2016, 215).[4] These works tend to posit the shared experience of continuing unfreedom and anti-Black sentiment as the basis for Black collectivity. In this regard, they differ significantly from the millennial works described in this study, which tend to be deeply suspicious of postulations of a Black collective identity and emphasize instead individual agency in bringing about change.

And yet, the emergence of a new structure of feeling does not signal the end of historiopoetic engagements with narratives of the past, nor of a post-black ethos. A significant number of artists, including Kara Walker, have continued to approach the past from this particular poetic and political vantage point well into the 2010s and 2020s.[5] In both her 2017 exhibition *Sikkema Jenkins and Co. is Compelled to present The most Astounding and Important Painting show of the fall Art Show viewing season!* and her 2020 exhibition *Drawings*,[6] Walker continues to put pressure on contemporary racial relations through the confrontational deployment of crude stereotypes and playful riffs on commodified narratives derived from dominant, counterhegemonic, and popular histories of slavery. The persistence of Walker's historiopoetic praxis is also apparent in the 2019 sculpture *Fons Americanus*, staged in Turbine Hall at the Tate Modern in London from September 2019 to April 2020—a sculpture that is in many ways reminiscent of *The Marvelous Sugar Baby* (2014). As "an allegory of the Black Atlantic" (Walker 2019, n.p.), *Fons Americanus* investigates in shape, materiality, and mise-en-scène the colonial commerce in bodies and goods connecting Europe with Africa and the Americas along with the monumental histories anchored in this triangular traffic. The diverse fountain figures signify on a spectrum of narratives of Blackness embedded in this colonial history and commodified in canonical artworks as well as popular culture, ranging from narratives of grotesque racialization to those of resistance. A number of motifs are direct echoes of Walker's previous works: the Black-girl fountain, the sculptural rendering of the foundering boat from Winslow Homer's *The Gulf Stream*, the elaborate title riff on past and present-day societies of spectacle, and the introduction of an unreliable narrator, the familiar "Celebrated Negress of the New World, Madame Kara E. Walker."[7]

Paul Beatty's Man Booker Prize–winning *The Sellout* (2015), furthermore, offers a pertinent example of how artists in the 2010s continued to deploy historiopoetic techniques on behalf of a post-black ethos. The novel's satiric conceit of reinstating slavery and segregation in the fictional town of Dickens, California, clearly mocks celebratory narratives of national progress toward a post-racial society and points up the pervasive entrenchment of racism in contemporary culture. At the same time, the novel also refuses to return "to a romanticized group identity" (Leader-Picone 2020, 77). As scholar Cameron Leader-Picone comments, "while Beatty critiques American progress narratives, his prescription for liberation is individualistic and highlights the ultimate targets of his satire: discourses of authenticity" (66). The novel ends with the eponymic narrator's advocacy of an "unmitigated blackness"—a Blackness that, as the Sellout insists, "doesn't sell"; it "is simply not giving a fuck" (Beatty 2015, 277). Resistant to concrete definition and somewhat opaque in its meanings, the novel's unmitigated Blackness asserts the power of performance both on the diegetic and formal level—in the narrator's and his sidekick Hominy Jenkins's performances of slavery and in Beatty's own imaginative, irreverent, and humorous poetic interventions into sacrosanct discourses of racial progress, collective struggle, and notions of authenticity. In short, while *The Sellout* perceptively traces the afterlife of slavery in contemporary life, it does not posit the Black subject's fundamental and perpetual unfreedom as its conclusion. Rather, it emphasizes the moments of possibility inherent in the ludic engagement with canonical, countermnemonic, and popular tropes, narratives, and iconographies that have come out of the history of slavery.[8]

In the remainder of this coda, I want to extend the discussion to two other prominent contemporary works that cogently underscore the continuing viability of a historiopoetic approach to the past: Branden Jacobs-Jenkins's Obie Award–winning play *An Octoroon* (2014), and Colson Whitehead's Pulitzer Prize and National Book Award–winning novel *The Underground Railroad* (2016). Both target canonical and popular discourses through which knowledges of slavery have been mediated: antebellum melodrama and the slave narrative, as well as the national mythology of the Underground Railroad. Both also liberally entangle the known "facts" of these discourses with their own creative interventions to refocus questions of freedom and identity from a present-day perspective. And despite a stark difference in tone and approach—high-spirited parody and humor in Jacobs-Jenkins, sober homage and refiguration in Whitehead—both ultimately affirm their protagonists' capacities for autopoiesis despite and against the pervasive endurance of structures of slavery that both works also foreground.

AN OCTOROON (2014)

Branden Jacobs-Jenkins is clearly heir to the poetics of Parks and Walker. *An Octoroon* forms part of a series of plays with which the playwright investigates the racial legacies of theatrical/dramaturgical forms in American theater.[9] His preceding play, *Neighbors* (2010), targets the endurance of minstrelsy; *An Octoroon* turns to the racial politics of nineteenth-century melodrama; and his subsequent play, *Appropriate* (2014), exposes the implied whiteness of realism.[10] In his bold and boisterous adaptation of Dion Boucicault's 1859 theater hit, *The Octoroon*, Jacobs-Jenkins zooms in on the political ambivalence and ethical dilemma that undergird Boucicault's play. While the emotional teleology of Boucicault's melodrama moves audiences toward an indictment of slavery on the basis of promoting empathy for the protagonist, the beautiful "octoroon" Zoe, the play's crude, minstrelsy-style portrayal of other enslaved characters lends support to proslavery arguments. The project of raising empathy and understanding for alterity is thus closely linked with the propagation of essentializing stereotypes; rather than promoting racial equality, the form ultimately reinforces existing power relations.[11] Jacobs-Jenkins's *An Octoroon* mocks the racial politics of nineteenth-century melodrama in an uproarious parody. Beyond that, so I suggest, it also intervenes in contemporary discourses of authenticity (with regard both to representing the experience of slavery and to representing Blackness) and advocates the imaginative agency of the individual.

While claims of truthfulness and authenticity were very much at the heart of Boucicault's antebellum melodrama about slavery, *The Octoroon, or Life in Louisiana*, they are strikingly absent from Jacobs-Jenkins's adaptation.[12] *An Octoroon* is, like works by Parks and Walker, first and foremost a play about acting, performing, and staging.

During the play's prologue, we watch an African American actor put on whiteface, a European American actor put on redface, and a Native American actor getting ready to play a Black character. With this framing device, Jacobs-Jenkins not only riffs on the antebellum tradition of white actors' performing in blackface and on Boucicault's own performances in the role of the Native American character, Wahnotee, he also throws into question present-day public and institutional expectations of a "Black playwright" and a "Black play": "Hi, everyone. I'm a 'black playwright,'" Jacobs-Jenkins's stage persona, BJJ, greets the audience at the start of the show, following up with the statement, "I don't know what exactly that means" (2015, 7). This focus on the performance of identity categories is sustained throughout the play as we watch actors set, dismantle, and reset the stage for their various scenes as well as cite their characters in Brechtian fashion rather than attempting to embody them in Method-style acting. Moreover, the constant doubling of roles leads to such amusingly absurd and highly theatrical situations as when BJJ performs, in whiteface, at one and the same time both hero and villain in a physical struggle with himself.

Furthermore, like Beatty in *The Sellout*, Jacobs-Jenkins presents slavery itself as a performance. While Boucicault starts his first act with a brief minstrelsy performance (we encounter several "slave" characters, played by white actors, speaking in a made-up Black vernacular and engaging in slapstick routines), Jacobs-Jenkins opens *An Octoroon* with a ten-minute portrait of the enslaved women Minnie and Dido (two very minor characters in Boucicault), who, in the playwright's words, are "hanging out . . . just shooting the shit, gossiping" (2014, n.p.). As one of them sweeps the patio, they chat about more effective work methods, their personal backgrounds, old and new masters, the romantic involvements of friends and acquaintances, the prospects of running away. Notably, this conversation is carried out in idiomatic contemporary Black English. In the stage directions, the playwright comments, "I don't know what a real slave sounded like. And neither do you" (2015, 17). Instead of attempting to simulate historicity, he decides to make his characters "sound like people that I know" (2014, n.p.). It is only upon the entrance of a "white" person (played by an African American actor) that they switch to a version of Boucicault's minstrelsy dialect. Such code-switching underlines that they consider "slave" to be an act put on for white people and not as an identity that defines them. As Minnie remarks quite explicitly in a later scene, "I know we slaves and evurt-hang, but you are not your job. You gotta take time out of your day to live life for you" (2015, 58).

In scenes like this one, Jacobs-Jenkins, moreover, provides the enslaved with a degree of interiority (something completely lacking in Boucicault), even as this interiority is, once again, blatantly made up from the playwright's own contemporary perspective, driven by his desire "to imagine what slaves might be talking about outside of a white gaze" (Ashe and Saal 2020a, 218), to see how they negotiate their relationship to their work and, as he states quite provocatively, to capture "what I imagined to be just the boredom of being a slave" (2014, n.p.). The playwright's imaginative rendering of the inner lives of the enslaved also includes Minnie's explicit lusting after a "fine-ass white man" (2015, 42)—this particular character, Captain Ratts, was ironically played by the playwright himself in the 2014 Soho Rep. production. In his rendering of Minnie and Dido, Jacobs-Jenkins undercuts in a humorous manner not only entrenched racist stereotypes of enslaved African Americans but also normative expectations of how slavery ought to be represented. He presents us with two characters who admit to sexual desires for their white owner and who attempt to claim their time and to carve out a life within slavery.

This, however, does not mean that *An Octoroon* reduces slavery to fun and games. On the contrary, the play exposes slavery as a brutal system of physical exploitation and sexual abuse. Throughout the play, the stage is covered in cotton balls, which metonymically index the hardship of field labor and the profitability of an exploitative system; acts of gratuitous violence (e.g., M'Closky's callous murder of the child Paul and his striking Dido for ruining one of his tableau scenes) along with references to sexual exploitation and the destruction of social bonds in the sale of friends and family members repeatedly puncture the boisterous spirt of the adaptation. And, of course, there is the plight of the eponymous character, the octoroon Zoe, who just as in Boucicault's original, serves Jacobs-Jenkins as the emotional anchor of the melodrama. Set up as the embodiment of beauty and virtue, Zoe's sale drives home the inherent inhumanity of slavery as an economic, legal, and ideological system. The scenes depicting Zoe's grief over having to forego her white suitor's (George) love as well as her horror at her impending sexual enslavement to the overseer M'Closky are, in contrast to all other scenes, played straight—that is, not as a humorous riff on melodramatic acting but for the force of their emotional impact on the audience. They tend to be rendered very movingly and often involve a believable display of tears on the part of the actors.[13]

Above all, Jacobs-Jenkins uses the melodramatic convention of the coup de théâtre—a sudden turn of events—to remind us of the horrific physical reality that undergirds representations of slavery in the antebellum period as well as today. In the "sensation scene" of the fourth act, which in nineteenth-century melodrama tended to clinch both the moral and emotional trajectory of a play in a spectacular display of theatrical technology,[14] he suddenly halts *An Octoroon*'s playful, parodic mode. Against the upstage wall of the theatre, he projects a documentary photograph of a public lynching of two African American men. In a sort of Barthesian *punctum*, Jacobs-Jenkins provokingly underscores that the collusion of fact and fiction in representations of slavery and perceptions of Blackness—the main target of his metatheatrical riff—continues to have concrete consequences in people's lives. In her review of the production, Jenna Clark Embrey describes the impact of this scene: "When the photograph first appears, the audience let out an apologetic yawp, and then went silent. It was as if the photograph jolted us into remembering what we had been laughing at all this while, and the image wrenched our remorse into the forefront" (2015, n.p.). Note that as the overhead projector slowly brings the photograph into focus, it zooms in first, not on the murdered bodies, but on a group of white spectators looking out at the camera. Because audiences share the camera's perspective, the white mob's gaze inevitably interpellates them into the picture and thus into the scene of lynching. The recoil of the audience that Embrey describes might thus bespeak not only the feeling of "remorse" but also the discomfort of feeling implicated in the history of slavery—either as the victim or as the perpetrator of the camera's threatening racializing gaze. Additionally, the photograph of violated Black bodies brings into focus the fraught racial legacy of the medium of photography—its deployment, for instance, on behalf of colonial fantasies as well as its complex use as documentary evidence of racial violence in the twentieth and twenty-first centuries. In short, Jacobs-Jenkins cleverly refunctions Boucicault's old-fashioned "sensation scene" to drive home to contemporary audiences the long history of scopic dynamics and visual discourses that have colluded in mapping across individual, living bodies the abstraction that Harvey Young calls "phenomenal blackness" (2010, 7), an abstraction at the heart of systems of racial discrimination.

Despite Jacobs-Jenkins's emphasis on the endurance of a shared experience of phenomenal blackness, *An Octoroon* refrains from cultivating a sense of Black political collectivity. Although the play's community of slaves is portrayed as sharing a complex emotional, social, and political life (they set up a "Runaway Plannin' Committee"), it is also shown as lacking a sense of solidarity. The "house slaves" bicker with the "field slaves," so that the field slaves refuse to inform the others of their plans for escape; a husband uses the opportunity for flight to abandon his pregnant wife for another woman; and Dido and Minnie decide not to intervene in Zoe's suicidal plans: "These people ain't our problem anymore," Minnie insists at the end of the play (42). Instead, she looks forward to her own planned escape to life on a steamboat, which she imagines not in terms of enslavement but in terms of emotional and sexual freedom: "coasting up and down the river, lookin' fly, wind whipping at our hair and our slave tunics and shit, and we surrounded by all these fine, muscle-y boat niggas who ain't been with a woman in years" (42).

Although, thanks to the play's deployment of dramatic irony, the audience knows at this point that Minnie's particular vision of freedom is not going to happen, the play nonetheless ends on a hopeful note: with a depiction of Minnie's and Dido's care for each other, their capacity to imagine change, as well as their willingness to act on this imagination. When Minnie and Dido doll up to attract the interest of a new master, they do so not because they are flippant or naïve with regard to the meaning of slavery but because they have faith in change and their own agency in bringing it about: "We 'bout to be on a boat, and it may not be heaven, but it's sho' as hell different than this here swamp and that's got to mean something" (58). Even as unbeknownst to them their dreams of a life on a boat have already been thwarted by the financial rescue of the perversely named plantation "Terrebonne," it is their detached attitude toward servitude ("You know I be getting so bored"), their care for each other ("we gotta be good to one anutha"), and their creative skills ("finish telling me about the rabbit") that close the play.[15] In the tradition of historiopoiesis, then, the play asserts, against the obvious endurance of the structures of slavery, the imagination as "a powerful form of agency," to borrow Shockley's phrase again (2013, 146).

There are many parallels between Walker's, Beatty's, and Jacobs-Jenkins's take on the contemporary legacies of slavery with regard to form, tone, and objective. Their approach could be fittingly summed up with Douglas A. Jones Jr.'s assessment of another historiopoetic work, Terrance Hayes's humorous poem "The Avocado" (2010), about which, Jones writes, the "irreverent and ironic treatment of slave history reanimates the past in a way that does not seek affective or psychic redress of slavery's injuries, for such repair is impossible"; instead, these works strive "to encourage new conceptual horizons with which to reconceive and thus inhabit our postslavery present" (2016, 43). This shared insistence on the ongoing need for investigating, troubling, and refiguring the established signs of the various histories informing perceptions of Blackness continued to be as relevant in the 2010s as in the 1990s. It is an ongoing fight against the closure of representation. It is also a push for "new conceptual horizons," with regard to approaching the past as well as imagining the future.

THE UNDERGROUND RAILROAD

Upon its publication in 2016, Colson Whitehead's novel *The Underground Railroad* was hailed by reviewers as remarkably different from the author's earlier work, which had been described as "post-soul historiographic metafiction" (Maus 2014, 10). Boris Kachka, for instance, commends Whitehead in an interview for leaving behind the "comic riffs and wild inventions" of his previous writing, to which Whitehead responds, "I do feel older and wiser," stressing his greater maturity (2016, n.p.). This brief exchange suggests that Whitehead has finally "grown up" by recognizing the gravity of his subject matter. Yet, a closer look at his 2016 novel reveals that, the change in tone notwithstanding, this award-winning novel continues to be firmly embedded in the post-soul/post-black ethos of his earlier fictions. Like the novels *The Intuitionist* (1999), *John Henry Days* (2001), or *Apex Hides the Hurt* (2006), it presents a self-aware metafictional text that imaginatively reworks, in the words of critic Derek Maus, "'the forms and contents of the past' in order to question how and why they arose to begin with and to determine whether or not they need to be reaffirmed, revised, or abandoned entirely" (2014, 10). Concretely, *The Underground Railroad* targets contemporary understandings of slavery as they have been articulated and mediated through the genre of antebellum slave narratives as well as through the national mythology of the Underground Railroad. Whitehead's historiopoetic interventions into these entrenched and cherished representational legacies of the past are most apparent in his critical Signifyin(g) on the classic plot structure of slave narratives (the teleological movement from enslavement to freedom) as well as in his liberal collusion of fact and fiction, such as the literalization of the eponymous metaphor and the anachronistic jamming of diverse historical events occurring over the course of more than a hundred years into a few years in the 1850s.

When the protagonist Cora flees from the horrific exploitation and violence of a Georgia plantation, she is ushered into a vast network of covert helpers and secret stations that is literally situated underground and that uses various actual vehicles of railroad transportation—a boxcar, a flatcar, a velvety passenger carriage, a handcar—to assist the fugitives in their escape. In giving concrete mechanical shape to a rather diffuse concept, Whitehead not only realizes his own childhood fantasy of what the Underground Railroad might mean but also playfully challenges what Kathryn Schulz calls America's "most evocative national metaphor" (2016, n.p.). Named for the first time in a newspaper article of 1839 and gaining popularity in abolitionist writing throughout the 1840s, the concept of the Underground Railroad began to take on mythological dimensions especially after the Civil War when (white) Americans attempted to integrate the horrific history of slavery into the national historiography. As Schulz maintains, the Underground Railroad provided a perfect discursive vehicle for putting issues of guilt, shame, and trauma aside by valorizing stories of heroic resistance (Black and white), interracial solidarity, and successful escapes to freedom. Historian William Henry Siebert's study *The Underground Railroad from Slavery to Freedom* (1898) was seminal in corroborating this particular perspective. It depicted a vast and well-organized network of dedicated and predominantly white agents. In reality, however, as later scholarship has shown, the network was neither as vast and organized nor as white as Siebert suggests and as generations of Americans subsequently chose to believe. Whitehead tackles this popular myth in various ways. In his novel, the underground railroad, even as it relies on an interracial network of solidarity for its operation, is above all the product of Black labor. It is also a rather haphazard arrangement, composed of mostly rickety vehicles, temporary stations, random schedules, ineffective communication, lack of information about destinations, and sudden dead ends. As the heterodiegetic narrator, focalizing Cora's perspective, remarks early on, "The steel ran south and north presumably, springing from some inconceivable source and shooting toward a miraculous terminus" (67).

The inconspicuous adverb "presumably" signals Whitehead's most radical intervention into both the popular, national mythology of the Underground Railroad and the plot structure of slave narratives, which the novel otherwise emulates closely. Whitehead's subterranean railroad does not necessarily take its passengers to freedom; it is not even clear whether such a "miraculous terminus" called "freedom" exists at all. Instead, it takes Cora on a meandering and troubling ride through what one of the agents calls various "state[s] of possibility" (68): from Georgia to South Carolina and North Carolina, to Tennessee and Indiana. The plot closely follows the tracks of Cora's railway journey: each chapter explores a new "state of possibility," each "with its own customs and ways of doing things" (68)—all of which, however, sooner or later corroborate Cora's continuing unfreedom. South Carolina's allegedly "more enlightened attitude toward colored advancement" (91) turns out to cover up a devious biopolitical scheme of medical experiments on African Americans, including the compulsory sterilization of women. North Carolina effectively "abolished slavery" in a statewide genocide of people of color. Tennessee has been burnt up by its own history of murdering and displacing the Native American population. Even the freedom of Valentine Farm, a free Black community in Indiana, proves to be temporary and frail, endangered by both internal disagreement over communal belonging and the resentment of white neighbors.

Yet, despite these repeated setbacks, the plot promises, in line with the conventions of the slave narrative, to end Cora's journey with the attainment of liberty, as suggested by the title of the novel's final chapter, "The North"—a vague geo-mythological denomination conventionally referring to the attainment of freedom by arrival in the non-slave-holding "free" states of the United States or in Canada. In her winding pilgrimage from Georgia to Indiana, Cora has indeed been moving "northward" (147) or "into northness" (302), as the narrator states at various points. But when after a narrow escape from the massacre at

Valentine Farm, a last brutal encounter with the slave catcher in pursuit of her, and another arduous journey underground, Cora finally arrives at the end of a long tunnel, she finds herself in a place without any geographic coordinates: "She didn't know what Michigan or Illinois or Canada looked like. Perhaps she wasn't in America anymore but had pushed beyond" (305). As readers, we never learn what her exact location in this last chapter is; the novel concludes with Cora joining a wagon train on its journey west, across Missouri to California. Throughout the novel, "the North" thus remains an evocative concept, but one that cannot be filled with salutary meaning; it is marked at best by constant deferral, by continuing movement rather than arrival.

The novel's sudden twist of plot trajectory from north to west indicates a signal departure from the conventional plot structure of the antebellum slave narrative and its successor, the twentieth-century neo–slave narrative,[16] which the novel otherwise emulates closely by tracing the Black subject's abduction from Africa and experience of the Middle Passage, life under slavery with a particular focus on what Saidiya Hartman calls "the scene of subjection" (1997), the plans for escape and the details of the flight from south to north, the acquisition of literacy and other benchmarks in the struggle for emancipation.[17] All these plot elements are present, mostly in Whitehead's description of Cora, sometimes outsourced to other characters, such as her African grandmother, Ajarry. Yet, when the novelist denies his protagonist physical arrival in a "free" state, Whitehead not so much breaks with the tradition of the slave and neo–slave narratives he cites but reinforces a critique already inherent in many of them. Authors such as Olaudah Equiano, Harriet Jacobs, and later Ishmael Reed have long disrupted the common equation of geographic location with legal, physical, and psychological freedom by pointing out the persistence of anti-Black racism in the North. Whitehead builds on such critique by stressing not only the geographic but also the temporal ubiquity of unfreedom. His underground railroad takes Cora across space as well as across time, transporting her, quite anachronistically, from the antebellum period to events in the late nineteenth and twentieth centuries—such as the mass lynching that began in the wake of the Reconstruction period and continued well into the 1960s as well as the infamous "Tuskegee Study of Untreated Syphilis in the Negro Male" (1932–1972)—events that poignantly underscore the afterlife of slavery.[18]

A second distinctive departure from the genre conventions of antebellum slave narratives (and neo–slave narratives) occurs in Whitehead's choice of third-person narration—or more precisely, heterodiegetic narration with variable focalization—in place of the classic first-person voice. Antebellum slave narratives sought to emphasize with their choice of autodiegetic narration the firsthand experience and hence authenticity and truthfulness of their accounts of slavery, and the neo–slave narratives of the 1970s to 1980s similarly used this technique to recover the "unwritten interior life" of the enslaved (Morrison 1998, 192). Whitehead's narrative of slavery, however, is not primarily interested in questions of realism, verisimilitude, and interiority. Although we do get some very naturalistic depictions of slavery (particularly in the opening chapters "Ajarry" and "Georgia") and partial insight into the emotional and psychological life of Black characters (more so with Ajarry, Mable, and Caesar than Cora)—as well as, quite surprisingly, their white antagonists Ridgeway, Stevens, and Ethel—their perspectives remain mediated by the detached voice of heterodiegetic narration. This voice, as critic Adam Kelly observes, is not "the revelatory truth-telling found in Brown's and Douglass's antebellum slave narratives, or the heightened and poetic register that Toni Morrison brought to the story of slavery in *Beloved*," but "the recounting of dry, hard facts in the apparently neutral language of the market, the language of price and exchange" (2018, 23)—a point to which I will return shortly.

Furthermore, also in contrast to slave narratives and neo–slave narratives, the novel's protagonist appears throughout the novel more as an allegorical figure than as a realistic character. Her decency and selflessness, particularly in the opening chapters, set her apart from the majority of the other characters in the novel, which Whitehead describes as representative of "a traumatized populace under siege" (quoted in Kachka 2016, n.p.). Above all, several times throughout the novel, Cora is metaphorically aligned with the underground railroad. When Caesar contemplates asking Cora along on his flight, he observes, "She wasn't a rabbit's foot to carry with you on the voyage but the locomotive itself. He couldn't do it without her" (2016, 234). When in a later moment Cora struggles with the slave catcher, Ridgeway, the narrative voice (this time from the perspective of external focalization) remarks, "Her scream came from deep inside her, a train whistle echoing in a tunnel"

(226). And finally, as Cora makes her ultimate escape from Ridgeway, the novel shifts to her perspective: "She discovered a rhythm, pumping her arms, throwing all of herself into movement. Into northness. Was she travelling through the tunnel or digging it? Each time she brought her arms down on the lever, she drove a pickax into the rock, swung a sledge onto a railroad spike" (304). These passages illustrate that Cora is not just a stray passenger on the underground railroad; she *is* the allegorical embodiment of the movement toward freedom that the railroad presents—no matter how haphazardly and inadequately this movement can be realized within the given structures and with the available tools.

Whitehead's refiguration of the protagonist from a realist figure in classic (neo-)slave narratives (conveying a sense of verisimilitude and inviting identification) into an allegorical figure (a trope of abstraction and critical distancing) presents a significant historiopoetic intervention in an otherwise rather deterministic sketch of a ubiquitous and enduring system of slavery. In all other aspects, the novel firmly establishes the entanglement of Black enslavement and white supremacy at the heart of American capitalism. Throughout the novel, Whitehead refers to "the ruthless engine of cotton," which, fueled by a vast system of racialized forced labor, generates free enterprise and national growth. Ridgeway, for instance, realizes that he and his blacksmith father, who disdains his son's work as a slave catcher, are ultimately both serving King Cotton: "The crop birthed communities, requiring nails. And braces for houses, the tools to build the houses, roads to connect them, and more iron to keep it all running. Let his father keep his disdain and his spirit, too. The two men were parts of the same system, serving a nation rising to its destiny" (76). Slavery, displacement, and genocide, as Whitehead also demonstrates with frequent references to Native American communities, are at the heart of American nationhood and intrinsic to its foundational economic system. The freedom postulated as the plot's ultimate goal by the genre of the slave narrative is, according to the logic of *The Underground Railroad*, impossible to attain with the given socioeconomic system.[19] But even as the novel thus shares significant concerns with Afro-pessimist theory, it does not subscribe to its central premise that the present is irrevocably tied to the past, that the past is coeval with the present, and that the Black subject is always already positioned as slave.[20] With Cora, Whitehead creates a resilient and determined protagonist, who, despite repeated setbacks and disillusionment, continues to journey on—to be sure, at first only by flight *from*; later on, however, by moving *through* and *toward*.

The concluding chapter firmly establishes Cora as the allegorical locomotive of underground desire and movement, pushing onward, regardless. Like many other late twentieth- and early twenty-first-century narratives of slavery, *The Underground Railroad* does not spell out what the terminus of such persistent movement might look or feel like; it lingers instead in what Margo Natalie Crawford calls the "ad hoc territory" of the unknown (2016, 71). Crawford establishes the poetics of unknowability and opacity as one of the distinctive features of what she calls "post-neo-slave narratives." These narratives do not seek to recuperate the past by filling in its gaps and silences or to memorialize its suffering. "If the neo-slave narrative builds on the form of nineteenth-century slave narratives, the post-neo-slave narrative may be the narratives that stop building *on* and begin to improvise more fully in . . . 'ad hoc territory'" (71). Like *An Octoroon* and other contemporary works, *The Underground Railroad* insists that there is value in movement, even as that movement entails confronting and traversing the space of the unknown and navigating an opaque, shifting and changing territory. When pumping a handcar through a pitch-dark tunnel and wondering whether she is actually riding or digging the railroad, Cora considers the implications of the enormous labor accomplished by those who, like her now, built this subterranean landscape of possibility: "Who are you after finishing something so magnificent—in constructing it you have also journeyed through it, to the other side. On one end there was who you were before you went underground, and on the other end a new person steps out into the light. The up-top world must be so ordinary compared to the miracle beneath, the miracle you made with your sweat and blood. The secret triumph you keep in your heart" (303–4). Cora's musings on the meaning of Black identity (rendered in free indirect discourse) insist, like Minnie in *An Octoroon*, on the value of movement.[21] Movement is here conceptualized as productive of spatial and temporal difference (the spatial difference of "the other side" and the temporal difference between the past and the present moment) as well as of inner growth and emancipation ("on the other end a new person steps out into the light"). It is not just a movement *from* or *to*, but a movement *through*—a preposition suggestive of prevailing and overcoming.

Whitehead's novel does not spell out the terms of the "miracle beneath," nor the direction of the movement it generates; it does not suggest that subterranean change might uproot the "up-top" world.[22] Once she resurfaces, Cora must continue her track toward the yet unknown. But in her movement "through" the underground, she has also come to differentiate the present from the past. "I was in Georgia. I ran away," she tells the African American wagoner who offers her a ride west, choosing the grammatical construction of the simple past, which clearly delineates its subjects as things of the past (rather than as continuing into the present). She also wonders where her companion "escaped from, how bad it was, and how far he travelled before he put it behind him" (306). These final lines underscore two things: first, the need to bear witness to the trauma of slavery (Cora's desire to learn of Ollie's pain) and, second, the perspective that the pain of the past does not need to be melancholically revisited but can be worked through. Clearly, Whitehead's novel refuses to support naïve narratives of national progress in race relations and zooms in on the endurance of the ideological legacies of slavery. But it also insists that while the present continues to be informed by the past, it is not identical with it. The past can be "put behind"—not in the sense of being ignored, repressed, or forgotten, but rather in the sense of being put in perspective.

To be sure, compared to the more straightforwardly reparative works of the 1990s (e.g., early Parks, Dunye, and Kincaid), *An Octoroon* and *The Underground Railroad* appear to be less exuberant in their affirmation of autopoiesis and change. As they bring into focus the structural confines imposed on Black subjectivities by the enduring ideological and representational afterlife of slavery, they nevertheless also underscore on the diegetic level the value of imaginative movement as productive of difference and of difference as generative of possibility—even as the emerging field of possibility remains unknown. On the nondiegetic level, these two works, moreover, continue the historiopoetic praxis of putting playful pressure on entrenched verbal and visual signs, of troubling ossified narratives, tropes, icons, and *lieux de mémoire* that continue to delimit discourses of Black identity so as to restore movement to the field of representation and open up new conceptual horizons for approaching the past, inhabiting the present, and moving toward the future.

NOTES

PREFACE

1. See, e.g., Diawara 1999; Garrett 2002; Goings 1994; Lee 1998; and "Change the Joke and Slip the Yoke: Conversations on the Use of Black Stereotypes in Contemporary Visual Practice," a symposium at Harvard University, March 18–19, 1998.

2. When Walker was attacked by a number of critics for her use of crude, racializing stereotypes, Gates famously came to her and other artists' defense, insisting that "in drawing upon this peculiarly American repertoire of debased, racist images—these artists are seeking to liberate both the tradition of representation of the black in popular and high art forms and to liberate our people from residual, debilitating effects that the proliferation of those images undoubtedly has had upon the collective unconscious of the African American people, and indeed on our artists themselves and their modes of representation" (quoted in Bowles 1997, 5).

3. "Melancholic historicism" is Stephen Best's term, which he coined in reference to a body of scholarship emerging in the 1990s; I use it to refer to a body of *artistic* work that became the basis for this scholarship. See Best 2012, 460.

4. My use of the term "poetic" is derived from the term *"poiesis,"* which stresses processes of making. See chapter 1 for a detailed explanation.

5. Each artist has also explored other media in their work: Parks has written several film scripts (e.g., Spike Lee's *Girl 6,* 1996 and Rashid Johnson's *Native Son,* 2019) and has written and performed her own blues songs for her plays (e.g., *Father Comes Home from the Wars*). Walker has worked with video (*Testimony: Narrative of a Negress Burdened by Good Intentions,* 2004; *8 Possible Beginnings or: The Creation of African-America, a Moving Picture by Kara E. Walker,* 2005) as well as in theater, supplementing her visual work with short puppet shows and theatrical skits (*Fibbergibbit and Mumbo Jumbo: Kara E. Walker in Two Acts,* 2004). In 2015 she directed and designed the production of Vincenzo Bellini's opera *Norma* at La Fenice in Venice.

6. For a discussion of the relevance of verbal narratives to the production and refiguration of memory, see Neumann 2010; for a discussion of relevance of images, see Sontag 1990 and Hirsch 2012; for relevance of performance, see D. Taylor 2003 and Roach 1996.

7. In some of her installations, Walker uses overhead projectors to interject the shadows of gallery visitors among the silhouettes on the wall, integrating her audiences in the antebellum landscapes and implicating them in the racialized plots. On the performative aspect of Walker's work, see Cox 2007 and Peabody 2013.

8. For the past thirty years, scholars have paid close and steady attention to African American literature's turn to slavery in the late 1960s, pursuing three distinctive though related angles of analysis: (a) to define, describe, and historicize a new genre in Black writing termed "neo–slave narratives" (see Bell 1987 and Rushdy 1999); (b) to establish and examine the relevance of this new genre for contemporary Black politics and identity (see Beaulieu 1999; Byerman 2005; Eyerman 2001; Keizer 2004; McDowell and Rampersad 1987); and (c) to consider the transatlantic reach and diasporic particularities of this turn to history (see Diedrich, Gates, and Petersen 1999 and Keizer 2004). Most of these studies focus on the by now classic canon of literary neo–slave narratives, including works by Octavia Butler, Charles Johnson, Toni Morrison, Ishmael Reed, and Sherley Anne Williams. In the visual arts, Howardena Pindell, Faith Ringgold, and Betye Saar have been considered foremost in rendering the traumatic dimension of slavery (see Bernier 2008). Few scholarly works have kept up with more recent cultural productions, including Bernier 2008; Copeland 2013; Eckstein 2006; Keizer 2008; Shaw 2004; Ward 2011. With a focus on Walker and Parks, this study maps some of the more recent developments in African American culture from the 1990s through the 2000s.

9. There has been a flurry of essays on both Parks and Walker, investigating their provocative renditions of history, some of them brought together in useful collections. For example, for Parks: Kolin 2010; Kolin and Young 2014; Wetmore and Smith-Howard 2007; and for Walker: Berry, English, Patterson, and Reinhardt 2003; Dixon 2002; and Vergne 2007. To date, there have been only two book-length studies on Parks (Geis 2008; J. Larson 2012) and only one on Walker (Shaw 2004).

10. See Holtzman 2007; Miyamoto 2012.

11. See, in particular, Keizer 2011.

12. See Keizer 2008.

13. See Bell 1987; Rushdy 1999 for foundational definitions of the genre.

14. See Nyong'o 2014.

CHAPTER 1

1. The term "useable past," which by now is widely used in historiographic and memory studies, was first coined by the American cultural critic Van Wyck Brooks in his 1918 article "On Creating a Useable Past," published in *The Dial*, April 11, 1918, 337–41. Brooks argues that the nation's literary past should be approached from the point of view of the "creative impulse," while bearing the question of relevance for the present in mind. See Van Wyck Brooks 1993.

2. Transcript from *MoMAudio Collection*, https://www.moma.org/audio/playlist/232/2979.

3. See Alberro 1996; note also Walker's title, *Harper's Pictorial History of the Civil War (Annotated)* (2005).

4. The appeal of Mitchell's novel extends well into the twenty-first century. According to a 2014 poll, it continues to be the second most widely read book in the United States (see Schuessler 2014).

5. According to Yasmil Raymond, footwear (or the lack thereof) in Walker's silhouettes is heavily invested with meaning, typically connoting property and power and differentiating slaves from masters. See Raymond 2007, 350.

6. Walker comments on drawing the swan motif from Greek mythology in Lott 2000, 73.

7. See Thompson and Copeland's special issue of *Representations* (2011), "New World Slavery and the Matter of the Visual." For studies of various visual representations of slavery in the late twentieth century, particularly since the 1990s, see Schmidt-Linsenhoff 2010; Sims, Husler, and Copeland 2006; and Keizer 2008.

8. From quite early on, the field of literary studies became interested in twentieth-century fictional engagements with slavery, especially with the corpus of prose texts conceptualized as "neoslave narratives" (Bell 1987) or "neo–slave narratives" (Rushdy 1997, 1999), which was investigated thoroughly with regard to its poetics and politics (see Bell 1987; Dubey 2010; Rushdy 1999; Spaulding 2005). While visual art works representing slavery, especially of the nineteenth and the twentieth century, have also been the subject of comprehensive studies (Bernier 2008; M. Wood 2000), they have not yet been considered in terms of a shared aesthetics to the same extent that literary narratives have. To my knowledge, no equivalent term has been coined for visual narratives of slavery. Viktoria Schmidt-Linsenhoff (2010) uses the term "afterimages of slavery" to describe contemporary refigurations of images of slavery. More recently, Janet Neary uses "visual slave narratives in contemporary art" to refer to a specific body of works (Glenn Ligon, Ellen Driscoll, Kara Walker) that seeks to "decode the visual work performed in original, literary slave narratives" (2014, 158). Neary's point of reference is once again the literary (neo-)slave narratives.

9. I here use the term "reading" in Roland Barthes's sense of "ranging over" a multidimensional space of writing 1978, 147.

10. See White 2010a, 112–25. See Koselleck 1985, 145.

11. "Jedes historisch eruierte und dargebotene Ereignis lebt von der Fiktion des Faktischen, die Wirklichkeit selber ist vergangen" (Koselleck 1985, 153). On the basis of the original German statement, I have slightly modified Keith Tribe's translation, *Futures Past*, which uses the term "actuality" in place of "facticity."

12. See Koselleck 2004, 128. White also identifies storytelling as the preferred mode of historiography, for instance, in "Storytelling: Historical and Ideological" (1996), included in his collection *The Fiction of Narrative: Essays on History, Literature, and Theory* (2010a, 273–92).

13. While Nora's investigation into the intersection of history and memory starts by setting up a binary distinction between a personal, affective, mutable access to the past through memory and the objective, causal structuring accomplished by the discipline of history, he then proceeds to trouble this distinction with the concept of *lieu de mémoire*, in which these two approaches to the past intersect (1989, 8–9).

14. Under the influence of New Left social history, historians of slavery have since the late 1960s increasingly paid attention to crafting histories from "the bottom up." According to Ashraf Rushdy, "the study of African American slavery was invigorated by a new respect for the truth and value of slave testimony, the significance of slave cultures, and the importance of slave resistance (1999, 3–4)." Rushdy sees this shift in historiographic praxis as an important condition for the emergence of the genre of neo–slave narratives.

15. Writing this book during a time when leading politicians tend to invent their own realities through verbal discourse, I hasten to add that such mendacity is where I draw the line between imagined historiographies and "alternative facts" that no longer bear any plausible relation to verified knowledge of the past.

16. During the 1930s, the Federal Writers' Project of the Works Progress Administration under President Roosevelt conducted thousands of interviews to collect such testimonies. See the collection "Born in Slavery: Slave Narratives from the Federal Writers' Project, 1936 to 1938" at the Library of Congress, https://www.loc.gov/collections/slave-narratives-from-the-federal-writers-project-1936-to-1938/about-this-collection/.

17. Timothy Spaulding writes similarly about what he calls the postmodern slave narrative: "the past history of slavery in these texts is real and present, subject to reinterpretation in direct and concrete ways" (2005, 19). While Madhu Dubey challenges Spaulding's reading (and also Rody's reading in *The Daughter's Return*) of postmodern and fantastic literatures of slavery as reinforcing rather than undermining historical authority, she agrees that in speculative fictions of slavery "the break from narrative realism . . . does not detract in any way from the reality effect of the past" (2010, 786).

18. In "Site of Memory," Morrison writes, "The exercise [of recording a slave's inner life] is also critical for any person who is black, or who belongs to any marginalized category, for, historically, we were seldom invited to participate in the discourse, even when we were its topic" (191).

19. Alice Walker describes her search for Hurston's grave in the essay "Looking for Zora," included in her book *In Search of Our Mother's Garden* (1983, 93–116).

20. For a discussion of contemporaneity of past and present, see Hartman 2002.

21. Best's 2012 essay, "On Failing to Make the Past Present," is reprinted in his 2018 monograph *None Like Us: Blackness, Belonging, Aesthetic Life*. In *None Like Us*, Best explicates his reasons for advocating a break with a melancholic historicist approach to the past in more detail and complexity.

22. In *None Like Us*, Best investigates, in addition to his reading of *A Mercy*, a number of other contemporary art works that are characterized by an "aesthetics of the intransmissible" (2018, 22), including works from the early 2000s by Ghanaian artist El Anatsui and US artist Mark Bradford. He writes on this score that "these works of art inspire me to the view that contemporary artists are in the process of enacting a kind of thought that literary critics are not yet willing to entertain, that they may be enacting a 'style' of freedom: freedom from constraining conceptions of blackness as authenticity, tradition, and legitimacy; of history as inheritance, memory, and social reproduction; of diaspora as kindship, belonging, and dissemination" (22–23). I concur with Best but suggest that this enactment of a certain "freedom" from the past started some fifteen years earlier.

23. Crawford uses a phrase from Davis 2005, 378–79.

24. Spillers writes this with regard to Ishmael Reed's novel *Flight to Canada* (1976). Parks's and Walker's work function much like Reed's.

25. I invoke the term "historiopoiesis" based on the etymology of its components and with a view to bringing the term "history" into a productive conversation with "poetics." The term has been sporadically used by a couple of authors before me, but so far only Claude Calame has attempted to theorize it. In *Poetic and Performative Memory in Ancient Greece* (2009), Calame advances the concept of history as a narrative practice embedded in processes of poetic construction and figuration. His use of the term is in this regard close to mine, although we have developed these notions independently. For my first discussion of the term, see Saal 2015.

26. I am paraphrasing Muhlack's definition of historiography (*Geschichtsschreibung*) as "die sprachliche Vermittlung historischer Erkenntnis" (1982, 607).

27. My discussion of the term *historía* is indebted to conversations with Marcus Folch, associate professor of classics at Columbia University.

28. Austin discusses the performative capacity of language in his study *How to Do Things with Words* (1975). See the section "Words Workin" in chapter 2 for a discussion of the artists' relationship to Austin's theory.

29. For perceptive readings of Dunye's film with regard to questions of authority and authenticity, history and fictionality, see, for instance, Reid-Pharr 2006; Zimmer 2008; and Ashe 2020.

30. Along the lines of Hartman's concern with the reiteration of violence in representations of the traumata of slavery, critics might object (and have objected) that Walker's ludic engagements with the various mediations and articulations of slavery present a second order of violence and are as obscene and prurient as much of the written and visual evidence of the lives of the enslaved contained in the archive. Yet, as I suggest in my discussion of Walker's (and Parks's) confrontational use of racializing stereotypes in chapter 4, these artists tap into "the traffic between fact, fantasy, desire, and violence" that, according to Hartman, has been "taken for granted" (2008, 5) in order to thematize this traffic, expose its affective powers, submit it to critique, and ideally bring about a change in perception.

31. I would like to thank Jason Merchant, professor of linguistics at the University of Chicago, for helping me with the proper grammatical terminology.

32. Georg Wilhelm Friedrich Hegel notoriously claims that the African continent "is no historical part of the World; it has no movement or development to exhibit" (2007, 99). For discussion of temporal structures of repetition, immediacy, and immanence in Black culture, see Snead 1984.

33. For a perceptive analysis of the various poetic techniques that Kincaid uses in her fabrication of personal and collective histories, see Purk 2014.

34. See Saal 2020 and Hatch 2013.

35. For a reading of Ligon's work in terms of fugitivity, see Copeland 2011; for a reading in the tradition of the slave narratives, see Connor 1996.

36. For discussion of Obadike's performance, see Elam 2005. Obadike's post, having raised a bid of $152.50, was closed within four days by eBay for "inappropriateness." For information on the piece, see http://blacksoundart.com/#/ice/. ayo discontinued her project when she received threats of violence. After taking her project off the web, ayo turned it into the satirical *How to Rent a Negro* (2005). For information on ayo's website, see https://anthology.rhizome.org/rent-a-negro.

37. For other examples, consider Young Jean Lee's *The Shipment* (2009) and

Branden Jacobs-Jenkins's *Neighbors* (2010), in which the actors on stage repeatedly halt their performance of racial stereotypes to stare out at the audience. See Saal 2020.

38. For other examples, see Ashe and Saal 2020c.

39. See Rushdy 1999 on the various sociohistorical and political factors that marked the experience of the generation of artists that brought forth the neo–slave narratives, such as the influence of the civil rights and Black Power movement, the establishment of Black Studies programs at universities, and the rise of New Left social histories.

40. "Post-soul" was first used by Nelson George in *Buppies, B-Boys, Baps & Bohos: Notes on Post-Soul Black Culture* (1992). Neal narrowly limits the marker post-soul to "folks born between the 1963 March on Washington and the Bakke case" (the challenge of affirmative action in 1978) (2002, 3). Ashe, by contrast, simply insists that the artists he qualifies as "post-soul" were born or came of age after the civil rights movement and "have no lived, adult experience with that movement" (Ashe 2007, 611).

41. Soyica Diggs Colbert (2017), for instance, points to the many ways in which post–civil rights artists craft "webs of affiliation" to connect performances of Blackness across time periods by challenging concepts of Blackness and concepts of linearity in historical movement.

42. Tate's article "Cult-Nats Meet Freaky-Deke" is included in *Flyboy in the Buttermilk*, along with other articles in which he traces a shift in experience and sensibility in Black popular culture of the late 1980s.

43. The quotation is from a conversation between Ellis, Danzy Senna, and Omar Wasow in *enigma* in 1992. See Ashe 2003, xi.

44. Ashe borrows the term "cultural mulattoism" from Ellis, who makes it a cornerstone of his New Black Aesthetic. Ellis defines the "cultural mulatto" as someone "educated by a multi-racial mix of cultures" capable of navigating both the Black and the white world without attempting to please either, but who is, significantly, "still black" (1989, 235).

45. This is, for instance, the case with the essay collection edited by Houston A. Baker and K. Merinda Simmons, *The Trouble with Post-Blackness* (2015). In this collection, much of the scholarly discontent with the term "post-black" seems to be based on a rather selective reading of Touré's *Who's Afraid of Post-Blackness?* (2011) that tends to ignore the crucial passage in which Touré stresses, "Let me be clear: Post-Black does not mean 'post-racial.' Post-racial posits that race does not exist or that we're somehow beyond race and suggests colorblindness: It's a bankrupt concept that reflects a naïve understanding of race in America" (12). For a perceptive reading of Baker and Simmons's critique of post-black, see Maus 2020.

46. For a discussion of nuances between the terms, see Paul Taylor 2007.

47. In *The Crossing* (2017), a satirical take on the Trump inauguration, Kara Walker not only parodies Emmanuel Leutze's famous 1851 academic painting *George Washington Crossing the Delaware* but also pays homage to Robert Colescott's earlier riff on Leutze in his painting *George Washington Carver Crossing the Delaware: Page from an American History Textbook* (1975). For an analysis of Colescott's Signifyin(g) on Leutze, see Mercer 2007.

CHAPTER 2

1. Dates in parenthesis refer to the year of the official stage premiere, not the year of print publication. *Imperceptible Mutabilities in the Third Kingdom*, directed by Liz Diamond, opened at BACA Downtown in Brooklyn in September 1989. *The Death of the Last Black Man in the Whole Entire World*, directed by Beth A. Schachter, premiered also at BACA Downtown in Brooklyn in September 1990. *Venus* opened under the direction of Richard Foreman at the Yale Repertory Theatre in March 1996 and was moved to the Joseph Papp Public Theater in New York City in April 1996. *The America Play*, also directed by Liz Diamond, premiered in New York City at the Public Theater as a co-production of the New York Shakespeare Festival, Yale Repertory Theater, and the Theater for a New Audience in February 1994. *Topdog/Underdog*, directed by George C. Wolfe, opened at the Public Theater in New York City in November 2006. *Father Comes Home from the Wars (Parts 1, 2 & 3)* was first produced at the Public Theater in New York City in October 2014 under the direction of Oskar Eustis. *White Noise*, also directed by Oskar Eustis, opened at the Public Theatre on March 19, 2019.

2. For further discussion of the gothic as one of the prevalent, if not *the* dominant mode, of historiography in American literature, see also Lloyd-Smith 2004 and Savoy 2008.

3. Teresa Goddu adds that "the Gothic as a genre emerged simultaneous and in dialogue with the rise of New World slavery and the construction of racial categories" (2013, 71). See also Toni Morrison's analysis of the spectral Africanist presence in Euro-American literature, *Playing in the Dark: Whiteness and the Literary Imagination* (1992).

4. For discussion of uses of the gothic in Black literature, see Goddu 2013 and Weinauer 2017.

5. Note that although in this particular phrasing of Parks's claims on theater the crucial words "new" and "make" are still framed by quotation marks, these quotation marks disappear in later rephrasings of the statement.

6. For discussion of the relationship of performance to past and present, see Carlson 2001.

7. For a discussion of the influence of the Lincoln myth on American memory culture, see K. Ryan 1999.

8. Douglass's reading of Lincoln's legacy has been consolidated in many other iterations, which in turn have also become *lieux de mémoire*, including Martin Luther King's "I Have a Dream" speech in 1963 during the March on Washington at the site of the Lincoln Memorial. With this event, Lincoln's alignment with the long civil rights movement has become firmly entrenched in the public imagination.

9. Kara Walker tackles the Lincoln myth in *The Emancipation Approximation*, 1999–2000.

10. In a talk with critic Joshua Shenk, Parks comments on how the Lincoln mythology continues to haunt African Americans well into the present: "It's like Lincoln created an opening with that hole in his head. We've all passed through it into now, you know, like the eye of a needle. Everything that happens, from 1865 to today, has to pass through that wound" (quoted in Shenk 2002, 5).

11. Though technically not a Founding Father, Lincoln is often aligned with this trope in popular iconographies and the popular imagination. In the Freedman's

Memorial, his right hand rests on a plinth that bears a portrait of George Washington in profile.

12. This description of the set is based on the video recording of the performance of February 1994, available in the Theatre on Film and Tape Archive of the Billy Rose Theater Division of the New York Public Library at Lincoln Center.

13. On reparative dramaturgy, see Colbert 2011.

14. The public display of Baartman's body continued well after her death in the wide dissemination of an autopsy report and the preservation and display of various body parts in formaldehyde jars at the Musée de l'Homme, a natural history museum, in Paris until the 1970s. See also chapter 4.

15. For a prominent example of this critical opinion, see J. Young, 1997. See chapter 4 for a discussion of the controversy over Parks's representation of Baartman.

16. For a discussion of Parks's play in terms of an archaeology of discourse, see Ford 2010 and D. Thompson 2007.

17. For a discussion of Parks's use of historical sources, see Innes 1999 and Worthen 1999.

18. For an extended discussion of the figure of the Hottentot Venus in the Western imagination, see Gilman 1985.

19. For a discussion of visual aspects of the play, see Solomon 1990.

20. This description is based on a video recording of the performance available in the Theatre on Film and Tape Archive of the Billy Rose Theater Division of the New York Public Library at Lincoln Center in New York City.

21. The themes of displacement, alienation, and fragmentation/dismemberment, along with the anxiety of misrecognition, are all taken up and developed further in Part 3: Open House and Part 4: Greeks (or The Slugs). For close readings of the play, see Solomon 1990; Geis 2008, 44–74; and Saal 2013.

22. There are further revisions of the motif of jumping throughout the play in the form of repeated references to being tossed overboard from the slave ships in the choral section, "Third Kingdom," and falling, in the last part, "Greeks."

23. There is an interesting parallel between Kin-Seer's and Venus's last lines. See discussion in chapter 4.

24. For an explication of the meanings of the names in *Death of the Last Black Man*, see Rayner and Elam 1994 and Geis 2008, 60–72.

25. On the nexus of empire and writing, see Jehlen 1994.

26. On Signifyin(g) in Parks, see Frank 2002.

27. In African American culture the Ohio River is often figured in biblical terms as the River Jordan in an analogy between the escape of African Americans from bondage into freedom and the exodus of the Israelites from slavery in Egypt.

28. For a discussion of Parks's refiguration of stereotypes, see J. Wood 2001.

29. For a discussion of the play *Death of the Last Black Man* as a public ritual of burial and mourning, see Rayner and Elam 1994.

30. Jacques Derrida (1982) also disagrees with Austin, but for different reasons. As he points out in his response to Austin, all performatives are always already citational; the distinction between the "ordinary" and "non-ordinary" context of speech acts is therefore negligible. Speech on stage is different from ordinary speech not in essence but in degree.

31. In a send-up of Old Testament genealogies, Ham skillfully refigures the history of social death inflicted on Black people chiefly by riffing on standard and vernacu-

lar uses of grammatical pronouns and appellations: "MeMines gived out 2 offspring one she called Mines after herself thuh uther she called Themuns after all them who comed before . . . Mines joined up with Wasshisname and from that union came AllYall" (Parks 1995c, 122). Establishing a family tree of African American genealogical descent, Ham refigures a "Histree" of violence (emblematically illustrated by the tree branch and noose attached to Black Man's neck throughout the second part of the play) as "Ham's Begotten Tree" (121). Thanks to his verbal acuity, he creates diverse lines of descent and a history of Black presence where there had been none. His dazzling parody of Old Testament genealogies also effectively debunks the misuse of biblical mythologies (the story of Ham and his descendants) to justify slavery. As Ham insists, "Ham. Is. Not. Tuh. BLAME!" (124). In mimicking the minstrelsy stump speech, Ham subverts blackface vaudeville entertainment.

32. For history of this stereotype, see Bogle 1989.

33. Visual artist Titus Kaphar also conceives of his ironic historiopoetic interventions into the history of visual representations of slavery as "amendments." See Stanley 2009.

34. While her husband and son are gravediggers by profession, Lucy has made a name for herself as a "confidence" (198), a keeper of a dying person's last words. And though she attempts to remain faithful to them, she also admits that the meaning of these last words often becomes clear only in the act of interpretation. As she admits with some pride, "I put thuh puzzle pieces in place" (177).

35. For analyses of figure of Mr. Smith in the play's concluding section, see Saal 2013 and Geis 2008, 44–74.

36. Consider also Parks's *Red Letter Plays*, in which she refigures the character of Nathaniel Hawthorne's Hester Prynne differently in two separate plays: *In the Blood* (1999) and *Fucking A* (2000). Parks takes up the motif of the returning war veteran in several of her plays: *Imperceptible Mutabilities*, various segments of *365 Days / 365 Plays* (2006), *The Book of Grace* (2010), and *Father Comes Home from the Wars* (2014).

37. See her interview with Solomon 1990. In her essay "From Elements of Style," Parks comments that she considers form "an integral part of the story"; "not merely a docile passive vessel, but an active participant in the sort of play which ultimately inhabits it" (1995e, 8-7).

38. For a discussion of the function of representation in realism, see Barthes 1989.

39. In the playbill to *Topdog/Underdog*, Parks writes, "This is a play about family wounds and healing." The note is reprinted in the fourth edition of *Topdog/Underdog* (2003).

CHAPTER 3

1. Transcript from *MoMAudio Collection*, https://www.moma.org/audio/playlist/232/2979.

2. Here and elsewhere in this chapter, I use the verb "refunction" analogous to Bertolt Brecht's use of the German term *Umfunktionierung*—that is, as entailing the process of both appropriating and repurposing of cultural means of production (e.g., apparatus, media, genres, etc.) for the sake of shifting power relations. For a discussion of Brecht's concept, see, e.g., Mueller 2006, 103.

3. See, for instance, the Negress's verbal appearance in the title of the silhouette installation *Slavery! Slavery! Presenting a GRAND and LIFELIKE Panoramic Journey into Picturesque Southern Slavery or "Life at 'Ol' Virginny's Hole' (sketches from Plantation Life)" See the Peculiar Institution as never before! All cut from black paper by the able hand of Kara Elizabeth Walker, an Emancipated Negress and a leader in her Cause* (1997), as well as her visual appearance, knife in hand, in *Virginia's Lynch Mob* (1998).

4. See Alberro 1996; note also the title of Walker's 2005 *Harper's Pictorial History of the Civil War (Annotated)*.

5. Although originally developed in the field of literary studies, the concept of Signifyin(g) can be usefully transferred to the visual arts. Henry Louis Gates Jr. defines Signifyin(g) in literature as the double-voiced practice of repeating and revising (with a signal difference) words, tropes, and texts—a poetic technique that disrupts previous semantic orientations, reveals processes of meaning production, and generates new meanings. In the visual arts, Norman Bryson points to a similar practice of modifying established visual signs and drawing them into unprecedented combinations with other signs. In this manner, the visual artist exposes the discursive work of the image and returns it to society "as fresh and renewing currents of discourse" (1991, 70).

6. See Sheets 2002 for Walker's account of the genesis of the figure of the Negress.

7. See her interviews with Alberro 1996 and Saltz 1996.

8. For a discussion of relevance of slave narratives, see Gates 1985a.

9. The Negress also features prominently in Walker's video and film work, such as *Testimony: Narrative of a Negress Burdened by Good Intentions* (2004), as well as in her writings, e.g., *Letter from a Black Girl* (1998).

10. For a discussion of how the politics of sentimentality, especially of fellow feeling, are entangled with an aesthetics of pleasure, consumption, and moral self-satisfaction, see Berlant 1998.

11. See, e.g., *A Thrilling Sketch of the Life of the Distinguished Chief Okah Tubbee Alias, Wm. Chubbee, Son of the Head Chief, Mosholeh Tubbee, of the Choctaw Nation of Indians* (1848) and *Interesting Account of Thomas Anderson, a Slave, Taken from His Own Lips* (1854). For similar titles, see the comprehensive catalogue of slave narratives on the Documenting the American South website, provided by the University of North Carolina at Chapel Hill, http://docsouth.unc.edu/neh/chron.html.

12. For a discussion of the pact between author, narrator, and audiences in slave narratives, see Olney 1985.

13. For a reading of Walker's uses of the genre of the historical romance, see Peabody 2016.

14. Sojourner Truth had her famous 1894 photograph (made in support of her abolitionist commitment) stamped with the lines: "I Sell the Shadow to Support the Substance. Sojourner Truth."

15. In his noted treatise *Laokoon oder* über *die Grenzen der Malerei und Poesie* (*Laocoon, or On the Limits of Painting and Poetry*, 1766), Gotthold Ephraim Lessing insists on the essential difference between the poetic and pictorial arts. According to Lessing, when it comes to depicting events, the visual arts must resort to spatial structuring devices, while the poetic arts structure them in temporal sequence. Therefore, it is the provenance of the visual arts to render bodies and objects in spatial proximity, while poetry's strength is rendering action. Lessing's concept

remained influential well into the twentieth century, when his strict division of the arts was challenged by mass media, on the one hand, and the historical avantgarde movement, on the other hand. For Lessing's theory, see Lessing 1994; for a contemporary challenge of his theory, see Baetens 2010.

16. See Armstrong 1997, 104; Lott 2000, 72; Reinhardt 2003; and Peabody 2016.

17. See Chatman 1978 and W. Wolf 2010 for a delineation of these narrative constituents. The exact definition of narrative continues to be under debate. See M. L. Ryan 2007.

18. See Kukkonen 2011, 37. Much of the transmedial scholarship on narrativity takes its cue from Roland Barthes's insight that narrative can come in "countless" forms and media, "as if all substances could be relied upon to accommodate man's stories" (1975, 237).

19. This phrase is included in a poster accompanying the opening of Walker's 1997 exhibit at the Renaissance Society of Chicago, *Presenting Negro Scene Drawn Upon My Passage Through the South and Refigured for the Benefit of Enlightened Audiences Wherever Such May Be Found, by Myself, Missus K. E. B. Walker, Colored*. The full text of the poster advertisement reads: "The Renaissance Society / Is Given The Opportunity To Present To You / Our Negro Brethren / [Works Of Certain Interest] / Created / Entirely By A Young / Negress / Of Unusual Ability / Silhouettes / Cut / From Black Paper / By / Madam K. E. B. Walker / Upon Her Return From / The South / This Female Artist Is Wont To Illustrate / Lascivious Subjects / [Miscegenation Is Key Among Them] / Therefore, / It Is Ill-Advised For Ladies & Children / To Attend This Exhibition / January 12–February 21, '97 / A Reception Will Be Held / January The Twelfth from 4–7 pm!" See http://renaissancesociety.tumblr.com/page/9.

20. With the phrase "with a humble heart" in one of her titles, Walker Signifies on the language of humility that frequently marked early Black autobiographical writing—consider, for instance, the opening apologias in Olaudah Equiano's *The Interesting Narratives of the Life of Olaudah Equiano, or Gustavus Vassa, the African, written by Himself* and Harriet Jacobs's *Incidents in the Life of a Slave Girl, Written by Herself* for any possible literary shortcomings in their works—a humility clearly not warranted by the professional skills of their writings and in stark contrast to the blatant lack thereof in the most famous autobiographical narrative of the time, Benjamin Franklin's *Autobiography*, which quite unapologetically espouses the merits of vanity.

21. For a discussion of unreliability in narration, see Booth 1983 and A. Nünning 1997.

22. For a discussion of the difference between fallible/foolish and deceitful/untrustworthy narrators, see V. Nünning 2015 and Olson 2003.

23. For a discussion of how Walker's satires confound and resist the politics of respectability, see Murray 2020.

24. In Walker's *Freedom: A Fable by Kara Elizabeth Walker—A Curious Interpretation of the Wit of a Negress in Troubled Times*, the Negress fails to articulate her vision to her people and is promptly abandoned by them.

25. For a discussion of the concept of "true womanhood," see Welter 1966.

26. Walker also diffracts the expectations and projections of African American audiences. In her provocative Signifyin(g) on the iconic status of historical figures such as John Brown (for instance, with the gouache *John Brown*, 1996, discussed in

Shaw 2004, chap. 3) or fictional figures such as Kunte Kinte in *Camptown Ladies* (1998).

27. Bodily excrement, such as feces, blood, semen, and milk, plays a crucial role in Walker's artwork, symbolizing not just notions of racial abjection and debasement but also fluidity and rebirth (see Raymond 2007). Walker repeatedly links excrement and bodily fluids explicitly with history. See Lott 2000 and Kara Walker 1997.

28. *World's Exposition* could be considered as companion piece to two other Walker silhouettes, *Cut* (1998) and *Burn* (1998), which critics have read as artistic expressions of defeat and self-mutilation (see Shaw 2004 on *Cut*) or as illustrating the duality of pain and possibility (see Bibler 2010 on *Burn*). The Negress as artist also appears in a number of other silhouette installations—as a cutter of profiles in *Virginia's Lynch Mob* (1998) and as a Degas-like dancer in *Presenting Negro Scenes* (1997).

29. In his 1925 essay, "The New Negro," included in the anthology *The New Negro*, Locke postulates a break with the "Old Negro" of the past, whom he considers to be "more of a myth than a man" (Locke 1994, 47) and proclaims the emergence of the "New Negro," a new, noble subject, filled with self-respect and racial pride and ready to assume (Cultural) leadership. As Henry Louis Gates Jr. and Gene Andrew Jarrett remark, this figure has been a "utopian construct," a discursive figure constructed and advanced by African American artists and intellectuals from the slave narratives onward (Gates and Jarrett 2007, 4).

30. My use of the term *Blickmaschine* takes its cue from the exhibition *Blickmaschinen oder wie Bilder entstehen* ("Gaze Machines or How Pictures Are Made"), curated by Nike Bätzner, Eva Schmidt, and Werner Nekes, at the Museum für Gegenwartskunst in Siegen, Germany, November 23, 2008–May 10, 2009. The exhibition focused on precinematic apparatuses, such as the magic lantern, camera obscura, and kaleidoscope, and on contemporary art works that engage this tradition. The catalogue accompanying the exhibition does not theorize the term but uses it merely in reference to these apparatuses. See Museum für Gegenwartskunst Siegen 2008.

31. For an example of her critique of Western visual arts, see also Walker's installation *Endless Conundrum, An African Anonymous Adventuress* (2001), in which she peels back the layers of racist assumptions undergirding European modernist art from Pablo Picasso to Henri Matisse to Constantin Brancusi.

32. See Wilson 1994 and Lisa G. Corrin's introductory essay to the volume.

33. In the United States, silhouette portraits first began to appear in the 1760s and 1770s and became extremely popular in the 1780s. By the early 1800s, a great number of stationary and itinerant profilists were available for cutting "shades." The craze subsided in the 1810s but was revived in the 1830s, probably thanks to Édouart. See Knipe 2002 for further details on the history of silhouette portraiture in the United States.

34. The year of Édouart's birth varies. Some cite 1789 (see Knipe 1999, 2002), others 1788. Édouart himself lists his date and place of birth in a letter to Miss Catherine Hutton of 1837 as follows: "I was the sixteenth and last child of my family; born the 27th January 1788 at Dunkerque département du Nord, France" (quoted in Oliver 1977, xii). Édouart started cutting silhouettes in 1826; he sailed for America in 1839 and stayed on the continent until 1849.

35. See Oliver 1977. Oliver estimates that Édouart, during his ten-year tour of the United States from 1839 to 1849, cut around 3,800 silhouette portraits.

36. Édouart is known as a meticulous recordkeeper, keeping doubles of all the profiles he cut, marked with the names of his sitters and the date of the sitting. *The Magic Lantern* is exceptional in this regard. The name of the family is still unknown, and the date is listed by the Met as ca. 1835. Given its subject matter, the magic lantern projection of a Wild West scene, this silhouette was probably cut during Édouart's sojourn in the United States between 1839 and 1849. During this decade, Édouart traveled widely along the East Coast and, during the winter and spring of 1844 also to the South, visiting New Orleans, Natchez in Mississippi, and Louisville and Lexington in Kentucky (see Oliver 1977, xiv).

37. The handwritten caption to Édouart's gouache refers to the image as a "Gallantie Show." Gallantee showmen were itinerant showmen, traveling around the country, hoping to be invited into large houses or theaters to provide an hour of entertainment. They would often travel in pairs, the operator of a magic lantern along with a musician. While the operator worked the images (hand-painted on long glass slides) through the projection apparatus and provided a narrative, the musician would accompany him on a lute or small barrel organ. I am grateful to David Evans of the Magic Lantern Society of the US & Canada for sharing his insights into the operations of a gallantee show with me.

38. I would like to thank William Merrill Decker of the English Department of Oklahoma State University for pointing out this particular semantic field.

39. Both Walker and Rothschild refer to a particular technique of silhouette making, the hollow-cut silhouette. These are typically cut from a light-colored piece of paper so that the center of the sheet, the "positive," drops away and leaves the "negative," the contour of the image, which is then pasted on a dark background. This technique was quite popular in the United States. Another technique involved drawing or painting a silhouette profile on a light-colored surface—paper, ceramic, or plaster, as in a silhouette medallion. There is also the cut-out technique, in which a figure is cut out from a dark material, typically blackened paper, and mounted on a light-colored surface, sometimes also on a lithograph or gouache, as in the work of Auguste Édouart. See Knipe 1999.

40. The paper for cut-out silhouettes was typically thin, white on one side and blackened on the other (Knipe 1999). Walker has used mostly black paper, although some of her later silhouettes are cut from white paper. See Christina Sharpe's chapter on Walker in her *Monstrous Intimacies: Making Post-Slavery Subjects* (2010) for an interesting theory on Walker's later choice of white paper for some of her cut-outs.

41. Copley's *Watson and the Shark* and Turner's *Slave Ship (Slavers Throwing Overboard the Dead and Dying, Typhoon Coming On)* are the only two works in the *After the Deluge* exhibition not originally located in The Met; they were lent to the exhibition by the Museum of Fine Arts in Boston.

42. For a discussion of the politics of media coverage of Hurricane Katrina, see Tierney, Bevc, and Kuligowski 2006.

43. For a detailed discussion of Wilson's archaeological approach, see Corrin 1994.

44. See Vergne 2007 and Shaw 2004 for a more detailed explication of this genealogy.

45. Lavater published his studies in *Physiognomische Fragmente zur Beförderung der Menschenkenntniß und Menschenliebe* in four volumes between 1775 and 1778. A translation, *Essays in Physiognomy: For the Promotion of Knowledge and the Love of Mankind,* was first published in the United States in 1794 in Boston. An abridged version, *The Pocket Lavater,* appeared in 1800 and helped popularize Lavater's theories along with the silhouette. Thus, the popularity of physiognomic studies coincides with the popularity of the silhouette form between the 1770s and the 1820s. See Knipe 1999.

46. For a discussion of one example, the 1796 pencil drawing of *Flora,* which accompanied a 1796 bill of sale, see Shaw 2004, 22–23.

47. For a discussion of the Zealy /Agassiz daguerreotypes and general consideration of the role of photography in processes of racialization, see Wallis 1995 and Rogers 2010.

48. For a discussion of the role of mid- to late nineteenth-century police photography in making the body morally legible, see Sekula 1986.

49. Weems created this body of work at the invitation of the J. Paul Getty Museum in Los Angeles and in response to the museum's concurrent exhibition, *Hidden Witness: African Americans in Early Photography,* showing photographs of African Americans from the period of slavery through emancipation to more recent times.

50. For thoughtful readings of Weems's installation, see Bernier 2008 and Copeland 2010.

51. For a discussion of stereotypes as sites of both phantasmatic projection and frozen knowledge, see Bhabha 1994 (in particular, the essay "The Other Question").

52. A reproduction of the sketch is included in Vergne 2007, 15.

CHAPTER 4

1. As early as 1997, Walker's works were included in the Whitney Museum Biennial. The same year, the Whitney hosted the solo exhibit, *Kara Walker: My Complement, My Enemy, My Oppressor, My Love* (October 1997–February 1998), and Walker received the prestigious MacArthur genius grant—making her, at the age of twenty-seven, the youngest recipient of the award. In the summer of 1997, the artist Betye Saar mounted a letter campaign against Walker's art: "I am writing you, seeking your support in spreading awareness about the negative images produced by the young African-American artist, Kara Walker" (quoted in Bowles 1997, 4). See Bowles's article for fuller discussion of the controversy.

2. Scholars have variously referred to Baartman by her Afrikaans first name "Saartjie," its non-diminutive version "Sara," or Anglicized version "Sarah"—all of which are examples of colonial naming practices; her original name remains unknown. I have elected to use the name she was commonly known by during her lifetime: Saartjie. For a discussion of naming praxis and its politics, see Holmes 2007.

3. Pindell has continued to oppose the works of Kara Walker. In 2009 she set up a digital discussion forum (http://karawalker-no-yes.blogspot.com) and published a collection of opinion pieces, *Kara Walker-no, Kara Walker-yes, Kara Walker-?* (2009). In 2017, the National Museum of African American History and Culture exhibited artworks by Saar (*Let Me Entertain You*) and Walker (*No World*) alongside each other, thus emphasizing the need for dialogue—a gesture that Walker

deeply appreciated, as she points out in an Instagram post of the two artworks. Saar, however, held on to her basic opposition to Walker's work (see Sargent 2017). Sargent's essay includes an overview of the Saar-Walker controversy as well as similar controversies (such as the temporary covering over of one of Walker's drawings at the Newark Public Library in 2012) and stakes out a more measured approach to the dilemma posed by Walker's work.

4. For further expressions of appreciation, see also Wallace 1996; Sims, Dalton, and Harris 1997; and Garrett 2002.

5. In the 1990s, this controversy is carried out, for instance, in a special issue of the academic journal *IRAAA: International Review of African American Art* (fall 1997, issue 14, number 03) and at a symposium at Harvard University, entitled "Change the Joke and Slip Yoke," in March 1998.

6. Like Saar and Pindell, Harris at first vehemently opposed Walker's art. Unlike them, however, he later published a more nuanced and measured reading of Walker's art. See Harris 2011.

7. In his groundbreaking study of Black collectibles, Kenneth Goings similarly concludes that the images created by African American artists from the 1960s onward to contest negative images of Blackness merely ended up producing new stereotypes, "however positive, replacing the old ones" (1994, 89).

8. For discussions of the risk of working with stereotypes, see Kumanyika, Hitt, Neary, and Ashe 2020 and Saal 2020.

9. See reviews by Hartigan 1996 and Brustein 1996.

10. The Black female body has frequently been troped as the allegorical figure of Venus, according to Roman mythology the goddess of beauty, love, sexuality, desire. See, for instance, Thomas Stothard's etching *The Voyage of the Sable Venus from Angola to the West Indies* (1794). Saartjie Baartman's stage name "The Hottentot Venus" is also derived from this iconography. For an overview of the history of rendering Black women in the iconography of the "Black Venus," see Hobson 2005. For an excellent discussion of the role of photography and live displays in Western culture in shaping and promoting this iconography, see Willis and Williams 2002.

11. For a discussion of the varied and complex history of concepts of theatricality, see Postlewait and Davis 2003.

12. On the stage-audience relationship, see Erika Fischer-Lichte's *Ästhetik des Performativen* (2004), translated as *The Transformative Power of Performance* (2008).

13. On the role of disgust and shame in the encounter with stereotypes, see Nyong'o 2002; on indifference, see Diawara 1999; on the role of carnivalesque laughter, see Mercer 2007.

14. According to Janell Hobson, after Baartman at least three other women of color were exhibited in Western Europe in 1822, 1829, and 1838 (2005, 46–47). For a history of such human displays in Europe and North America, see Fusco 1994. See also Deborah Willis's and Carla Williams's documentation of the racializing "anthropological" gaze in early photography, *The Black Female Body* (2002).

15. As Hazel Carby has shown, white antebellum literature tended to render Black female sexuality as a direct threat to the "conjugal sanctity" of the white mistress and master. Sexual desire and agency were ascribed to the Black woman rather than white master, with the master rendered as "prey to the rampant sexuality of his female slaves" (1987, 27).

16. See also Keizer 2008 for a reading of Walker's *Emancipation Approximation*.

17. Juliette Bowles, for instance, strongly objects to Walker's "gleeful display of so many little and prepubescent Black girls being sexually abused or hypersexed" (1997, 15). For an assertion of Black female sexuality and desire, see also Walker's textual work, e.g., *Letter from a Black Girl* (1998).

18. Ferguson makes this remark with regard to Walker's art. Shawn-Marie Garrett similarly describes Parks's work as an "unseemly obsession with unearthing hushed-up secrets, performing what's been buried or hidden away, revealing the carnal, physical body, and getting its hands (yes) dirty—in front of an audience, as part of a ritualized, shared event" (2000, 133).

19. For a discussion on representing violence in art and scholarship, see chapter 1.

20. See Carla Williams, *Venus* (1994); Lyle Ashton with Renee Cox, *Venus Hottentot 2000* (1994); Renée Green, *Sa Main Charmante* (1989) and *Permitted* (1989); Carrie Mae Weems, *The Hottentot Venus* (1997). These artworks along with other artistic engagements with Venus are included in Deborah Willis's edited volume *Black Venus 2010* (2010). In Walker's work, Venus is sometimes directly referred to in some of her silhouette vignettes, most prominently in *Camptown Ladies* (1998); it also informs Walker's fashioning of the figure of "The Negress."

21. As part of Napoleon's 1814 campaign, the Battle of Paris took place in late March. Baartman most likely arrived in Paris shortly after, in April 1814 (see Holmes 2007). While alliance forces occupied Paris, it is unclear whether Scottish soldiers were among them. The cartoonist probably chose Scottish soldiers to draw out the analogy between kilt and loincloth.

22. In the Foreman production, the entire cast remains onstage throughout the play. There are few scenes in which the Venus is not the focus of the gaze. Even in the play-within-the-play, *For the Love of Venus*, the Bride-to-Be functions as a surrogate for the Venus figure. My observations are based on the video recording of a May 1996 performance at the Public Theater, available in the Theatre on Film and Tape Archive, Billy Rose Theater Division of the New York Public Library.

23. Parks's play-within-the-play is loosely based on the burlesque *Le Vénus hottentote, ou haine aux françaises* (The Hottentot Venus, or The Hatred of French women), which opened in Paris in November 1814—six months after Baartman's arrival in the French metropolis. For an English translation of the play, see Sharpley-Whiting 1999; for a discussion of the play, see Mitchell 2010.

24. Zine Magubane (2010) observes that British debates over Baartman's status as free agent or enslaved subject dovetailed easily with projects of imperial expansion, entailing the conversion of slave labor into a "free" market economy. Consider also Robin Mitchell's reading of the cultural function of the popular 1814 play *Le Vénus hottentote, ou haine aux françaises* (*The Hottentot Venus, or the Hatred of French Women*), which was based on the sensational display of Baartman in Paris. Mitchell observes, "The Hottentot Venus became the terrain for projecting all that was dangerous for French national identity, such as gender inappropriateness, class transgressions, and racial miscegenation. At the same time, command over her made up for the losses in the Caribbean colonies and gave further justification for the African colonial project" (2010, 43).

25. At the time Parks's play opened in 1996, parts of Baartman's body were still kept in formaldehyde in jars at the Musée de l'Homme in Paris, even though

removed to a basement shelf. Baartman's remains were repatriated to South Africa in the spring of 2002 and buried in Eastern Cape province.

26. Foreman drew strings across the stage to break up the visual field (Garrett 2010, 80).

27. In Renee Cox's enactment, *Venus Hottentot 2000*, in collaboration with Lyle Ashton Harris, enormous metallic breast and buttock plates are somewhat haphazardly attached to Cox's body with the help of thin strings, highlighting the stark contrast between the live body of the performer and her cyborg-like costume, while the metallic sheen provides a sort of mirror in which onlookers can find themselves reflected—thus enhancing the notion that whatever we "see" in this outfit is our own projection.

28. Catanese points out that the request of the Griqua people of South Africa for the repatriation of Baartman's remains was "intimately linked to their struggle for taxonomic and political differentiation" (2010, 53), involving, among other things, claims to land and recognition. See also Sara Warner's essay on South Africa's interest in Baartman's remains as part of their Truth and Reconciliation project as well as her discussion of Diana Ferrus's poem "I've Come to Take You Home" (Warner 2008).

29. These are also the ingredients of recent historiographic and artistic attempts to recover the biography of Saartjie Baartman, for instance, in Rachel Holmes's biography *The Hottentot Venus: The Life and Death of Saartjie Baartman* (2007) and the film *Vénus noire*, dir. Abdellatif Kechiche (2010).

30. The trope of chocolate, a staple of the colonial plantation economy, is used throughout the play in conjunction with the Venus. Her body is repeatedly equated with chocolate (*Petits Coeurs, Enfant de Bruxelles, Capezzoli die Veneri*, 104). As she indulges in the taste of chocolate, her "chocolatized" body is consumed by the insatiable appetite of mass audiences as well as "scientific" observers. See L. Wright 2002 on the Venus's self-cannibalization.

31. Fried famously declares that "art degenerates as it approaches the condition of theater" (1998, 164), referring to the loss of the alleged disinterestedness and purposelessness of "true" art. The problem of theater for Fried is the problem of an audience: "For theater has an audience—it exists for one—in a way the other arts do not; in fact this more than anything else is what modernist sensibility finds intolerable in theater in general" (163).

32. In *Embodied Avatars*, Uri McMillan provides a nuanced reading of a number of Piper's radical performances of objecthood as acts of extreme self-alienation. In *Untitled Performance for Max's Kansas City*, Piper walked around a fashionable, bohemian bar in SoHo with her eyes blindfolded, her ears and nose plugged, and her hands gloved so as to minimize all sensory experience of her environment and transform herself into an art object. See McMillan 2015, 111–12.

33. The company was founded in 1856 as the American Sugar Refinery Company on the Brooklyn site. Most buildings had to be rebuilt in 1882 after a major fire, among them the building that would house Walker's sugar sculpture.

34. The sugar Sphinx had, over the course of nine weekends, an audience of 130,554 visitors. See Sutton 2014.

35. The consumption is not only visual. Documentary footage of the installation reveals visitors attempting to touch the sculpture and to lick remnants of the smaller molasses sculptures attending the Sugar Baby.

36. Fried's vehement dismissal of theatricality seems based on a rather crude and stereotypical understanding of theater as mass entertainment. In a brief passage, he salutes the attempt of theater artists such as Brecht and Artaud to "defeat" conventional perceptions of theater and to establish "a drastically different relationship to its audience" (1998, 163). Brecht and Artaud are, of course, known for their anticulinary approach to theater, which is, to a great extent, achieved through the foregrounding of theater's theatricality. In other words, from the perspective of theater makers, theatricality has long been a trademark of a "modernist sensibility" (163).

37. In the nineteenth century, the United States was the world's fastest growing population and second biggest consumer of sugar (after Britain), consuming much more sugar than it produced. Cuba was its largest import source; by 1865, 65 percent of Cuban sugar was exported to the United States. Cuba abolished slavery only in 1886. In 1999, the Domino Refinery became the site of a twenty-month strike, the longest in the history of New York City.

38. For development plans and their evolution, see the site "Domino" on NY.Curbed.com (https://ny.curbed.com/domino/archives). The website also includes a reportage on the fight over including affordable housing units; see, for instance, https://ny.curbed.com/2014/3/4/10136820/city-planning-set-to-approve -two-trees-domino-development.

39. In an interview with *Art 21*, Walker describes the Domino Refinery as a "cathedral to industry" (Walker 2014, n.p.).

40. Sugar was still a luxury commodity in the seventeenth century, reserved for displays of wealth and power. By the eighteenth century it had become quite affordable for the middle class, and in the course of the nineteenth century, thanks to the rise of the tea industry, it became a staple of nutrition of the lower classes.

41. See Holcomb 2016, 36–62.

42. In his study of Black collectibles and American stereotypes, Kenneth Goings writes that bandanas and "large breasts" typically symbolized the "Old South mammy" (1994, 65). He adds that although the bandanas initially signified a connection to Africa, where the practice of wearing them originated, during antebellum times they quickly turned into a "badge of servility" (65–66).

43. Kriz also includes Phillis Wheatley's poem "On Being Brought from Africa to America" (1773) in her discussion of metropolitan efforts at refinement to illustrate the extent to which artists of the time, even the enslaved, were cognizant of their position within this imperial geography (2008, 3).

44. For a discussion of the function of Blackness in Manet's paintings *Olympia* and *Nana*, see Gilman 1985.

45. Fanon writes, "For not only must the black man be black; he must be black in relation to the white man" (2008, 82–83).

46. Silke Hackenesch (2017) discusses how, in addition to sugar, chocolate has served as a major trope for sexualizing and commodifying otherness.

47. See, e.g., Munro 2014, Powers 2014, Callahan 2014, and Goodman 2014.

48. On a smaller scale, this dynamic was already enacted at the inaugural gala dinner at the Sugar Baby installation, hosted by Creative Time and Walker on May 5, 2014, a few days before the opening of the exhibit. Creative Time announced the event as "a night full of daring art, impeccable company, delicious dining, and unexpected fun." In its gleaming whiteness, the Sphinx presided regally over these proceedings, and one wondered who was to be consumed by whom. See Creative Time 2014.

49. In some cultures, the hand sign of the fig (*figa*) is used to ward off evil or to make an obscene gesture. With her usual sense of humor, Walker comments on her use of the sign: "The hand gesture means good luck and fuck you" (Walker 2014, n.p.).

50. This is how Walker describes the focus of the video in the wall notes accompanying the screening of the film at the New York City gallery Sikkema Jenkins & Co. in November 2014.

51. The film opens with a shot of a sign at the door stating, "Please do not touch the artwork but do share pictures on social media with #karawalkerdomino."

CODA

1. See, for example, Ashe 2020; Elam 2005; Ford 2010; Purk 2014; Reid-Pharr 2006.

2. See chapter 1 for definitions and uses of these two terms.

3. For discussions of these various developments, see Alexander 2010; Goffman 2014; Marable 2006; Ridgeway 2009.

4. Robert J. Patterson is one of the three editors of *The Psychic Hold of Slavery*, which underscores this particular strand of thought in conceptualizing slavery. See also the essays by editors Soyica Diggs Colbert 2016b and Aida Levy-Hussen in the same volume.

5. For discussions of contemporary artworks that continue to operate in the spirit of historiopoiesis, see, e.g., Ashe and Saal 2020a. The evolution of Parks's dramatic engagements with history in her work is harder to gauge than Walker's. With *Father Comes Home from the Wars* (2014) and *White Noise* (2019), she continues to investigate questions of freedom and agency in light of the past of slavery. While *Father Comes Home from the Wars* continues to play with verbal signs, the materiality of language, genre conventions (epic) and myths (the hero's return), *White Noise* strikingly lacks the playwright's trademark dramaturgy of Rep & Rev, her playful foregrounding of the materiality and mediality of language. It might very well signal a departure in the evolution of her oeuvre, but at this point it is simply too early to endorse such a statement.

6. *Kara Walker: Drawings* was exhibited from March 5–14 and September 8–30, 2020, at Sikkema Jenkins & Co. in New York City. The full title of the 2017 show is *Sikkema Jenkins and Co. is Compelled to present The most Astounding and Important Painting show of the fall Art Show viewing season! Collectors of Fine Art will Flock to see the latest Kara Walker offerings, and what is she offering but the Finest Selection of artworks by an African-American Living Woman Artist this side of the Mississippi. Modest collectors will find her prices reasonable, those of a heartier disposition will recognize Bargains! Scholars will study and debate the Historical Value and Intellectual Merits of Miss Walker's Diversionary Tactics. Art Historians will wonder whether the work represents a Departure or a Continuum. Students of Color will eye her work suspiciously and exercise their free right to Culturally Annihilate her on social media. Parents will cover the eyes of innocent children. School Teachers will reexamine their art history curricula. Prestigious Academic Societies will withdraw their support, former husbands and former lovers will recoil in abject terror. Critics will shake their heads in bemused silence. Gallery Directors will wring their hands at the sight of throngs of the gallery-curious*

flooding the pavement outside. The Final President of the United States will visibly wince. Empires will fall, although which ones, only time will tell.

7. The sculpture's full title is: *Fons Americanus: It is With an Overabundance of Good Cheer and Great Enthusiasm that We Present the Citizens of the Old World (Our Captors, Saviors and Intimate Family) A Gift and Talisman Toward the Reconciliation of Our Respective Mother-lands, Afrique and Albion. Witness! the Fons Americanus: The Daughter of Waters An Allegorical Wonder. Behold! the Sworling Drama of the Merciless Seas, Routes and Rivers, upon which our dark fortunes were traded and on whose frothy shores lay prostrate Captain, Slave and Starfish, alike. Come, One and All, to Marvel and Contemplate The Monumental Misrememberings of Colonial Exploits Yon. Gasp Plaintively, Sigh Mournfully, Gaze Knowingly, And Regard the Immaterial Void of the Abyss etc. etc. in a Delightful Family Friendly Setting. Created by that Celebrated Negress of the New World, Madame Kara E. Walker, NTY.*

8. See Leader-Picone 2020 for Beatty's Signifyin(g) on these narratives.

9. *An Octoroon* premiered at the Soho Rep. in Manhattan under the direction of Sarah Benson on May 4, 2014. My observations are based on the video recording of a June 2014 performance at the Soho Rep, Theatre on Film and Tape Archive, Billy Rose Theater Division of the New York Public Library.

10. For a discussion of Jacobs-Jenkins's interest in the racial legacies of theatrical forms, see his interview with Ashe and Saal (2020a); here the playwright also stresses the formative influence of both Parks and Walker on his work.

11. The dynamic between humanist intent and racializing form is also apparent in Harriet Beecher Stowe's novel *Uncle Tom's Cabin* (1852).

12. Boucicault wrote his play in the wake of Harriet Beecher Stowe's bestselling novel *Uncle Tom's Cabin* (1852) and apparently as a corrective to the latter, considering Stowe's portrayal of plantation life too harsh. *The Octoroon* heavily borrows from Maryne Reid's novel *The Quadroon* (1856) and draws on Boucicault's own observations of slavery, which he made during a sojourn in New Orleans between 1855 and 1856 (see Foster 2016, 287).

13. *An Octoroon* not only debunks melodrama (for its racializing assumptions), it also pays homage to it in many ways. See Jacobs-Jenkins's comments on the emotional power of melodrama in the interview with Ashe and Saal 2020a, 221. See also Foster 2016 for a discussion of Jacobs-Jenkins's play *An Octoroon* as "meta-melodrama."

14. In Boucicault, the villain is exposed thanks to the evidence of a daguerreotype machine—still a technological sensation in 1859—but escapes arrest by blowing up a steamboat. The explosion was rendered on stage through various light effects.

15. The folkloric figure of Br'er Rabbit makes a repeated cameo appearance throughout the play. In the Soho Rep. production, it was played by Jacobs-Jenkins himself. At various moments in the production, he enters the stage to help with scene shifts and to pick up props, but quite often he simply stares at the audience, showing that he is watching them—most powerfully at the end of the play.

16. Rushdy defines neo–slave narratives as "contemporary novels that assume the form, adopt the conventions, and take on the first-person voice of the antebellum slave narrative" (1999, 3).

17. See Olney 1985 for a description of the "master plan" of typical plot elements in classic slave narratives.

18. For a discussion of the histories indexed by Cora's various experiences, see Dischinger 2017.

19. Adam Kelly even refers to *The Underground Railroad* as Whitehead's "most Marxist novel yet and one of the most Marxist novels in the mainstream literary landscape" (2018, 29).

20. See Hartman 2002 and Wilderson 2010.

21. Morrison's novel *A Mercy* (2008) contains a similar moment, when Florens's mother abandons her child to an unknown future in the hope for difference. See Best 2012, 470, for a perceptive reading of this scene as indicating a shift in Morrison's oeuvre. See chapter 1 for a discussion of the implications of this shift.

22. The novel also refuses to endorse a Black political collectivity. The slave community on Randall plantation comes together only in festive moments, such as Jockey's birthday, or in the marginal community of outsiders, the Hobbs women. Their everyday lives under slavery are marked by small turf fights (Cora's garden lot) and intraracial violence (Cora's rape). Even the utopia of Valentine Farm is anchored in a fragile sense of community. In his speech, Lander contests the very notion of a collective "we" born out of a shared experience of subjugation and exploitation. Yet the novel also makes clear that individual agency and inner freedom do not suffice. They require the support of shifting networks of intra- and interracial solidarity.

BIBLIOGRAPHY

WORKS OF SUZAN-LORI PARKS

Plays

1995a. *The America Play*. In *The America Play and Other Works*, 157–99. New York: Theatre Communications Group. First performed in 1994.

1995b. *The Death of the Last Black Man in the Whole Entire World*. In *The America Play and Other Works*, 99–131. New York: Theatre Communications Group. First performed in 1990.

1995c. *Imperceptible Mutabilities in the Third Kingdom*. In *The America Play and Other Works*, 23–71. New York: Theatre Communications Group. First performed in 1989.

1997. *Venus*. New York: Theatre Communications Group. First performed in 1996.

2001a. *Fucking A*. In *The Red Letter Plays*, 113–225. New York: Theatre Communications Group. First performed in 2000.

2001b. *In the Blood*. In *The Red Letter Plays*, 1–112. New York: Theatre Communications Group. First performed in 1999.

2001c. *Topdog/Underdog*. New York: Theatre Communications Group. First performed in 2001.

2006. *365 Days / 365 Plays*. New York: Theatre Communications Group. First performed in 2006.

2015. *Father Comes Home from the Wars: Parts 1, 2 & 3*. New York: Theatre Communications Group. First performed in 2014.

2016. *The Book of Grace*. New York: Theatre Communications Group. First performed in 2010.

2021. *White Noise*. New York: Theatre Communications Group. First performed in 2019.

Prose

1995d. "An Equation for Black People Onstage." In *The America Play and Other Works*, 19–22. New York: Theatre Communications Group.

1995e. "From Elements of Style." In *The America Play and Other Works*, 6–18. New York: Theatre Communications Group.

1995f. "Possession." In *The America Play and Other Works*, 3–5. New York: Theatre Communications Group.

2004. *Getting Mother's Body: A Novel of Love, Lies, and the Blues*. New York: Harper Perennial. First published 2003, Random House (New York).

2005. "New Black Math." *Theatre Journal* 57, no. 4 (December): 576–83.

WORKS OF KARA WALKER

Art

1992. *Working Drawing*. Ink on paper. Sikkema Jenkins & Co., New York.

1994. *Gone: An Historical Romance of a Civil War as it Occurred b'tween the Dusky Thighs of One Young Negress and Her Heart*. Cut paper on wall. Museum of Modern Art, New York.

1995. *The Battle of Atlanta: Being the Narrative of a Negress in the Flames of Desire—A Reconstruction*. Seventeen paper silhouettes. Hammer Museum, Los Angeles.

1995. *The End of Uncle Tom and The Grand Allegorical Tableau of Eva in Heaven*. Cut paper on wall. Collection of Jeffrey Deitch, New York.

1996. *Being the True Account of the Life of the Negress*. Cut paper and adhesive on wall. Collection of Dakis Joannou, Athens, Greece.

1996–97. *Negress Notes (Brown Follies)*. Twenty-four watercolors. Collection of Michael and Joan Salke, Naples, FL.

1997. *Freedom: A Fable by Kara Elizabeth Walker—A Curious Interpretation of the Wit of a Negress in Troubled Times, with Illustrations*. Bound volume of offset lithographs and five laser-cut, pop-up silhouettes on wove paper. Norton Family Foundation, Santa Monica, CA.

1997. *Presenting Negro Scenes Drawn upon My Passage through the South and Reconfigured for the Benefit of Enlightened Audiences, Wherever Such May Be Found, by Myself, Missus K. E. B. Walker, Colored*. Paper and watercolor on paper. Museum of Contemporary Art, Chicago.

1997. *Slavery! Slavery! Presenting a GRAND and LIFELIKE Panoramic Journey into Picturesque Southern Slavery or "Life at 'Ol' Virginny's Hole' (sketches from Plantation Life)" See the Peculiar Institution as never before! All cut from black paper by the able hand of Kara Elizabeth Walker, an Emancipated Negress and a leader in her Cause*. Cut paper and adhesive on wall. Collections of Peter Norton and Eileen Harris Norton, Santa Monica, CA.

1997. *World's Exposition*. Cut paper on wall. Collection of Jeanne Greenberg and Nicolas Rohatyn, New York.

1998. *Camptown Ladies*. Cut paper and adhesive on wall. Rubell Family Collection, Miami, FL.

1998. *Letter from a Black Girl*. Transfer text on wall. Collection of the artist.

1998. *Untitled (Girl with Bucket)*. Cut paper on wall. Private Collection, New York.

1998. *Virginia's Lynch Mob*. Cut paper on wall. Montclair Art Museum, NJ.

1999. *No mere words can Adequately reflect the Remorse this Negress feels at having been Cast into such a lowly state by her former Masters and so it is with a Humble heart that she brings about their physical Ruin and earthly Demise.* Cut paper and adhesive. San Francisco Museum of Modern Art.

1999–2000. *Emancipation Approximation*. Series of twenty-seven silkscreen prints on paper. Figge Art Museum, Davenport, IA.

2001. *American Primitives*. Typewriting on index cards. Series of thirty-six plus eight framed text panels. Collection of Rachel and Jean-Pierre Lehmann, New York.

2001. *Endless Conundrum, An African Anonymous Adventuress*. Cut paper on wall. Walker Art Center, Minneapolis.

2002. *For the Benefit of All the Races of Mankind: An Exhibition of Artifacts, Remnants, Effluvia EXCAVATED from the Black Heart of a Negress*. Installation with cut paper and wall projections. Kunstverein Hannover, Hannover, Germany.

2005. *8 Possible Beginnings or: The Creation of African-America, a Moving Picture by Kara E. Walker*. Black & white video with sound, 15:57 min. Walker Art Center, Minneapolis.

2005. *Harper's Pictorial History of the Civil War (Annotated)*. Portfolio of fifteen lithograph and screenprints. Museum of Modern Art, New York.

2006. *Kara Walker [at The Met]: After the Deluge*. Exhibition March 21–August 6, 2006. Metropolitan Museum of Art, New York.

2014. *An Audience*. Digital video with sound, 27:18 minutes.

2014. *A Subtlety, or the Marvelous Sugar Baby, an Homage to the unpaid and overworked Artisans who have refined our Sweet tastes from the cane fields to the Kitchens of the New World on the Occasion of the demolition of the Domino Sugar Refining Plant*. Polystyrene foam and sugar. Exhibition, May 10–July 6, 2014. Domino Sugar Refinery, Brooklyn.

2017. *The Crossing. New Yorker*, February 13 and 20, 2017. http://www.newyorker.com/magazine/2017/02/13/the-crossing-kara-walker.

2017. *Sikkema Jenkins and Co. is Compelled to present The most Astounding and Important Painting show of the fall Art Show viewing season!* Exhibition, September 7–October 14, 2017. Sikkema Jenkins & Co., New York.

2019. *Fons Americanus*. Sculpture, recyclable or reusable materials including wood, cork, metal, acrylic and cement composite. Tate Modern, London.

2020. *Drawings*. Exhibition, March 5–14 and September 8–30, 2020. Sikkema Jenkins & Co., New York.

Exhibition Catalogues

2002. *Kara Walker*. Edited by Stephan Berg. Catalogue of an exhibition held at the Kunstverein Hannover, Freiburg, Breisgau, June 9–August 4, 2002. Freiburg: Kunstverein Hannover / Modo.

2002. *Kara Walker: Pictures from Another Time*. Edited by Annette Dixon. Published in conjunction with the exhibition "Kara Walker: An Abbreviated Emancipation," at Ann Arbor, University of Michigan Museum of Art, March 9–May 26, 2002. Ann Arbor: University of Michigan Press.

2007. *After the Deluge: A Visual Essay by Kara Walker*. Catalogue of an exhibition at the Metropolitan Museum of Art, March 21–August 6, 2006. New York: Rizzoli International Publications.

2007. *Kara Walker: My Complement, My Enemy, My Oppressor, My Love*. Edited by Philippe Vergne. Minneapolis: Walker Art Center; Ostfiltern, Germany: Hantje Cantz.

2011. *Kara Walker: A Negress of Noteworthy Talent*. Edited by Olga Gambari. Turin: Fondazione Merz.

Interviews

1996. "Kara Walker." Interview with Alexander Alberro. *Index* 1, no. 1 (February). http://www.indexmagazine.com/interviews/kara_walker.shtml.

1996. "Kara Walker." Interview with Elizabeth Armstrong, July 23, 1996. In *No Place (Like Home)*, edited by Douglas Fogle, 102–13. Catalogue of an exhibition held at the Walker Art Center, March 9–June 8, 1997. Minneapolis: Walker Art Center.

1997. "The Big Black Mammy of the Antebellum South Is the Embodiment of History." Essay. In *Kara Walker: The Renaissance Society at the University of Chicago, January 12–February 23, 1997*. Chicago: Renaissance Society of the University of Chicago.

2002. "Interview with Kara Walker about the Exhibition." Interview with Silke Boerma. In */Kara Walker/*, edited by Stephan Berg, 165–73. Freiburg: Kunstverein Hannover / Modo.

2011. "Conversations: Hilton Als & Kara Walker." Interview. Hammer Museum, December 11, 2011. https://hammer.ucla.edu/programs-events/2011/12/hilton-als-kara-walker/#.

2011. "The Melodrama of *Gone with the Wind*." Interview. *Art 21* (November). http://www.art21.org/texts/kara-walker/interview-kara-walker-the-melodrama-of-gone-with-the-wind.

2014. "A Subtlety, Or the Marvelous Sugar Baby." Interview. *Art 21* (23 May). https://art21.org/watch/extended-play/kara-walker-a-subtlety-or-the-marvelous-sugar-baby-short/.

2019. "I'm an Unreliable Narrator." Transcript of video for *Fons Americanus* exhibition at the Tate Modern, London, September 2019. https://www.tate.org.uk/art/artists/kara-walker-2674/kara-walkers-fons-americanus#introduction.

Abu El-Haj, Nadia. 2001. *Facts on the Ground: Archaeological Practice and Territorial Self-Fashioning in Israeli Society*. Chicago: University of Chicago Press.

Achilles, Jochen. 2010. "Does Reshuffling the Cards Change the Game? Structures of Play in Parks's *Topdog/Underdog*." In *Suzan-Lori Parks: Essays on the Plays and Other Works*, edited by Philip C. Kolin, 103–23. Jefferson, NC: McFarland.

Ackermann, Marion, and Helmut Friedel, eds. 2001. *SchattenRisse: Silhouetten und Cutouts*. Ostfildern: Hatje Cantz.

Alberro, Alexander. 1996. "Kara Walker." *Index* 1, no. 1 (February): 25–28. http://www.indexmagazine.com/interviews/kara_walker.shtml.

Alexander, Michelle. 2010. *The New Jim Crow: Mass Incarceration in the Age of Colorblindness*. New York: New Press.

Als, Hilton. 2011. "Conversations: Hilton Als & Kara Walker." Hammer Museum, December 11, 2011. https://hammer.ucla.edu/programs-events/2011/12/hilton-als-kara-walker/.

Armstrong, Elizabeth. 1997. "Kara Walker." Interview with Liz Armstrong, July 23, 1996. In *No Place (Like Home)*, edited by Douglas Fogle, 102–13. Catalogue of an exhibition held at the Walker Art Center, March 9–June 8, 1997. Minneapolis: Walker Art Center.

Artaud, Antonin. 1994. *The Theater and Its Double*. Translated by Mary Caroline Richards. New York: Grove.

Ashe, Bertram D. 2003. Foreword to Trey Ellis, *Platitudes*, vii–xxvi. Boston: Northeastern University Press.

———. 2007. "Theorizing the Post-Soul Aesthetic: An Introduction." *African American Review* 41 (4): 609–23.

———. 2020. "*Plantation Memories*: Cheryl Dunye's Representation of a Representation of American Slavery in *The Watermelon Woman*." In *Slavery and the Post-Black Imagination*, edited by Bertram D. Ashe and Ilka Saal, 182–97. Seattle: University of Washington Press.

Ashe, Bertram D., and Ilka Saal. 2020a. "An Audience Is a Mob on Its Butt: An Interview with Branden Jacobs-Jenkins." In *Slavery and the Post-Black Imagination*, edited by Bertram D. Ashe and Ilka Saal, 198–228. Seattle: University of Washington Press.

———. 2020b. "Introduction." In *Slavery and the Post-Black Imagination*, edited by Bertram D. Ashe and Ilka Saal, 3–20. Seattle: University of Washington Press.

———, eds. 2020c. *Slavery and the Post-Black Imagination*. Seattle: University of Washington Press.

Austin, J. L. (1975) 1997. *How to Do Things with Words*. 2nd ed. Cambridge, MA: Harvard University Press.

Baetens, Jan. 2010. "Image and Narrative." In *Routledge Encyclopedia of Narrative Theory*, edited by David Herman, Manfred Jahn, and Marie-Laure Ryan, 236–37. New York: Routledge.

Baker, Houston A., and K. Merinda Simmons, eds. 2015. *The Trouble with Post-Blackness*. New York: Columbia University Press.

Baraka, Amiri [Leroi Jones]. 1964. *Dutchman and The Slave*. New York: Morrow Quill Paperbacks.

Barthes, Roland. 1975. "Introduction to the Structural Analysis of Narrative." *New Literary History* 6, no. 2 (Winter): 237–72.

———. 1978. "Death of the Author." In *Image-Music-Text*, translated by Stephen Heath, 142–48. New York: Hill & Wang.

———. 1989. "The Reality Effect." In *The Rustle of Language*, translated by Richard Howe and edited by François Wahl, 141–48. Berkeley: University of California Press.

Beatty, Paul. 2015. *The Sellout*. New York: Farrar, Straus & Giroux.

Beaulieu, Elizabeth Ann. 1999. *Black Women Writers and the American Neo-Slave Narrative*. Westport, CT: Greenwood.

Bell, Bernard W. 1987. *The Afro-American Novel and Its Tradition*. Amherst: University of Massachusetts Press.

Berlant, Lauren. 1998. "Poor Eliza." In "No More Separate Spheres!," edited by Cathy N. Davidson. Special issue, *American Literature* 70, no. 3 (September): 635–68.

Bernier, Celeste-Marie. 2008. *African American Visual Arts*. Edinburgh: Edinburgh University Press.

Berry, Ian, Darby English, Vivian Patterson, and Mark Reinhardt, eds. 2003. *Kara Walker: Narratives of a Negress*. Cambridge, MA: MIT Press. Exhibition catalogue.

Best, Stephen. 2012. "On Failing to Make the Past Present." *Modern Language Quarterly* 73, no. 3 (September): 453–73.

———. 2018. *None Like Us: Blackness, Belonging, Aesthetic Life*. Durham, NC: Duke University Press.

Bhabha, Homi K. 1994. *The Location of Culture*. New York: Routledge.

Bibler, Michael P. 2010. "The Flood Last Time: 'Muck' and the Uses of History in Kara Walker's 'Rumination' on Katrina." *Journal of American Studies* 44, no. 3 (August): 503–18.

Boerma, Silke. 2002. "Interview with Kara Walker about the Exhibition." In */Kara Walker/*, edited by Stephan Berg, 165–73. Freiburg: Kunstverein Hannover / Modo.

Bogle, Donald. 1989. *Toms, Coons, Mulattoes, Mammies, and Bucks: An Interpretive History of Blacks in American Films*. New York: Continuum.

Booth, Wayne C. 1983. *The Rhetoric of Fiction*. 2nd ed. Chicago: University of Chicago Press.

Boucicault, Dion. 1997. "*The Octoroon*." In *Early American Drama*, edited by Jeffrey Richards, 444–94. New York: Penguin.

Bowles, Juliette. 1997. "Extreme Times Call for Extreme Heroes." *IRAAA: International Review of African American Art* 14 (3): 2–15.

Bradley, David. (1981) 1990. *The Chaneysville Incident*. New York: Harper.

Brogan, Kathleen. 1998. *Cultural Haunting: Ghosts and Ethnicity in Recent American Literature*. Charlottesville: University of Virginia Press.

Brooks, Van Wyck. 1993. "On Creating a Usable Past." In *The Early Years*, rev. ed, edited by Claire Sprague, 219–26. Boston: Northeastern University Press.

Brown, Vincent. 2008. "Eating the Dead: Consumption and Regeneration in the History of Sugar." *Food and Foodways* 16 (2): 117–26.

Brown, William Wells. (1858) 2006. "The Escape: or, A Leap of Freedom: A Drama in Five Acts." In *The Works of William Wells Brown: Using His "Strong, Manly Voice,"* edited by Paula Garrett and Hollis Robbins, 264–308. Oxford: Oxford University Press.

——. (1847) 2006. "A Lecture Delivered before the Female Anti-Slavery Society of Salem." In *The Works of William Wells Brown: Using His "Strong, Manly Voice,"* edited by Paula Garrett and Hollis Robbins, 3–18. Oxford: Oxford University Press.

Brustein, Robert. 1996. "Resident Theater Hopes." *New Republic* 240, no. 2 (May 20): 28.

Bryson, Norman. 1991. "Semiology and Visual Interpretation." In *Visual Theory*, edited by Norman Bryson, Michael Ann Holly, and Keith Moxey, 61–73. Cambridge: Polity.

Bush, Jason. 2007. "Who's Thu Man?! Historical Melodrama and the Performance of Masculinity in *Topdog/Underdog*." In *Suzan-Lori Parks: A Casebook*, edited by Kevin J. Wetmore Jr. and Alycia Smith-Howard, 73–88. New York: Routledge.

Butler, Octavia. 1979. *Kindred*. New York: Doubleday.

Byerman, Keith. 2005. *Remembering the Past in Contemporary African American Fiction*. Chapel Hill: University of North Carolina Press.

Calame, Claude. 2009. *Poetic and Performative Memory in Ancient Greece*. Cambridge, MA: Harvard University Press.

Callahan, Yesha. 2014. "Reactions to Kara Walker's *A Subtlety* Prove a Black Woman Will Be Sexualized, Even in Art." *The Root*, May 28, 2014. https://thegrapevine.theroot.com/reactions-to-kara-walker-s-a-subtlety-prove-a-black-wom-1790885464.

Cameron, Dan. 1997. "Rubbing History the Wrong Way." *On Paper: The Journal of Prints, Drawings, and Photography* 2, no. 1 (September–October): 10–14.

Carby, Hazel V. 1987. *Reconstructing Womanhood: The Emergence of the Afro-American Novelist*. Oxford: Oxford University Press.

Carlson, Marvin. 2001. *The Haunted Stage: The Theatre as Memory Machine*. Ann Arbor: University of Michigan Press.

Catanese, Brandi Wilkins. 2010. "Remembering Saartjie Baartman." *Atlantic Studies* 7, no. 1 (March): 47–62.

Chatman, Seymour. 1978. *Story and Discourse*. Ithaca, NY: Cornell University Press.

Chaudhuri, Una. 2002. "*Topdog/Underdog* at the Public Theater." *Theatre Journal* 54, no. 2 (May): 289–91.

———. 2014. "For Posterior's Sake." In *Suzan-Lori Parks in Person: Interviews and Commentaries*, edited by Philip C. Kolin and Harvey Young, 55–57. New York: Routledge.

Coates, Ta-Nehisi. 2015. *Between the World and Me*. New York: Random House.

———. 2017. "The First White President." *Atlantic* (October). https://www.theatlantic.com/magazine/archive/2017/10/the-first-white-president-ta-nehisi-coates/537909/.

Colbert, Soyica Diggs. 2011. *The African American Theatrical Body*. Cambridge: Cambridge University Press.

———. 2016a. "Black Rage: On Cultivating Black National Belonging." *Theatre Survey* 57, no. 3 (September): 336–57.

———. 2016b. "Do You Want to Be Well?" In *The Psychic Hold of Slavery: Legacies in American Expressive Culture*, edited by Soyica Diggs Colbert, Robert J. Patterson, and Aida Levy-Hussen, 1–16. New Brunswick, NJ: Rutgers University Press.

———. 2017. *Black Movements: Performance and Cultural Politics*. New Brunswick, NJ: Rutgers University Press.

Connor, Kimberly Rae. 1996. "*To Disembark*: The Slave Narrative Tradition." *African American Review* 30, no. 1 (Spring): 35–57.

Copeland, Huey. 2010. "In the Wake of the Negress." In *Modern Women: Women Artists at the Museum of Modern Art*, edited by Cornelia Butler and Alexandra Schwartz, 480–97. New York: Museum of Modern Art.

———. 2011. "Glenn Ligon and Other Runaway Subjects." *Representations* 113, no. 1 (Winter): 73–110.

———. 2013. *Bound to Appear: Art, Slavery, and the Site of Blackness in Multicultural America*. Chicago: University of Chicago Press.

Copeland, Huey, and Krista Thompson. 2011. "Perpetual Returns: New World Slavery and the Matter of the Visual." In "New World Slavery and the Matter of the Visual." Special issue, *Representations* 113, no. 1 (Winter): 1–15.

Corrin, Lisa G. 1994. "Mining the Museum: Artists Look at Museums, Museums Look at Themselves." Introduction to *Mining the Museum: An Installation by Fred Wilson*, edited by Lisa G. Corrin, 1–23. Baltimore: Contemporary; New York: New Press.

Cox, Lorraine Morales. 2007. "A Performative Turn: Kara Walker's *Song of the South* (2005)." *Women & Performance: A Journal of Feminist Theory* 17 (1): 59–87.

Crawford, Margo Natalie. 2016. "The Inside-Turned-Out Architecture of the Post-Neo-Slave Narrative." In *The Psychic Hold of Slavery: Legacies in American Expressive Culture*, edited by Soyica Diggs Colbert, Robert J. Patterson, and Aida Levy-Hussen, 69–85. New Brunswick, NJ: Rutgers University Press.

Creative Time. 2014. "Creative Time Honoring Kara Walker." Creative Time, May 6, 2014. https://creativetime.org/events/benefit-2014/.

D'Aguiar, Fred. 1997. "The Last Essay about Slavery." In *The Age of Anxiety*, edited by Sarah Dunant and Roy Porter, 125–47. London: Virago.

BIBLIOGRAPHY

Davis, Colin. 2005. "État Présent: Hauntology, Specters, and Phantoms." *French Studies* 59 (3): 373–79.

Derrida, Jacques. 1982. "Signature Event Context." In *Margins of Philosophy*, translated by Alan Bass, 307–30. Chicago: University of Chicago Press.

DesRochers, Rick. 2014. "The Mythology of History, Family and Performance." In *Suzan-Lori Parks in Person: Interviews and Commentaries*, edited by Philip C. Kolin and Harvey Young, 107–9. New York: Routledge.

Diamond, Liz. 1993. "Perceptible Mutability in the Word Kingdom." *Theater* 24, no. 3 (Fall): 86–87.

Diawara, Manthia. 1999. "The Blackface Stereotype." Introduction to David Levinthal, *Blackface*, 7–17. Santa Fe, NM: Arena.

Diedrich, Maria, Henry Louis Gates Jr., and Carl Pedersen, eds. 1999. *Black Imagination and the Middle Passage*. New York: Oxford University Press.

Dietrick, Jon. 2007. "Making It 'Real': Money and Mimesis in Suzan-Lori Parks's *Topdog/Underdog*." *American Drama* 16, no. 1 (Winter): 47–74.

Dischinger, Matthew. 2017. "States of Possibility in Colson Whitehead's *The Underground Railroad*." *Global South* 11, no. 1 (Spring): 82–99.

Dixon, Annette, ed. 2002. *Kara Walker: Pictures from Another Time*. Published in conjunction with the exhibition "Kara Walker: An Abbreviated Emancipation," at Ann Arbor, University of Michigan Museum of Art, March 9–May 26, 2002. Ann Arbor: University of Michigan Press.

Doran, Robert. 2010. Introduction to *The Fiction of Narrative: Essays on History, Literature, and Theory, 1957–2007*, by Hayden White. Baltimore: Johns Hopkins University Press.

Douglass, Frederick. 2018. "The Freedman's Monument to Abraham Lincoln (1876)." In *The Speeches of Frederick Douglass: A Critical Edition*, edited by John R. McKivigan, Julie Husband, and Heather L. Kaufman, 337–55. New Haven, CT: Yale University Press.

Drukman, Steven. 1995. "Suzan-Lori Parks and Liz Diamond." *TDR: The Drama Review* 39, no. 3 (Fall): 56–75.

———. 1996. "A Show Business Tale/Tail." *American Theatre* 13, no. 5 (May): 4–5.

Du Bois, W. E. B. (1903) 1989. *The Souls of Black Folk*. New York: Penguin Books.

Dubey, Madhu. 2010. "Speculative Fictions of Slavery." *American Literature* 82, no. 4 (December): 779–805.

Dunye, Cheryl, dir. 1996. *The Watermelon Woman*. First Run Features.

DuVernay, Ava, dir. 2016. *13th*. Netflix.

Eckstein, Lars. 2006. *Re-membering the Black Atlantic: On the Poetics and Politics of Literary Memory*. Amsterdam: Rodopi.

Elam, Harry J., Jr. 2005. "Change Clothes and Go: A Postscript to Postblackness." In *Black Cultural Traffic: Crossroads in Global Performance and Popular Culture*, edited by Harry J. Elam Jr. and Kennell Jackson, 379–88. Ann Arbor: University of Michigan Press.

Elam, Harry J., Jr., and Alice Rayner. 1998. "Body Parts: Between Story and Spectacle in *Venus* by Suzan-Lori Parks." In *Staging Resistance: Essays on Political*

Theatre, edited by Jeanne Colleran and Jenny Spencer, 265–82. Ann Arbor: University of Michigan Press.

Ellis, Trey. 1989. "The New Black Aesthetic." *Callaloo* 12, no. 1 (Winter): 233–43.

Embrey, Jenna Clark. 2015. "Where the Light Falls: The Performance of Reaction in Branden Jacobs-Jenkins's *An Octoroon*." *Culturebot*, May 17, 2015. https://www.culturebot.org/2015/03/23484/where-the-light-falls-the-performance-of-reaction-in-branden-jacobs-jenkins-an-octoroon/.

Equiano, Olaudah. (1789) 2001. *The Interesting Narratives of the Life of Olaudah Equiano, or Gustavus Vassa, the African, written by Himself.* Edited by Werner Sollers. Norton Critical Edition. New York: Norton.

Erll, Astrid. 2011. *Memory in Culture.* Translated by Sara B. Young. New York: Palgrave Macmillan.

———. 2014. "Generation in Literary History: Three Constellations of Generationality, Genealogy, and Memory." *New Literary History* 45, no. 3 (Summer): 385–409.

Eyerman, Ron. 2001. *Cultural Trauma: Slavery and the Formation of African American Identity.* Cambridge: Cambridge University Press.

Fabre, Geneviève, and Robert O'Meally. 1994. Introduction to *History and Memory in African-American Culture*, edited by Geneviève Fabre and Robert O'Meally, 3–17. New York: Oxford University Press.

Fanon, Frantz. (1952) 2008. *Black Skin, White Masks.* Translated by Charles Lam Markmann. London: Pluto.

Ferguson, Roderick A. 2009. "A Special Place within the Order of Knowledge: The Art of Kara Walker and the Conventions of African American History." *American Quarterly* 61, no. 1 (March): 185–92.

Ferguson, Russell, Martha Gever, Trinh T. Minh-ha, and Cornel West, eds. 1990. *Out There: Marginalization and Contemporary Cultures.* New York: New Museum of Contemporary Art.

Fiedler, Leslie. (1960) 2003. *Love and Death in the American Novel.* Normal, IL: Dalkey Archive.

Fischer-Lichte, Erika. 2004. *Ästhetik des Performativen.* Frankfurt am Main: Suhrkamp.

———. 2008. *The Transformative Power of Performance: A New Aesthetics.* Translated by Saskya Iris Jain, with an introduction by Marvin Carlson. New York: Routledge.

Ford, Kianga K. 2010. "Playing with Venus: Black Women Artists and the Venus Trope in Contemporary Visual Art." In *Black Venus 2010: They Called Her "Hottentot,"* edited by Deborah Willis, 96–106. Philadelphia: Temple University Press.

Foster, Verna. 2005. "Suzan-Lori Parks's Staging of the Lincoln Myth in *The America Play* and *Topdog/Underdog*." *JADT: Journal of American Drama and Theatre* 17, no. 3 (Fall): 24–35.

———. 2016. "Meta-Melodrama: Branden Jacobs-Jenkins Appropriates Dion Boucicault's *The Octoroon*." *Modern Drama* 59, no. 3 (Fall): 285–305.

Foucault, Michel. (1972) 2010. *The Archaeology of Knowledge*. Translated by A. M. Sheridan Smith. New York: Vintage.

Fraden, Rena. 2005. "A Mid-Life Crisis: Chiastic Criticism and Encounters with the Theatrical Works of Suzan-Lori Parks." *Journal of American Drama and Theatre* 17, no. 3 (Fall): 36–56.

Frank, Haike. 2002. "The Instability of Meaning in Suzan-Lori Parks's *The America Play*." *American Drama* 11, no. 2 (Summer): 4–20.

Fried, Michael. (1967) 1998. "Art and Objecthood." In *Art and Objecthood: Essays and Reviews*, 148–72. Chicago: University of Chicago Press.

Fusco, Coco. 1994. "The Other History of Intercultural Performance." *TDR: The Drama Review* 38, no. 1 (Spring): 143–67.

Gaines, Ernest. (1971) 2009. *The Autobiography of Miss Jane Pittman*. New York: Dial Press.

Gambari, Olga, ed. 2011. *Kara Walker: A Negress of Noteworthy Talent*. Turin: Fondazione Merz. Exhibition catalogue.

Gamble, Clive. 2008. *Archaeology: The Basics*. 2nd ed. New York: Routledge.

Garrett, Shawn-Marie. 2000. "The Possession of Suzan-Lori Parks." *American Theatre* 17, no. 8 (October): 22–26, 132–34.

———. 2002. "Return of the Repressed." *Theater* 32, no. 2 (Summer): 27–43.

———. 2010. "'For the Love of the Venus': Suzan-Lori Parks, Richard Foreman, and the Premiere of *Venus*." *Suzan-Lori Parks: Essays on the Plays and Other Works*, edited by Philip C. Kolin, 76–87. Jefferson, NC: McFarland.

Gates, Jr. Henry Louis. 1985a. "Preface." *The Slave's Narrative*, edited by Charles T. Davis and Henry Louis Gates Jr., v–vii. Oxford: Oxford University Press.

———. 1985b. "The Language of Slavery." Introduction to *The Slave's Narrative*, edited by Charles T. Davis and Henry Louis Gates Jr., xi–xxxiv. Oxford: Oxford University Press.

———. *The Signifying Monkey*. 1988. New York: Oxford University Press.

Gates, Henry Louis, Jr., and Gene Andrew Jarrett. 2007. Introduction to *The New Negro: Readings on Race, Representation and African American Culture*, edited by Henry Louis Gates Jr. and Gene Andrew Jarrett, 1–20. Princeton, NJ: Princeton University Press.

Geis, Deborah R. 2008. *Suzan-Lori Parks*. Michigan Modern Dramatists Series. Ann Arbor: University of Michigan Press.

George, Nelson. (1992) 2001. *Buppies, B-Boys, Baps & Bohos: Notes on Post-Soul Black Culture*. New York: Da Capo.

Gilman, Sander L. 1985. *Difference and Pathology: Stereotypes of Sexuality, Race, and Madness*. Ithaca, NY: Cornell University Press.

Gilroy, Paul. 1993. *The Black Atlantic: Modernity and Double Consciousness*. Cambridge, MA: Harvard University Press.

Glissant, Édouard. (1989) 1999. "The Known, the Uncertain." In *Caribbean Discourse: Selected Essays*, translated by J. Michael Dash, 13–95. Charlottesville: University of Virginia Press.

Goddu, Teresa. 2013. "The African American Slave Narrative and the Gothic." In *A Companion to American Gothic*, edited by Charles L. Crow, 71–83. Oxford: Wiley Blackwell.

Goffman, Alice. 2014. *On the Run: Fugitive Life in an American City*. Chicago: University of Chicago Press.

Goings, Kenneth W. 1994. *Mammy and Uncle Mose: Black Collectibles and American Stereotyping*. Indianapolis: Indiana University Press.

Golden, Thelma. 2001. Introduction to *Freestyle*, edited by Christine Y. Kim and Franklin Sirmans, 14–15. New York: Studio Museum in Harlem.

Goodman, Matthew Shen. 2014. "'We Are Here': People of Color Gather at Kara Walker Show." *Art in America Magazine*, June 20, 2014. http://www.artinamericamagazine.com/news-features/previews/we-are-here-people-of-color-gather-at-kara-walker-show-/.

Gordon, Avery. 1997. *Ghostly Matters: Haunting and the Sociological Imagination*. Minneapolis: University of Minnesota Press.

Hackenesch, Silke. 2017. *Chocolate and Blackness: A Cultural History*. Frankfurt am Main: Campus.

Hall, Stuart. 1996. "The After-life of Frantz Fanon: Why Fanon? Why Now? Why *Black Skin, White Masks*?" In *The Fact of Blackness: Frantz Fanon and Visual Representation*, edited by Alan Read, 13–37. London: Institute of Contemporary Art.

———. 1997a. "Old and New Identities, Old and New Ethnicities." In *Culture, Globalization, and the World-System: Contemporary Conditions for the Representation of Identity*, edited by Anthony D. King, 41–68. Minneapolis: University of Minnesota Press. First published 1991 by Department of Art and Art History, SUNY (Binghamton, New York).

———. 1997b. *Representation and the Media*. Produced and directed by Sut Jhally. Media Education Foundation. Transcript available at https://www.mediaed.org/assets/products/409/transcript_409.pdf.

Harris, Michael D. 2011. "Talking in Tongues: Personal Reflections on Kara Walker." *NKA: Journal of Contemporary African Art* 29 (Fall): 129–39.

Hartigan, Patty. 1996. "'Venus' as Victim." *Boston Globe*, March 27, 1996, 79.

Hartman, Saidiya V. 1997. *Scenes of Subjection: Terror, Slavery, and Self-Making in Nineteenth-Century America*. New York: Oxford University Press.

———. 2002. "The Time of Slavery." *South Atlantic Quarterly* 101, no. 4 (Fall): 757–77.

———. 2008. "Venus in Two Acts." *Small Axe* 12, no. 2 (June): 1–14.

Hatch, Ryan Anthony. 2013. "First as Minstrelsy, Then as Farce: On the Spectacle of Race in the Theater of Young Jean Lee." *CR: The New Centennial Review* 13, no. 3 (Winter): 89–114.

Hegel, Georg Wilhelm Friedrich. (1837) 2007. *The Philosophy of History*. Translated by John Sibree. New York: Cosimo.

Hine, Darlene Clark. 1989. "Rape and the Inner Lives of Black Women in the Middle West: Preliminary Thoughts on the Culture of Dissemblance." *Signs: Journal of Women in Culture and Society* 14, no. 4 (Summer): 912–20.

Hirsch, Marianne. 2012. *The Generation of Postmemory: Writing and Visual Culture After the Holocaust*. New York: Columbia University Press.

Hobbs, Robert. 2001. "Kara Walker: Slavery! Slavery!" In *Kara Walker: Slavery! Slavery! Catalogue for the 25th International Biennial of Sao Paulo*, 9–48. Washington, DC: International Arts & Artists.

Hobson, Janell. 2005. *Venus in the Dark: Blackness and Beauty in Popular Culture*. New York: Routledge.

Holcomb, Julie. 2016. *Moral Commerce: Quakers and the Transatlantic Boycott of the Slave Labor Economy*. Ithaca, NY: Cornell University Press.

Holmes, Rachel. 2007. *The Hottentot Venus: The Life and Death of Saartjie Baartman*. London: Bloomsbury.

Holtzman, Dinah. 2007. "'Save the Trauma for Your Mama': Kara Walker, the Art World's *Beloved*." *Les Carnets du Cerpac*, no. 6, 377–404.

hooks, bell. 1992. "Eating the Other." In *Black Looks: Race and Representation*, 21–40. Boston: South End.

Hutcheon, Linda. 1988. *A Poetics of Postmodernism: History, Theory, Fiction*. New York: Routledge.

———. 1994. *Irony's Edge: The Theory and Politics of Irony*. London: Routledge.

———. 2002. *The Politics of Postmodernism*, 2nd ed. New York: Routledge.

Innes, Christopher. 1999. "Staging Black History: Re-Imaging Cultural." *South African Theater Journal* 13 (1): 21–29.

Jacobs, Harriet. (1861) 2010. *Incidents in the Life of a Slave Girl, Written by Herself*. Edited with an introduction by Jennifer Fleischer. Boston: Bedford / St. Martin's.

Jacobs-Jenkins, Branden. 2016. *Appropriate*. New York: Dramatists Play Service. First staged in 2014.

———. 2014. "FEED Discussion with Raphael Martin and Sarah Benson." April 30, 2014, Soho Rep., https://www.youtube.com/watch?v=psqmqqvlCS8.

———. 2012. "Neighbors." In *Reimagining a Raisin in the Sun: Four New Plays*, edited by Rebecca Ann Rug and Harvey Young, 305–403. Evanston, IL: Northwestern University Press. First staged in 2010.

———. 2015. *An Octoroon*. New York: Dramatist's Play Service. First staged in 2014.

Jehlen, Myra. 1994. "The Literature of Colonialization." In *Cambridge History of American Literature*, vol. 1, edited by Sacvan Bercovitch, 11–168. Cambridge: Cambridge University Press.

Jiggetts, Shelby. 1996. "Interview with Suzan-Lori Parks." *Callaloo* 19, no. 2 (Spring): 309–17.

Jones, Douglas A., Jr. 2016. "The Fruit of Abolition: Discontinuity and Difference in Terrance Hayes's 'The Avocado.'" In *The Psychic Hold of Slavery: Legacies in American Expressive Culture*, edited by Soyica Diggs Colbert, Robert J. Patterson, and Aida Levy-Hussen, 39–54. New Brunswick, NJ: Rutgers University Press.

Kachka, Boris. 2016. "In Conversation with Colson Whitehead." *Vulture*, August 14, 2016. https://www.vulture.com/2016/08/colson-whitehead-author-of -the-underground-railroad-c-v-r.html.

Kalb, Jonathan, ed. 2004a. "Remarks on Parks: A Symposium on the Work of Suzan-Lori Parks, Part I: Critics and Scholars." *HotReview.org*, April 30, 2004. http://www.hotreview.org/articles/remarksparks1.htm.

——. 2004b. "Remarks on Parks: A Symposium on the Work of Suzan-Lori Parks, Part II: Directors." *HotReview.org*, April 30, 2004. http://www.hotreview.org/articles/remarksparks2.htm.

Keizer, Arlene R. 2004. *Black Subjects: Identity Formation in the Contemporary Narrative of Slavery*. Ithaca, NY: Cornell University Press.

——. 2008. "Gone Astray in the Flesh: Kara Walker, Black Women Writers, and African American Postmemory." *PMLA* 123, no. 5 (October): 1649–72.

——. 2011. "Our Posteriors, Our Posterity: The Problem of Embodiment in Suzan-Lori Parks's *Venus* and Kara Walker's *Camptown Ladies*." *Social Dynamics* 37, no. 2 (June): 200–12.

Kelly, Adam. 2018. "Freedom to Struggle: The Ironies of Colson Whitehead." *Open Library of Humanities* 4, no. 2 (October): 1–35.

Kincaid, Jamaica. 1996. *Autobiography of My Mother*. New York: Farrar, Straus & Giroux.

——. 2002. *Mr. Potter*. New York: Farrar, Straus & Giroux.

Kinnunen, Taina, and Marjo Kolehmainen. 2019. "Touch and Affect: Analyzing the Archive of Touch Biographies." *Body & Society* 25. 1: 29–56.

Knipe, Penley. 1999. "Shades and Shadow Pictures: The Materials and Techniques of American Portrait Silhouettes." In *The Book and Paper Group Annual*, vol. 18. Washington, DC: The American Institute for Conservation. http://cool.conservation-us.org/coolaic/sg/bpg/annual/v18/bp18–07.html#fn26.

——. 2002. "Paper Profiles: American Portrait Silhouettes." *Journal of the American Institute for Conservation* 41, no. 3 (Autumn–Winter): 203–23.

Kolin, Philip C., ed. 2010. *Suzan-Lori Parks: Essays on the Plays and Other Works*. Jefferson, NC: McFarland.

Kolin, Philip C., and Harvey Young, eds. 2014. *Suzan-Lori Parks in Person: Interviews and Commentaries*. New York: Routledge.

Koselleck, Reinhart. (1979) 1985. *Vergangene Zukunft: Zur Semantik geschichtlicher Zeiten*. Frankfurt am Main: Suhrkamp.

——. 2004. *Futures Past: On the Semantics of Historical Time*. Translated and with an introduction by Keith Tribe. New York: Columbia University Press.

Kriz, Kay Dian. 2008. *Slavery, Sugar, and the Culture of Refinement: Picturing the British West Indies, 1700–1840*. Paul Mellon Centre for Studies in British Art. New Haven, CT: Yale University Press.

Kukkonen, Karin. 2011. "Comics as a Test Case for Transmedial Narratology." *SubStance* 40. 1: 34–52.

Kumanyika, Chenjeraj, Jack Hitt, Chris Neary, and Bertram D. Ashe. 2020. "The Song: Living with 'Dixie' and the 'Coon Space' of Post-Blackness." In *Slavery and the Post-Black Imagination*, edited by Bertram D. Ashe and Ilka Saal, 124–39. Seattle: University of Washington Press.

Kuspit, Donald. 2004. "Kara Walker's Cakewalk." *Artnet Magazine*, November 4, 2004. http://www.artnet.com/magazine/features/kuspit/kuspit11 -4–03.asp.

Larson, Jennifer. 2012. *Understanding Suzan-Lori Parks*. Columbus: University of South Carolina Press.

Larson, Kay. 2014. "A Subtlety, or the Marvelous Sugar Baby." *Curator: The Museum Journal* 57, no. 4 (October): 505–11.

Leader-Picone, Cameron. 2020. "Whispering Racism in a Postracial World: Slavery and Post-Blackness in Paul Beatty's *The Sellout*." In *Slavery and the Post-Black Imagination*, edited by Bertram D. Ashe and Ilka Saal, 65–82. Seattle: University of Washington Press.

Lee, Josephine. 1998. *Performing Asian America: Race and Ethnicity on the Contemporary American Stage*. Philadelphia: Temple University Press.

Lee, Young-Jean. 2010. *The Shipment and Lear*. New York: Theatre Communications Group. First staged in 2009.

LeMahieu, Michael. 2012. "The Theater of Hustle and the Hustle of Theater: Play, Player, and Played in Suzan-Lori Parks's *Topdog/Underdog*." *African American Review* 45, nos. 1–2 (Spring–Summer): 33–47.

Lessing, Gotthold Ephraim. (1766) 1994. *Laokoon: Oder über die Grenzen der Malerei und Poesie*. Stuttgart: Reclam.

Levy-Hussen, Aida. 2016. "Trauma and the Historical Turn in Black Literary Discourse." In *The Psychic Hold of Slavery: Legacies in American Expressive Culture*, edited by Soyica Diggs Colbert, Robert J. Patterson, and Aida Levy-Hussen, 195–211. New Brunswick, NJ: Rutgers University Press.

Lindsey, Treva B., and Jessica Marie Johnson. 2014. "Searching for Climax: Black Erotic Lives in Slavery and Freedom." *Meridians: Feminism, Race, Transnationalism* 12. 2: 169–95.

Lloyd-Smith, Allan. 2004. *American Gothic Fiction: An Introduction*. New York: Continuum.

Locke, Alain. (1925) 1994. "The New Negro." In *The Portable Harlem Renaissance Reader*, edited by David Levering Lewis, 46–51. New York: Penguin.

Lott, Tommy. 2000. "Kara Walker Speaks: A Public Conversation on Racism, Art, and Politics with Tommy Lott." *Black Renaissance / Renaissance Noire* 3, no. 1 (Fall): 69–91.

Magubane, Zine. 2010. "Which Bodies Matter? Feminism, Poststructuralism, Race, and the Curious Theoretical Odyssey of the 'Hottentot Venus.'" In *Black Venus 2010: They Called Her "Hottentot,"* edited by Deborah Willis, 47–61. Philadelphia: Temple University Press.

Mannheim, Karl. (1952) 1998. "The Problem of Generations." In *Collected Works: Essays on the Sociology of Knowledge*, vol. 5, edited by Paul Kecskemeti, 276–320. New York: Routledge.

Marable, Manning. 2006. "Katrina's Unnatural Disaster: A Tragedy of Black Suffering and White Denial." *Souls: A Critical Journal of Black Politics, Culture, and Society* 8 (1): 1–8.

Maus, Derek C. 2014. *Understanding Colson Whitehead*. Columbia: University of South Carolina Press.

———. 2020. "Three Fifths of a Black Life Matters Too: Four Neo-Slave Novels from the Year Postracial Definitely Stopped Being a Thing." In *Slavery and the Post-Black Imagination*, edited by Bertram D. Ashe and Ilka Saal, 43–64. Seattle: University of Washington Press.

McDowell, Deborah E., and Arnold Rampersad, eds. 1987. *Slavery and the Literary Imagination*. Baltimore: Johns Hopkins University Press.

McMillan, Uri. 2015. *Embodied Avatars: Genealogies of Black Feminist Art and Performance*. New York: New York University Press.

Mercer, Kobena. 2007. "Tropes of the Grotesque in the Black Avant-Garde." In *Annotating Art's Histories: Pop Art and Vernacular Cultures*, edited by Kobena Mercer, 136–59. Cambridge, MA: MIT Press.

Mintz, Sidney. 1985. *Sweetness and Power: The Place of Sugar in Modern History*. New York: Viking.

Miranda, Carolina A. 2014. "Kara Walker on the Bit of Sugar Sphinx She Saved, Video She's Making." *Los Angeles Times*, October 3, 2014. http://www.latimes.com/entertainment/arts/miranda/la-et-cam-kara-walker-on-her-sugar-sphinx-the-piece-she-saved-video-shes-making-20141013–column.html#page=1.

Misrahi-Barak, Judith. 2014. "Post-*Beloved* Writing: Review, Revitalize, Recalculate." *Black Studies Papers* 1 (1): 37–55. http://elib.suub.uni-bremen.de/edocs/00103775-1.pdf.

Mitchell, Robin. 2010. "Another Means of Understanding the Gaze: Sarah Bartmann in the Development of Nineteenth-Century French National Identity." In *Black Venus 2010: They Called Her "Hottentot*," edited by Deborah Willis, 32–46. Philadelphia: Temple University Press.

Miyamoto, Keiko. 2012. "Toni Morrison and Kara Walker: The Interaction of Their Imaginations." *Japanese Journal of American Studies* 23: 231–61.

Morrison, Toni. 1987. *Beloved*. New York: Knopf.

———. (1992) 1993. *Playing in the Dark: Whiteness and the Literary Imagination*. New York: Vintage.

———. 1998. "The Site of Memory." In *Inventing the Truth: The Art and Craft of Memoir*, rev. ed., edited by William K. Zinsser, 185–200. New York: Houghton Mifflin.

———. 2008. *A Mercy*. New York: Knopf.

Moss, Thylias. 2004. *Slave Moth: A Narrative in Verse*. New York: Persea.

Moten, Fred. 2003. *In the Break: The Aesthetics of the Black Radical Tradition*. Minneapolis: University of Minnesota Press.

Mueller, Roswitha. 2006. "Learning for a New Society: the *Lehrstück*." In *The Cambridge Companion to Brecht*, edited by Peter Thompson and Glendyr Sacks, 101–18. Cambridge: Cambridge University Press.

Muhlack, Ulrich. 1982. "Theorie und Praxis der Geschichtsschreibung." In *Theorie der Geschichte: Beiträge zur Historik*, vol. 4, *Formen der Geschichtsschreibung*, edited by Reinhart Koselleck, Heinrich Lutz, and Jörn Rüsen, 607–20. München: dtv Wissenschaft.

Munro, Cait. 2014. "Kara Walker's Sugar Sphinx Spawns Offensive Instagram Photos." *Artnet* (May 30, 2014). https://news.artnet.com/art-world/kara -walkers-sugar-sphinx-spawns-offensive-instagram-photos-29989.

Murray, Derek Conrad. 2016. *Queering Post-Black Art: Artists Transforming African-American Identity after Civil Rights.* London: Taurus.

———. 2020. "The Blackest Blackness: Slavery and the Satire of Kara Walker." In *Slavery and the Post-Black Imagination,* edited by Bertram D. Ashe and Ilka Saal, 21–42. Seattle: University of Washington Press.

Museum für Gegenwartskunst Siegen. 2008. *Blickmaschinen oder wie Bilder entstehen: Die zeitgenössische Kunst schaut auf die Sammlung Werner Nekes.* Köln: Dumont.

Neal, Mark Anthony. 2002. *Soul Babies: Black Popular Culture and the Post-Soul Aesthetic.* New York: Routledge.

Neary, Janet. 2014. "Representational Static: Visual Slave Narratives of Contemporary Art." *Melus* 39, no. 2 (Summer): 157–97.

Neumann, Birgit. 2010. "The Literary Representation of Memory." In *A Companion to Cultural Memory Studies,* edited by Astrid Erll and Ansgar Nünning, 333–43. Berlin: De Gruyter.

Nichols, Charles H. 1985. "The Slave Narrators and the Picaresque Mode: Archetypes for Modern Black Personae." In *The Slave's Narrative,* edited by Charles T. Davis and Henry Louis Gates Jr., 283–98. Oxford: Oxford University Press.

Nora, Pierre. 1989. "Between Memory and History: *Les Lieux de Mémoire.*" Translated by Marc Roudebush. *Representations* 26 (Spring): 7–24.

Nünning, Ansgar. 1997. "'But Why *Will* You Say That I Am Mad?' On the Theory, History, and Signals of Unreliable Narration in British Fiction." *AAA—Arbeiten aus Anglistik und Amerikanistik* 22 (1): 83–105.

Nünning, Vera. 2015. "Conceptualising (Un)reliable Narration and (Un)trustworthiness." In *Unreliable Narration and Trustworthiness: Intermedial and Interdisciplinary Perspectives,* edited by Vera Nünning, 1–28. Berlin: De Gruyter.

Nussbaum, Felicity A. 2003. *The Limits of the Human: Fictions of Anomaly, Race and Gender in the Long Eighteenth Century.* Cambridge: Cambridge University Press.

Nyong'o, Tavia. 2002. "Racial Kitsch and Black Performance." *Yale Journal of Criticism* 15 (2): 371–91.

———. 2014. "Unburdening Representation." *TBS: The Black Scholar* 44, no. 2 (Summer): 70–80.

———. 2019. *Afro-fabulations: The Queer Drama of Black Life.* New York: New York University Press.

Oliver, Andrew. 1977. *Auguste Edouart's Silhouettes of Eminent Americans, 1839–1844.* Charlottesville: Published for the National Portrait Gallery, Smithsonian Institution, by University Press of Virginia.

Olney, James. 1985. "'I Was Born': Slave Narratives, Their Status as Autobiography and as Literature." In *The Slave's Narrative*, edited by Charles T. Davis and Henry Louis Gates Jr., 148–75. New York: Oxford University Press.

Olson, Greta. 2003. "Reconsidering Unreliability: Fallible and Untrustworthy Narrators." *Narrative* 11, no. 1 (January): 93–109.

Omi, Michael, and Howard Winant. 1986. *Racial Formation in the United States: From the 1960s to the 1980s*. New York: Routledge.

Ong, Han. 1994. "Suzan-Lori Parks." *Bomb Magazine*, April 1, 1994. https://bomb-magazine.org/articles/suzan-lori-parks/.

Patterson, Robert J. 2016. "Conclusion: Black Lives Matter, Except When They Don't: Why Slavery's Psychic Hold Matters." In *The Psychic Hold of Slavery: Legacies in American Expressive Culture*, edited by Soyica Diggs Colbert, Robert J. Patterson, and Aida Levy-Hussen, 212–20. New Brunswick, NJ: Rutgers University Press.

Peabody, Rebecca. 2013. "Close-Up: Afrosurrealism. The Art of Storytelling in Kara Walker's Film and Video." *Black Camera: An International Film Journal* 5, no. 1 (Fall): 140–63.

——. 2016. *Consuming Stories: Kara Walker and the Imagining of American Race*. Oakland: University of California Press.

Pearce, Michele. 1994. "Alien Nation." *American Theatre* 11, no. 3 (March): 26–27.

Pindell, Howardena. 2009. *Kara Walker-no, Kara Walker-yes, Kara Walker-?* New York: Midmarch Arts.

Piper, Adrian. 1999. *Out of Order, Out of Sight*. Volume 1: *Selected Writings in Meta-Art, 1968–1992*. Rev. ed. Cambridge, MA: MIT Press.

Postlewait, Thomas, and Tracy C. Davis. 2003. "Theatricality: An Introduction." In *Theatricality*, edited by Tracy C. Davis and Thomas Postlewait, 1–40. Cambridge: Cambridge University Press.

Powers, Nicholas. 2014. "Why I Yelled at the Kara Walker Exhibit." *Indypendent*, June 30, 2014. https://indypendent.org/2014/06/30/why-i-yelled-kara-walker-exhibit.

Purk, Antonia. 2014. "Writing Possibilities of the Past: Jamaica Kincaid's *Mr. Potter*." *Discourse: Journal for Theoretical Studies in Media and Culture* 36, no. 1 (Winter): 71–86.

Rankine, Claudia. 2014. *Citizen: An American Lyric*. New York: Graywolf Press.

Raymond, Yasmil. 2007. "Maladies of Power: A Kara Walker Lexicon." In *Kara Walker: My Complement, My Enemy, My Oppressor, My Love*, edited by Philippe Vergne, 347–69. Minneapolis: Walker Art Center; Ostfiltern, Germany: Hantje Cantz.

Rayner, Alice, and Harry J. Elam Jr. 1994. "Unfinished Business: Reconfiguring History in Suzan-Lori Parks's *The Death of the Last Black Man in the Whole Entire World*." *Theatre Journal* 46, no. 4 (December): 447–61.

Reed, Ishmael. 1976. *Flight to Canada*. New York: Simon & Schuster.

Reid-Pharr, Robert F. 2002. "Black Girl Lost." In *Pictures from Another Time*, edited by Annette Dixon, 27–41. Ann Arbor: University of Michigan Press.

——. 2006. "Makes Me Feel Mighty Real: *The Watermelon Woman* and the Critique of Black Visuality." In *F is for Phony: Fake Documentaries and Truth's Undoing*, edited by Alexandra Juhasz and Jesse Lerner, 130–40. Minneapolis: University of Minnesota Press.

Reinhardt, Mark. 2003. "The Art of Racial Profiling." In *Kara Walker: Narratives of a Negress*, edited by Ian Berry, Vivian Patterson, and Mark Reinhardt, 109–29. Cambridge, MA: MIT Press.

Ricoeur, Paul. 1981. *Hermeneutics and the Human Sciences*. Translated by John B. Thompson. Cambridge: Cambridge University Press.

Ridgeway, James. 2009. "The Secret History of Hurricane Katrina." *Mother Jones*, August 28, 2009. http://www.motherjones.com/environment/2009/08/secret-history-hurricane-katrina.

Roach, Joseph. 1996. *Cities of the Dead: Circum-Atlantic Performance*. New York: Columbia University Press.

Rody, Caroline. 2001. *The Daughter's Return: African-American and Caribbean Women's Fictions of History*. New York: Oxford University Press.

Rogers, Molly. 2010. *Delia's Tears: Race, Science, and Photography in Nineteenth-Century America*. New Haven, CT: Yale University Press.

Rooney, Kara. 2014. "A Sonorous Subtlety: Kara Walker with Kara Rooney." *The Brooklyn Rail: Critical Perspectives on Art, Politics, and Culture*, May 6, 2014. http://brooklynrail.org/2014/05/art/kara-walker-with-kara-rooney.

Rowell, Charles H. 2002. "Poetry, History, and Humanism: An Interview with Margaret Walker." In *Conversations with Margaret Walker*, edited by Maryemma Graham, 19–31. Jackson: University Press of Mississippi.

Rushdy, Ashraf H. 1997. "Neo-Slave Narrative." In *The Oxford Companion to African American Literature*, edited by William L. Andrews, Frances Smith Foster, and Trudier Harris, 533–35. New York: Oxford University Press.

——. 1999. *Neo-slave Narratives: Studies in the Social Logic of a Literary Form*. New York: Oxford University Press.

Ryan, Katy. 1999. "'No Less Human': Making History in Suzan-Lori Parks's *The America Play*." *Journal of Dramatic Theory and Criticism* 13, no. 2 (Spring): 81–94.

Ryan, Marie-Laure. 2007. "Toward a Definition of Narrative." In *The Cambridge Companion to Narrative*, edited by David Herman, 22–38. Cambridge: Cambridge University Press.

Saal, Ilka. 2013. "Suzan-Lori Parks." In *Methuen Drama Guide to Contemporary American Playwrights*, edited by Martin Middeke, Christopher Innes, Peter Paul Schnierer, and Matthew Roudané, 243–60. London: Methuen Drama.

——. 2015. "Of Diggin' and Fakin': Historiopoiesis in Suzan-Lori Parks and Contemporary African American Culture." In *African American Culture & Society Post Rodney King: Provocations & Protests, Progression & 'Post-Racialism,'* edited by Jo Metcalf and Carina Spaulding, 67–81. Farnham: Ashgate.

——. 2020. "Performing Slavery at the Turn of the Millennium: Stereotypes, Affect, and Theatricality in Branden Jacobs-Jenkins's *Neighbors* and Young

Jean Lee's *The Shipment.*" In *Slavery and the Post-Black Imagination*, edited by Bertram D. Ashe and Ilka Saal, 140–59. Seattle: University of Washington Press.

Saltz, Jerry. 1996. "Kara Walker: Ill-Will and Desire." *Flash Art: The International Art Review* 29, no. 191 (November–December): 82–86.

———. 2014. "Kara Walker Bursts into Three Dimensions, and Flattens Me." *New York Magazine*, June 2, 2014. http://www.vulture.com/2014/05/art-review -kara-walker-a-subtlety.html.

Saltzman, Lisa. 2006. *Making Memory Matter: Strategies of Remembrance in Contemporary Art*. Chicago: University of Chicago Press.

Sanneh, Kelefa, Kara Walker, Juliette Bowles, Don Bacigalupi, and Michael Ray Charles. 1998. "Stereotypes Subverted: The Debate Continues." *IRAAA: International Review of African American Art* 15 (2): 44–52.

Sargent, Antwaun. 2017. "Kara Walker Showed Me the Horror of American Life." *Vice Magazine*, November 12, 2017. https://www.vice.com/en_us/ article/59ywgz/kara-walker-showed-me-the-horror-of-american-life.

Sauter, Willmar. 2000. *The Theatrical Event: Dynamics of Performance and Perception*. Iowa City: University of Iowa Press.

Savoy, Eric. 1998. "The Face of the Tenant: A Theory of the American Gothic." In *American Gothic: New Interventions in a National Narrative*, edited by Robert K. Martin and Eric Savoy, 3–19. Iowa City: University of Iowa Press.

———. 2008. "The Rise of the American Gothic." In *The Cambridge Companion to Gothic Fiction*, 7th ed., edited by Jerrold E. Hogle, 167–88. Cambridge: Cambridge University Press.

Savran, David. 2014. "Suzan-Lori Parks." In *Suzan-Lori Parks in Person: Interviews and Commentaries*, edited by Philip C. Kolin and Harvey Young, 78–98. New York: Routledge.

Saxon, Theresa. 2021. "Performing Il/legibility: Staging Miscegenation in *Oroonoko* and *Inkle and Yarico* on the Late Eighteenth-Century Stage." In *American Cultures in Transnational Performance*, edited by Katrin Horn, Leopold Lippert, Ilka Saal, and Pia Wiegmink. London: Routledge.

Schechner, Richard. 2002. *Performance Studies: An Introduction*. London: Routledge.

Schmidt-Linsenhoff, Viktoria. 2010. "On and Beyond the Colour Line: Afterimages of Old and New Slavery in Contemporary Art since 1990." *Slavery in Art and Literature: Approaches to Trauma, Memory and Visuality*, edited by Birgit Haehnel and Melanie Utz, 59–91. Berlin: Frank & Timme.

Schuessler, Jennifer. 2014. "Wither Dan Brown? Poll Lists America's Favorite Books." *New York Times*, April 30, 2014. https://artsbeat.blogs.nytimes .com/2014/04/30/whither-dan-brown-poll-lists-americans-favorite -books/?_r=1.

Schulz, Kathryn. 2016. "The Perilous Lure of the Underground Railroad." *New Yorker*, August 15, 2016. https://www.newyorker.com/magazine/2016/08/22/ the-perilous-lure-of-the-underground-railroad.

Seigworth, Gregory J., and Melissa Gregg. 2010. "An Inventory of Shimmers." In
    The Affect Theory Reader, edited by Gregory J. Seigworth and Melissa Gregg,
    1–25. Durham, NC: Duke University Press.

Sekora, John. 1987. "Black Message / White Envelope." *Callaloo* 32 (Summer):
    482–515.

Sekula, Allan. 1986. "The Body and the Archive." *October* 39 (Winter): 3–64.

Sharpe, Christina. 2010. *Monstrous Intimacies: Making Post-Slavery Subjects*.
    Durham, NC: Duke University Press.

Sharpley-Whiting, Tracey Denean. 1999. *Black Venus: Sexualized Savages, Primal
    Fears, and Primitive Narratives in French*. Durham, NC: Duke University
    Press.

Shaw, Gwendolyn DuBois. 2004. *Seeing the Unspeakable: The Art of Kara Walker*.
    Durham: Duke University Press.

———. 2005. "'Moses Williams, Cutter of Profiles:' Silhouettes and African Ameri-
    can Identity in the Early Republic." *Proceedings of the American Philosophical
    Society* 149, no. 1 (March): 22–39.

Sheets, Hilary. 2002. "Cut It Out!" *Artnews* 101, no. 4 (April): 126–29. http://www.
    artnews.com/2002/04/01/cut-it-out/.

Shenk, Joshua Wolf. 2002. "Beyond a Black-and-White Lincoln." *New York
    Times*, April 7, 2002. http://www.nytimes.com/2002/04/07/theater/
    theater-beyond-a-black-and-white-lincoln.html.

Shockley, Evie. 2013. "Portrait of the Artist as a Young Slave: Visual Artistry as
    Agency in the Contemporary Narrative of Slavery." In *Contemporary African
    American Literature: The Living Canon*, edited by Lovalerie King and Shirley
    Moody-Turner, 137–54. Bloomington: Indiana University Press.

Sims, Lowery Stokes, Karen C. Dalton, and Michael D. Harris. 1997. "The Past Is
    Prologue but Is Parody and Pastiche Progress? A Conversation." *IRAA: Interna-
    tional Review of African American Art* 14 (3): 17–29.

Sims, Lowery Stokes, Kathleen Husler, and Cynthia R. Copeland. 2006. *Legacies:
    Contemporary Artists Reflect on Slavery*. Catalogue of an exhibition at the New
    York Historical Society, June 16, 2006–January 7, 2007. New York: New York
    Historical Society.

Snead, James A. 1984. "Repetition as a Figure of Black Culture." In *Black Litera-
    ture and Literary Theory*, edited by Henry Louis Gates Jr., 59–79. New York:
    Routledge.

Solomon, Alisa. 1990. "Signifying on the Signifyin': The Plays of Suzan-Lori Parks."
    Theater 21, no. 3 (Summer–Fall): 73–80.

Sontag, Susan. (1977) 1990. *On Photography*. New York: Doubleday Anchor.

Spaulding, A. Timothy. 2005. *Re-Forming the Past: History, the Fantastic and the
    Postmodern Slave Narrative*. Columbus: Ohio State University Press.

Spillers, Hortense J. 1987a. "Changing the Letter: The Yokes, the Jokes of Dis-
    course, or, Mrs. Stowe, Mr. Reed." In *Slavery and the Literary Imagination*,
    edited by Deborah E. McDowell and Arnold Rampersad, 25–62. Baltimore:
    Johns Hopkins University Press.

————. 1987b. "Mama's Baby, Papa's Maybe: An American Grammar Book." *Diacritics* 17, no. 2 (Summer): 65–81.

Stanley, Jason. 2009. "Titus Kaphar." *Bomb Magazine*, June 13, 2009. https://bombmagazine.org/articles/titus-kaphar/.

Subotnick, Ali. 2002. "Kara Walker." *Make: The Magazine for Woman's Art* 92: 25–27.

Sutton, Benjamin. 2014. "Beyoncé, Jay Z, and 130,552 Other People Visited Kara Walker's Sphinx."*Artnet News*, July 8, 2014. https://news.artnet.com/art-world/beyonce-jay-z-and-130552-other-people-visited-kara-walkers-sphinx-57075.

Tate, Greg. 1992. *Flyboy in the Buttermilk: Essays on Contemporary America.* New York: Simon & Schuster.

Taylor, Diana. 2003. *The Archive and the Repertoire: Performing Cultural Memory in the Americas.* Durham, NC: Duke University Press.

Taylor, Paul C. 2007. "Post-Black, Old-Black."*African American Review* 41, no. 4. (Winter): 625–40.

Thompson, Debby. 2007. "Digging the Fo'-fathers: Suzan-Lori Parks's Histories." In *Contemporary African American Women Playwrights*, edited by Philip C. Kolin, 167–84. New York: Routledge.

Thompson, Krista. 2012. "A Sidelong Glance: The Practice of African Diaspora History in the United States."*Art Journal* 70, no. 3 (Fall): 6–31.

Thompson, Krista, and Huey Copeland. 2011. "Perpetual Returns: New World Slavery and the Matter of the Visual." In "New World Slavery and the Matter of the Visual." Special issue, *Representations* 113 (Winter): 1–15.

Tierney, Kathleen, Christine Bevc, and Erica Kuligowski. 2006. "Metaphors Matter: Disaster Myth, Media Frames, and their Consequences in Hurricane Katrina." *Annals of the American Academy of Political and Social Science* 604 (March): 57–81.

Tompkins, Kyla Wazana. 2012. *Racial Indigestion: Eating Bodies in the 19th Century.* New York: New York University Press.

Touré. 2011. *Who's Afraid of Post-Blackness? What It Means to Be Black Now.* New York: Free Press.

Tucker-Abramson, Myka. 2007. "The Money Shot: Economies of Sex, Guns, and Language in *Topdog/Underdog*." *Modern Drama* 50, no. 1 (Spring): 77–97.

Vergne, Philippe. 2007. "The Black Saint Is the Sinner Lady." In *Kara Walker: My Complement, My Enemy, My Oppressor, My Love*, edited by Philippe Vergne, 7–25. Minneapolis: Walker Art Center; Ostfiltern, Germany: Hantje Cantz.

Wagner, Anne M. 2003. "Kara Walker: The Black-White Relations." In *Kara Walker: Narratives of a Negress*, edited by Ian Berry, Darby English, Vivian Patterson, and Mark Reinhardt, 91–108. Cambridge, MA: MIT Press.

Walker, Alice. 1983. *In Search of Our Mother's Garden: Womanist Prose.* New York: Harcourt Brace Jovanovich.

Walker, Margaret. 1966. *Jubilee.* New York: Houghton Mifflin Harcourt.

Wall, David. 2010. "Transgression, Excess, and the Violence of Looking in the Art of Kara Walker." *Oxford Art Journal* 33, no. 3 (October): 277–99.

Wallace, Michele. 1996. "The Hottentot Venus." *Village Voice*, May 21, 1996, 31.

Wallis, Brian. 1995. "Black Bodies, White Science: Louis Agassiz's Slave Daguerreotypes." *American Art* 9, no. 2 (Summer): 38–61.

Ward, Abigail. 2011. *Caryl Phillips, David Dabydeen, and Fred D'Aguiar: Representations of Slavery.* Manchester, UK: Manchester University Press.

Warner, Sara L. 2008. "Suzan-Lori Parks's Drama of Disinterment: A Transnational Exploration of Venus." *Theatre Journal* 60, no. 2 (May): 181–99.

Watts, Stephanye. 2014. "The Audacity of No Chill: Kara Walker in the Instagram Capital." *Gawker*, June 4, 2014. http://gawker.com/the-audacity-of-no-chill-kara-walker-in-the-instagram-1585944103.

Weinauer, Ellen. 2017. "Race and the American Gothic." In *The Cambridge Companion to American Gothic*, edited by Jeffrey Andrew Weinstock, 85–98. Cambridge: Cambridge University Press.

Welter, Barbara. 1966. "The Cult of True Womanhood: 1820–1860." *American Quarterly* 18, no. 2, part 1 (Summer): 151–74.

Wetmore, Kevin J., Jr. 2007. "It's an Oberammergau Thing: An Interview with Suzan-Lori Parks." In *Suzan-Lori Parks: A Casebook*, edited by Kevin J. Wetmore Jr. and Alycia Smith-Howard, 124–40. New York: Routledge.

Wetmore, Kevin J., Jr., and Alycia Smith-Howard, eds. 2007. *Suzan-Lori Parks: A Casebook.* New York: Routledge.

White, Hayden. 1990. *The Content of Form: Narrative Discourse and Historical Representation.* Baltimore: Johns Hopkins University Press.

———. 2010a. *The Fiction of Narrative: Essays on History, Literature, and Theory, 1957–2007*, edited and with introduction by Robert Doran. Baltimore: Johns Hopkins University Press.

———. 2010b. "The Practical Past." *Historein* 10 (May): 10–19.

Whitehead, Colson. 2016. *The Underground Railroad.* New York: Doubleday.

Wilderson, Frank B., III. 2010. *Red, White and Black: Cinema and the Structure of U.S. Antagonisms.* Durham, NC: Duke University Press.

Williams, Raymond. 1977. *Marxism and Literature.* Oxford: Oxford University Press.

Williams, Sherley Anne. (1986) 1999. *Dessa Rose.* New York: Quill.

Willis, Deborah, ed. 2010. *Black Venus 2010: They Called Her "Hottentot."* Philadelphia: Temple University Press.

Willis, Deborah, and Carla Williams. 2002. *The Black Female Body: A Photographic History.* Philadelphia: Temple University Press.

Wilson, Fred. 1994. *Mining the Museum: An Installation by Fred Wilson*, edited by Lisa G. Corrin. Baltimore: Contemporary; New York: New Press. Exhibition catalogue.

Wolf, Werner. 2010. "Pictorial Narrativity." In *Routledge Encyclopedia of Narrative Theory*, edited by David Herman, Manfred Jahn, and Marie-Laure Ryan, 431–35. New York: Routledge.

Womack, Ytasha L. 2010. *Post Black: How a New Generation Is Redefining African American Identity*. Chicago: Lawrence Hill.

Wood, Jacqueline. 2001. "Sambo Subjects: Declining the Stereotype in Suzan-Lori Parks's *The Death of the Last Black Man in the Whole Entire World*." *Studies in the Humanities* 28, nos. 1–2 (June–December): 109–20.

Wood, Marcus. 2000. *Blind Memory: Visual Representations of Slavery in England and America, 1780–1865*. Manchester, UK: Manchester University Press.

Worthen, W. B. 1999. "Citing History: Textuality and Performativity in the Plays of Suzan-Lori Parks." *Essays in Theatre / Études théâtrales* 18, no. 2 (November): 3–22.

Wright, Laura. 2002. "'Macerations' French for 'Lunch': Reading the Vampire in Suzan-Lori Parks's *Venus*." *Journal of Dramatic Theory and Criticism* 17, no. 1 (Fall): 69–86.

Wright, Michelle M. 2015. *Physics of Blackness: Beyond the Epistemology of the Middle Passage*. Minneapolis: University of Minnesota Press.

Young, Harvey. 2010. *Embodying Black Experience: Stillness, Critical Memory, and the Black Body*. Ann Arbor: University of Michigan Press.

Young, Jean. 1997. "The Re-objectification and Re-commodification of Saartjie Baartman in Suzan-Lori Parks's *Venus*." *African American Review* 31, no. 4 (Winter): 699–708.

Young, Kevin. 2012. *The Grey Album: On the Blackness of Blackness*. Minneapolis: Graywolf.

Zimmer, Catherine. 2008. "Histories of *The Watermelon Woman*: Reflexivity between Race and Gender." *Camera Obscura* 23 (2): 41–67.

Žižek, Slavoj. 1989. "Looking Awry." *October* 50 (Autumn): 30–55.

INDEX

abolitionism, 58–60, 98–104, 145–46, 169, 191

absence: and digging, 56–57, 61–62, 82–83; fabricated, 52, 58

Abu El-Haj, Nadia, 27, 81–82

Achilles, Jochen, 85

aesthetics, 2–3, 6, 8, 31–32, 45–48, 64–65, 148–50, 161–62, 166, 171, 201n7, 208n10

affect, 2–6, 10–11, 30, 32, 42–43, 138–41, 143–50, 157–58, 162–63, 175–78, 190, 203n30

Africa, African, 40–41, 118, 121–22, 150–52, 159, 173, 183, 203n32

African American: history, 1–2, 21–26, 28–29, 32–33, 47–49, 55–56, 61–62, 72–73, 83–84, 99–101, 136–37, 180–81; literature, 19, 73–74, 98–104, 120, 200n8; marginalization, 82–83; memory, 18–21, 99, 145–48; as Other, 53, 62–63, 68, 116–18, 137–38; profiling, 42, 126–27, 129, 130–31; trauma, 1–4, 8, 13, 29–33, 48–49, 60–61, 82–84, 99–100, 139–40, 144–45, 179, 191, 197, 200n8; writers, 17, 22–25, 99–104. *See also* America, American;

Black; Black female body; Black women; slavery

Africanist, 126–28

afro-fabulation, 37–40. *See also* counterfeiting; critical fabulation; storying

afro-pessimism, 182–83, 195–96

Agassiz, Louis, 130, 132

alienation, 52, 65–70, 206n21, 215n32; Brechtian, 157–59

allegory, 14–16, 29–30, 52–53, 83, 118–19, 125–26, 148–49, 163–75, 183–84, 194–96, 213n10

alterity, 73–74, 120, 124–25, 185. *See also* Other, Otherness

ambiguity, 82–83, 112–16, 125–26, 129, 146–48, 171–74

America, American, 48–49, 53–54, 58–59, 61–62, 66, 122–23, 128–29, 130, 140–41, 163, 167–68, 181–83, 191–97, 199n2, 204n45. *See also* United States

anamorphosis, 96–98, 99, 108–09, 116–17, 120–23. *See also* sidelong glance

anti-Blackness, 11, 38, 50, 181–83, 193. *See also* racism, racist archaeology, 8–9, 18–29, 35–37, 41–43, 56–58, 63–65, 79–84, 128–29, 140–41, 143–44, 152, 163; of discourse, 63; Foucauldian, 8–9, 63; literary, 22, 56; performative, 27, 35–37, 41–42, 79–84. *See also* diggers, digging; excavation, exhumation

archive, 18–29, 37–39, 56–57, 82–84, 111, 121–23, 133–34, 143–50, 180–81. *See also* repertoire

Artaud, Antonin, 129, 216n36

Ashe, Bertram D., 46–47, 204n40, 204n44

audience, 5–6, 10–11, 41, 43, 118–20, 139–40, 141–42, 152–63, 166–67, 173, 175–78, 185–89, 200n7, 203n37, 209n26, 215n31, 218n15. *See also* beholder, beholders; spectator

Austin, J. L., 34, 76, 79, 206n30

autobiography, 35–37, 41–42, 95, 98–103, 104, 159–60, 209n20. *See also* slave narratives

autodiegetic narrator, 24, 35–37, 96, 102–03, 106–07, 194

autopoiesis, 55, 61–62, 83–84, 91–93, 102–04, 182–85, 197

ayo, damali, 6, 43, 203n36; *Rent-A -Negro.com* (2003), 6, 43, 203n36

Baartman, Sara (Sarah, Saartjie), 27, 28, 63–65, 136–37, 144–45, 148, 150–63, 170, 206n14, 212n2, 213n10, 213n14, 214n24, 214n25, 215nn28–29

Ball, Thomas, 60

Beatty, Paul, 19, 184, 186, 190; *The Sell-out* (2015), 19, 184, 186

beholder, beholders, 2–3, 5–6, 30, 44, 60, 108–09, 116–17, 126, 130, 133–35, 138–43, 151–52, 154, 160–63, 166–67, 172–75, 176–78. *See also* audience; spectator

Best, Stephen, 7–8, 29–32, 199n3, 202nn21–22

Bhabha, Homi K., 138, 154

Bibler, Michael, 128

Birth of a Nation (1915), 105

Black: art/artists, 1–5, 6–8, 10–11, 27–29, 32–33, 35–37, 42–50, 59, 104, 109, 118, 120, 121–22, 130–35, 136–38, 149–50, 161–62, 180–85, 199n2, 200n8, 202n22, 204nn39–41, 210n29, 212n1, 212n3, 213n7; authority, 38; body, 11, 42–43, 71–72, 75–76, 96, 100–01, 104, 108–09, 116–20, 134–35, 140–41, 166–67, 171–73, 175–76; economic discrimination, 14, 85–91; history, 1–4, 8–10, 13–18, 19–29, 30–32, 38–39, 41, 47–50, 58–59, 61–62, 71–73, 74–76, 82–85, 94–96, 99, 104, 118–20, 136; identity, 4, 33, 40, 41, 44–47, 51, 65–66, 68, 72, 74–75, 99, 170, 181, 196, 197, 200n8; linguistic difference, 72–76; literature, 73–74, 99–101, 120, 200n8; nationalism, 138; radical performance, 161–62; rage, 182–83; subjectivity, 10, 65, 162; vernacular, 67–68, 72–76, 186–87. *See also* African American; Black female body; Black women; slavery

Black Arts movement, 28

Black Atlantic, 29, 183–84. *See also* Middle Passage

Black female body, 5, 28, 42, 98, 171; femininity, 10–11, 63–64, 112–15, 172–74; representation, 63–64, 140–41, 144–45, 163; sexualization, 105, 153–54, 213n10, 213n15. *See also* Black Venus; Black women

Black Lives Matter, 182

Black Power movement, 44, 46

Black Venus, 140–41, 143–50, 151–63. *See also* Venus

Black women, 28, 35–37, 63, 71–76, 95, 140–43, 157–58; body, 140–41, 143–50; dissemblance, 145; sexuality, 150–55, 213n10, 213n15; slavery, 163–175; and taboo, 115–16, 140–41, 144–48. *See also* Black female body; Black Venus; Venus

blackface, 171, 173, 186, 206n31

fugitive, 23–25, 74–75, 105, 115, 191–93; Slave Act, 59. *See also* runaways

Gaines, Ernest, 19, 22–24; *The Autobiography of Miss Jane Pittman* (1971), 19, 22
gallantee show. *See* magic lantern
Garrett, Shawn-Marie, 3, 139, 214n18
Gates Jr., Henry Louis, 3, 9, 46, 73–74, 83, 99, 102, 137, 199n2, 208n5, 210n29
gaze: beholder's, 96, 116–17, 159, 162, 174–75; and *Blickmaschine*, 10, 121; male, 172–73; of a figure, 116–17, 156–57; object of, 161; of oppressed, 121–22; of scientific racism, 132; white, 67, 137, 154, 160, 172–73, 187, 188–89
generation, 1, 4, 8, 11–12, 43–50, 137–38
genre, 5, 141–42; conventions, 5, 18, 96, 99, 107, 194; slave narrative, 95, 98–108, 191, 194–96, 202n14
gestus, 2, 18, 23, 34, 43–44
ghosts, 9–10, 23–24, 52–55, 57, 61–62. *See also* haunting
Gilman, Sander L., 144, 154
Gilroy, Paul, 19
Glissant, Édouard, 36
Golden, Thelma, 46–47
Gordon, Avery, 54
gothic, 52–54, 205n3
grammar, 67–68, 72–76; American, 74, 140
Great Hole of History, 8–9, 27, 52, 57–58, 61–62, 66, 79–82. *See also* diggers, digging; excavations, exhumation
Green, Renée, 32, 150
Gregg, Melissa, 138–39

Haley, Alex, 19; *Roots* (1977), 1, 19
Hall, Stuart, 138–41, 163, 169
Harris, Lyle Ashton, 42, 215n27
Harris, Michael D., 137, 213n6
Hartman, Saidiya, 38–39, 143–49, 193, 203n30

haunting, 9, 16, 23–24, 30–33, 52–56, 61–62, 80, 173
Hegel, G. W. F., 40–41, 203n32
Hill, Lauren, 182
Hine, Darlene Clark, 145
Hirsch, Marianne, 8, 18
historicism: melancholic, 4, 29–32, 39, 179
historiography, -ies, -ic, 34, 53–54, 61–62, 83–84, 107, 108–09, 145–48, 160, 168, 190–91; dominant, 2–3, 35, 57–58, 62–63; imaginative, 3–4, 21–24, 181; mass-cultural, 17; metafiction, 37–38, 190–91; production, 18–24, 36–38, 78–79, 82–83; of slavery, 5–7, 11–12, 15–24, 51, 94–95, 191–92
historiopoiesis, historiopoetic, 33–41, 43–44, 49–50, 56, 62–63, 70, 74–75, 83–84, 149, 179–85, 189–91, 195–97, 203n25; Parks's, 8–9, 54–55, 56, 62–63, 65, 70, 74–75, 83–85; Walker's, 8–9, 17–18, 36–37, 40–41, 94–96, 120–21, 134–35, 139–40, 183–84
history, historical, 3–4, 18–29, 41–44, 53–54, 59–61, 84–85, 133–35, 144, 170–71, 177–78, 200n9, 202n14, 202n18, 202n25; African American, 28–33, 41–44, 56, 58–59, 72–75, 98–101; amendment, 76–79; clichés of, 16, 29, 36, 43, 93; discipline of, 19–21, 24; making/construction of, 3–6, 8–9, 16–18, 26–27, 33–41, 54–55, 65, 78–82, 86, 118–20, 179–81; misreading of, 16–17, 94–95, 97; mythological, 14–16, 36–37, 58–60, 145; pictorial, 14–17, 96; record, 14–16, 20–23, 26–27, 35–36, 41, 76–77, 84, 160; reparative, 61–62, 83–84; representation, 34; revisionist, 24–25, 31, 191–92; validity, 35–37; white, 60; with a capital *H*, 36, 169
Homer, Winslow, 127, 133–34, 183; *The Gulf Stream* (1899), 127, 133, 183

Mannheim, Karl, 44

Maryland Historical Society, 121, 128–29

masculinity, 87–89

materiality, 5–6, 25, 41, 43–44, 135, 161, 166–67, 169, 174–75, 180, 183; of language, 69, 142, 217n5

Maus, Derek, 190–91

McMillan, Uri, 162, 215n32

mediality, 5–6, 25, 41–44, 122–23, 141–43, 155–56, 167–68, 180

melancholia, melancholic, 9, 29–33, 36, 52, 56, 178; historicism, 4–5, 29–30, 39, 179; iteration, 58, 61–62

melodrama, 42, 184, 185–86, 188–89, 218n13

memory: cultural/collective, 2, 12, 37, 58–59, 99, 111, 145–48; faulty, 35; post-, 8, 18–19; re-, 23–24, 29–32; studies, 7, 20–21, 200n1

metafiction, 23–24, 190–91; historiographic, 37–38

metaphor, 23, 66, 69–70, 83, 86–87, 138, 191–92, 194–95

metonymy, 80, 83, 138, 168, 174, 183, 187–88

Middle Passage, 16, 66, 68, 75, 193; epistemology, 48–49

mimesis, 38, 84, 141

minstrelsy, 3, 42, 76, 170, 185, 186–87, 206n31. *See also* stereotypes

Mintz, Sidney, 168–69

Mitchell, Margaret, 15–16, 94, 171; *Gone with the Wind* (1936), 15–16, 94; *Gone with the Wind* (1939 film), 15–16, 171

mockumentary, 19, 35

Morrison, Toni, 1, 21–24, 26–27, 29–32, 127, 194, 202n18; *A Mercy* (2008), 30–32, 219n21; *Beloved* (1987), 1, 21–22, 29–32, 194

Moss, Thylias, 6, 181

Moten, Fred, 11, 143, 161–62, 167

mourning, 30–31, 56, 132, 145

Murray, Derek Conrad, 47, 48

myth, mythology, 15–17, 29, 36–37, 71–72, 74–76, 82, 111, 128, 140; and Baartman, 144–45, 159–60; and Black women, 167, 170, 174–75; Lincoln, 58–61, 80–82, 84; "Old Negro," 120; plantation, 116; and the Underground Railroad, 184–85, 191–93

narration, 39, 96, 144, 149, 194; unreliable, 9–10, 37, 97–108, 120–21

narrative, 3–4, 53–54, 58–59, 94–96, 177–78; antebellum slave, 5, 7, 9–10, 75, 96–120, 184, 190–97; concepts, 105–06; construction, 5–6, 37–50, 83–84, 116, 135, 179–81, 183–84; contemporary of slavery, 7, 11; neo-slave, 7–8, 17–18, 21, 23–25, 30–33, 49, 145, 196, 200n8, 201n8, 202n14; post-neo-slave, 31–33, 196; structuring, 19–21, 75–76; subconscious, 121

Native American, 186, 192, 195

naturalism, 84–86, 90–93, 194

Neal, Mark Anthony, 44–46, 204n40

"Negress," the (alter ego), 10, 28, 36–37, 95–98, 101–03, 159, 181; narrator, 104–11; and the picaresque, 111–20

neo-slave narratives, 7–8, 17–18, 21, 23–25, 30–33, 49, 145, 196, 200n8, 201n8, 202n14

neoliberalism, 87, 168–69, 182

New Black Aesthetic, 56

New Orleans, 121, 127–28

Nichols, Charles, 112, 116

Nora, Pierre, 20, 201n13

North, the, 192–93

Nünning, Ansgar, 107–08

Nyong'o, Tavia, 38–39

Obadike, Keith, 6, 43, 44, 180, 203n36; *Blackness for Sale* (2001), 6, 43

Obama, Barack, 47

object, objects, 20–21, 27–29, 81–82, 97–98, 141–43; resistance, 160–63

objecthood, 141–43, 161–75

objectification, 118, 137, 143, 155, 158, 166–67, 181

Olney, James, 100, 102

O'Meally, Robert, 20–21

Other, Otherness, 53, 63, 64, 66, 68, 118, 137–41, 144, 171–75

Parks, Suzan-Lori: on the "black play," 54; *The America Play* (1994), 8–9, 14, 26–27, 36, 40, 51–52, 56–63, 79–84; characters, 9, 51–52, 56, 62, 69, 84–85, 158–60; criticism, 136–37, 139–40; *The Death of the Last Black Man in the Whole Entire World* (1990), 51, 55, 65, 70–72; digging, 8–9, 26–29, 55–65, 70–76, 79–83, 163; *Father Comes Home from the Wars* (2014/2015), 27, 51, 55, 85, 217n5; "From Elements of Style" (1995), 84; *Getting Mother's Body* (2003), 14, 26–27, 52, 56; *Imperceptible Mutabilities in the Third Kingdom* (1989), 2, 5, 9, 14, 51–52, 55, 65–66, 69, 72, 77–79, 84; on language, 36, 65–76; method, 8–9, 17–18, 36, 38–40, 55, 56, 62, 69–70, 74–75, 83–84; and the past, 3–4, 5–7, 13–14, 33–34, 37–38, 58–62, 70–73, 177–78; "Possession" (1995), 26; realism, 84–86, 91–93; *Sinner's Place* (1984), 55; stereotypes, 10–11, 136–38, 139–41, 150–63; themes, 8–9, 26–27, 32–33, 51–56; *Topdog/Underdog* (2001), 9, 13–14, 26–27, 51–52, 55, 77, 84–93; use of language, 55–56; *Venus* (1996), 5–6, 8–9, 10–11, 14, 27, 51–52, 55, 63–65, 75, 136–37, 139–42, 146–48, 150–63, 170, 176, 214n23; *White Noise* (2019), 51, 52, 55, 85, 217n5

parody, 3, 9–10, 42, 53, 101, 116, 137, 154, 185

past: affective attachment to, 30; attitudes toward, 8, 15–17, 29–33, 135; construction of, 37–41, 69–71; knowledge of, 18–29, 33–37, 121; meddling with, 8–10, 94–95, 96–98; and the present, 11, 41–50, 61–62, 179–80, 196–97; practical, 78–80, 86; political interest in, 8, 17–18, 29–33, 180–81. *See also* history, historical; slavery

performance, 4, 5–6, 8–11, 13–14, 39, 55, 60–61, 64–65, 84–93, 104–05, 112–16, 161–62, 184, 186–87; bodily, 5–6, 14, 19–21, 76–79; theatrical, 54, 141–43

performativity, performative, 4–5, 11, 17–18, 33–44, 54–57, 74–76, 79–93, 101–02, 105, 142–43, 163, 179–82

performer-spectator relations, 156–59, 161–63

photography, 77–78, 130–32, 188–89, 208n14

physiognomy, 129–30

picara, picaro, picaresque, 10, 95, 111–20

Pindell, Howardena, 137, 200n8, 212n3

Piper, Adrian, 161–62, 215n32; *Untitled Performance for Max's Kansas City* (1970), 161–62, 215n32

plantation, 14–17, 94–95, 112–16, 142, 190, 215n30, 218n12; labor, 142, 166–69, 175

poetic, poetics, poiesis, 1–2, 4–5, 6–8, 11–12, 33–41, 43–44, 49–50, 83–84, 179–84, 185–87, 196; devices, 18–20, 55, 69; of evasion, 145

possession, 9, 55–56, 80

post-Black, 8, 18, 46–50, 181, 183–84, 190–91, 204n45

post-neo-slave narratives, 31–33, 196

post-racial, post-racialism, 11, 47, 50, 182, 184, 204n45

post-soul, 8, 18, 44–49, 59, 181, 190–91, 204n40

postmemory, 8, 18–19

poststructuralism, 4, 29, 37–38

puns, punning, 40–41, 78, 81–83

race, racial, 9–10, 32–33, 167, 169, 180–81, 197; ambiguity, 125–27, 172–73; categorizations, 53, 143; cliché,

43-44; construction of, 5-6, 9-10, 68, 96, 120, 122-35, 152-58, 171-72; fantasies, 42-43, 152; identity, 125-27; ideology, 63; pathology, 128-30, 135; perceptions of, 4-5, 11, 42-43, 52-53, 63, 121-22; performances of, 118, 143, 173-74; profiling, 42, 126, 129-31; representations of, 95, 99, 172-74; stereotypes, 2-3, 10-11, 43-44, 71-72, 120, 136-41, 150, 170; violence, 70-72, 188-89

racialization, 5-6, 120-28, 135, 171-72

racism, racist, 137-42, 166-67; anti-Black, 11, 35-37, 48-50, 86-87, 98-99, 104, 105, 118-20, 181-83, 184, 193; hysteria, 128; scientific, 130, 132

Rankine, Claudia, 182

rape, 16, 113, 116, 117, 143-45

Rayner, Alice, 157, 161, 162-63

realism, 23, 42, 84-93, 185, 194

Reed, Ishmael, 49, 193; *Flight to Canada* (1976), 49

refinement, 170-74

Reid-Pharr, Robert, 111, 118-19, 170

rememory, 23-24, 29-31

Rep & Rev, 8-9, 55, 62, 69-76, 82-83, 142, 160, 217n5

repertoire, 20-21

repetition, 9, 54, 69-70, 134, 160, 177; and difference, 74, 83

ressurectionist, 52, 55-56, 63-65, 152-53, 156-59. *See also* archaeology; diggers, digging; excavation, exhumation

Ricoeur, Paul, 20

rights: civil, 8, 44, 46-47, 182; human, 99-100

Ringgold, Faith, 19, 32, 145; *Slave Rape Series* (1972-73), 19, 145

Roach, Joseph, 54

Robinson, Marc, 52-53, 63

Rody, Caroline, 24

romance: historical, 14-16, 94-95, 108

Rothschild, Eva, 126, 211n39

runaways, 115, 130, 189; broadsheets, 42

Saar, Betye, 1, 108-10, 137, 212n1; *The Liberation of Aunt Jemima* (1972), 1, 137

Saltz, Jerry, 175

satire, 3, 150-52, 177-78, 184

Sauter, Willmar, 141

Savoy, Eric, 53-54

Schechner, Richard, 54

science fiction, 23-24

scopic, 5-6, 42-43, 64-65, 96, 121, 126, 150-63, 188-89

Seigworth, Gregory, 138-39

Sekora, John, 100

sensation scene, 188-89

sensationalism, 103-04

sex, sexual, 113-15, 143-49, 167, 170-74, 213n15; abuse, 16, 107, 112, 145, 146, 158-59, 187, 214n17; agency, 146, 158-59; desire, 109-10, 150-52; dissemblance, 145; fetishization, 154, 156-57; power, 16, 146; roles, 105, 140-41; and slavery, 115-16, 145-48, 187-89

shame, 105, 139-40

Shaw, Gwendolyn DuBois, 131-32

Shockley, Evie, 181, 189

show, showing, 150-63; business, 158-59

sidelong glance, 9-10, 37, 95, 97-98, 121-23, 130-32

Siebert, William Henry, 191-92

Signifyin(g), 9-10, 46, 74-75, 83, 95, 97-99, 101, 104, 134, 180, 191, 208n5

silhouettes, shades, Schattenriß, 5-6, 9-10, 15-17, 94-99, 105-07, 116-20, 120-35, 145-49; cut-paper (technique), 9-10, 95-98, 105-06, 120-35, 210n33, 211nn39-40; Schattenriss, 120-21, 129-30; shade, 120-23, 129-30, 210n33; shadow tracing, 130. *See also* Walker, Kara

Simpson, Lorna, 32

slave narratives, 5, 9-10, 21-22, 75, 95-96, 98-104, 112, 184, 191-96

INDEX

wordplay. *See* puns, punning
Wright, Michelle M., 47–49

Young, Harvey, 11, 117, 132, 189

Young, Kevin, 38, 40, 42, 86

Zealy, Joseph T., 130, 132
Žižek, Slavoj, 97–98

STUDIES IN THEATRE HISTORY
AND CULTURE

Bloody Tyrants and Little Pickles: Stage Roles of Anglo-American Girls in the Nineteenth Century
by Marlis Schweitzer

Classical Greek Theatre: New Views of an Old Subject
by Clifford Ashby

Collusions of Fact and Fiction: Performing Slavery in the Works of Suzan-Lori Parks and Kara Walker
By Ilka Saal

Cracking Up: Black Feminist Comedy in the Twentieth and Twenty-First Century United States
by Katelyn Hale Wood

Czech Theatre Design in the Twentieth Century: Metaphor and Irony Revisited
edited by Joseph Brandesky

Embodied Memory: The Theatre of George Tabori
by Anat Feinberg

Fangs of Malice: Hypocrisy, Sincerity, and Acting
by Matthew H. Wikander

Fantasies of Empire: The Empire Theatre of Varieties and the Licensing Controversy of 1894
by Joseph Donohue

French Theatre Today: The View from New York, Paris, and Avignon
by Edward Baron Turk

From Androboros to the First Amendment: A History of America's First Play
by Peter A. Davis

Irish on the Move: Performing Mobility in American Variety Theatre
by Michelle Granshaw

The Jewish Kulturbund Theatre Company in Nazi Berlin
by Rebecca Rovit

Jews and the Making of Modern German Theatre
edited by Jeanette R. Malkin and Freddie Rokem

The Show and the Gaze of Theatre: A European Perspective
by Erika Fischer-Lichte

The Song Is You: Musical Theatre and the Politics of Bursting into Song and Dance
by Bradley Rogers

Stagestruck Filmmaker: D. W. Griffith and the American Theatre
by David Mayer

Staging Postcommunism: Alternative Theatre in Eastern and Central Europe after 1989
edited by Vessela S. Warner and Diana Manole

Strange Duets: Impresarios and Actresses in the American Theatre, 1865–1914
by Kim Marra

Susan Glaspell's Poetics and Politics of Rebellion
by Emeline Jouve

Textual and Theatrical Shakespeare: Questions of Evidence
edited by Edward Pechter

Theatre and Identity in Imperial Russia
by Catherine A. Schuler

Theatre, Community, and Civic Engagement in Jacobean London
by Mark Bayer

Theatre Is More Beautiful Than War: German Stage Directing in the Late Twentieth Century
by Marvin Carlson

Theatres of Independence: Drama, Theory, and Urban Performance in India since 1947
by Aparna Bhargava Dharwadker

The Theatrical Event: Dynamics of Performance and Perception
by Willmar Sauter

Traveler, There Is No Road: Theatre, the Spanish Civil War, and the Decolonial Imagination in the Americas
by Lisa Jackson-Schebetta